Also by David Sheff

*The Buddhist on Death Row: How One Man Found
Light in the Darkest Place*

Clean: Overcoming Addiction and Ending America's Greatest Tragedy

Beautiful Boy: A Father's Journey Through His Son's Addiction

*All We Are Saying: The Last Major Interview
with John Lennon and Yoko Ono*

China Dawn: The Story of a Technology and Business Revolution

Game Over: How Nintendo Conquered the World

YO KO

A BIOGRAPHY

DAVID SHEFF

SIMON & SCHUSTER

NEW YORK AMSTERDAM/ANTWERP LONDON
TORONTO SYDNEY/MELBOURNE NEW DELHI

Simon & Schuster
1230 Avenue of the Americas
New York, NY 10020

First Simon & Schuster hardcover edition April 2025

SIMON & SCHUSTER and colophon are registered trademarks of Simon & Schuster, LLC

For information about special discounts for bulk purchases, please contact
Simon & Schuster Special Sales at 1-866-506-1949 or business@simonandschuster.com.

Interior design by Wendy Blum

Manufactured in the United States of America

10 9 8 7 6 5 4 3 2 1

Library of Congress Cataloging-in-Publication Data has been applied for.

ISBN 978-1-9821-8824-5
ISBN 978-1-9821-8826-9 (ebook)

For Kyoko Ono and Sean Ono Lennon

AUTHOR'S NOTE

PORTIONS OF THIS BOOK WERE previously published in magazine articles I wrote or cowrote, including "The *Playboy* Interview with John Lennon and Yoko Ono," "The Betrayal of John Lennon," "The Night Steve Jobs Met Andy Warhol," "Yoko Ono: How She Is Holding Up," and others and in my book *All We Are Saying: The Last Major Interview with John Lennon and Yoko Ono.*

Over the years, I conducted many hours of interviews with Yoko for those articles and other projects. I also spent countless more hours talking with her about her life and work. In this book, if sources of Yoko's quotes aren't otherwise noted, they're from our conversations.

For clarity, I cleaned up and tightened some of the quotes and edited and condensed some of the interviews with Yoko, John, and others.

CONTENTS

YO
KO

PROLOGUE

Cut Piece

ON THE EVENING OF MARCH 21, 1965, New York's Carnegie Recital Hall was packed. The audience had gathered for a concert by the artist Yoko Ono, a rising star in the international avant-garde art and music scene.

Yoko walked onto the stage and sat in *seiza* posture, her legs folded beneath her body. *Seiza* —"proper sitting"—is the formal sitting position in Japan. It indicates deference.

Yoko was thirty-two years old, with long black hair parted on the side and tied back in a low bun. She was dressed all in black. Besides the artist, the stage was empty except for a pair of scissors on the floor in front of her.

Yoko was performing a work called "Cut Piece." The audience was invited to come onto the stage one at a time and cut off a piece of her clothing. People were at first diffident and polite when they approached Yoko and wielded the scissors. They trimmed material from the sleeve, neckline, and hem of her sweater and skirt.

But according to artist and filmmaker Eleanor Antin, who was in attendance, "The atmosphere changed to dark and unpleasant when several young men . . . started taking off large parts of her skirt and sweater, disclosing her bra, and getting back in line after each of their cuts. They couldn't stop laughing. I recall [the artist] Carolee Schneemann going up to one of them and slapping him in the face, which didn't faze him one bit. He was after Yoko—the offered sacrifice."

A man approached and stood over Yoko, mulling where to cut. "It's very delicate," he said. "It might take some time." After cutting away her slip and exposing her bra, he cut the bra straps. Someone in the audience remarked, "He's getting carried away." A woman called out, "For God's sake, stop being such a creep!" There was trepidation in Yoko's eyes.

Antin recalled, "Yoko made a slight gesture towards the wings, and the curtain immediately closed on her before her breast could be revealed. The piece was over."

AT THE DEBUT PERFORMANCE OF "Cut Piece," in Kyoto in 1964, a man mimed stabbing Yoko. The year after the New York performance, she presented it in London, where a group of predatory men rushed the stage and, within minutes, cut off her dress, then her underclothes, leaving her naked.

Schneemann later remarked, "It was an extremely dangerous piece, especially in the moment when it was done, because there was no sense of feminist presence or barriers. . . . Vile things were in the air then, so she was challenging those very dark impulses in this vulnerable position—and that was the indelible power of it."

In 2020, more than half a century after "Cut Piece" was first performed, the *New York Times* identified it as "one of the twenty-five most influential works of American protest art since World War II."

LIKE "CUT PIECE," THE SCORES for many of Yoko's works took the form of poetic instructions for actions and events. Sometimes she executed them herself, but the instructions for her "unfinished" works could be completed by anyone, and some, like "Cut Piece," required the participation of the viewer or listener. Inviting the audience to join in making a work of art challenged the very idea of what art was. At that time, almost every artist in every medium presented finished work, whether images, objects, plays, poems, or symphonies, but many of Yoko's scores asked the audience to complete them by performing physical or mental actions. For "Fly Piece," with the single-word instruction "Fly," people could come onto the stage and "fly" by jumping off ladders—or they could fly in their minds. For "Whisper Piece," a work about the fragility of human communication, the audience played the child's game of telephone. "Bag Piece" instructed participants to get into a cloth bag, in which they could do whatever they wanted—remove their clothes, dance, meditate, take a nap. The meaning, according to Yoko: "All of us are in a bag, you know. The point was the outline of the bag, the movement of the bag: how much we see of a person. Inside there might be a lot going on. Or maybe nothing's going on." "Earth Piece," which Yoko composed in 1963, was a deceptively simple instruction: "Listen to the sound of the Earth turning." I invite you to try it now. Put down this book and experience an Ono composition: Listen to the sound of the Earth turning.

The artist and musician Laurie Anderson observed, "Yoko had this revolutionary idea that art happens mainly in your head, which is where her work manifests." And art historian and curator Reiko Tomii said, "She is a conceptual artist who said, 'You don't need an object or material to create art.' Basically, all you need is your mind. You can construct a painting in your head. In your mind, you can create an event." It was a new concept of what art could be and who could make it.

YOKO CREATED THE FIRST OF her imagination exercises when she was twenty, but their roots go back to her childhood. She was born in Tokyo, a daughter of the Yasuda dynasty. The Yasudas were among the wealthiest, most influential families in Japanese business. As a child, she lived a life of extreme privilege—servants, elite schools, palatial summer and winter homes—until it was interrupted by war.

On the night of March 9, 1945, when Yoko was twelve, the United States dropped 1,665 tons of incendiary bombs on Tokyo. Much of the city was incinerated, and at least one hundred thousand people were killed. Her father was in Hanoi. Her mother and siblings hid in a bomb shelter dug into the garden of their mansion, but Yoko was sick with a fever and couldn't be moved from her bedroom. She watched the bombs fall—heard the whistling, the explosions; felt the earth shake—and she watched the city burn.

Yoko's mother decided to evacuate her children to a farming village in Nagano Prefecture, where she bought a small home. It wasn't fully constructed; the ceiling was unfinished. Money was worthless and food was scarce.

In Nagano, Yoko was with her younger brother, Keisuke (Kei), and she felt responsible for him. "We were starving, my brother looking extremely sad. I remember thinking, 'Why don't we make a menu that would really make us feel good?'" Yoko told Kei, "How about starting with ice cream?" She went on: "Lying on our backs, looking up at the sky through an opening in the roof, we exchanged menus in the air and used our powers of visualization to survive."

"We made those menus; we imagined the food," Kei said. "That was my sister's first conceptual art piece."

"CUT PIECE" MEANT DIFFERENT THINGS to different people. Many saw it as a feminist work about the vulnerability of women and the violence perpetrated on them.

"Canonized as one of the most chilling, spellbinding works of feminist art to date, 'Cut Piece' eloquently conveys an experience familiar to many women—that of being inside a body upon which others feel entitled to act," according to critic Zoë Lescaze.

However, Yoko refused to be pinned down about the meaning of "Cut Piece." For her, the work was about anything anyone said it was. That was the point of her unfinished art. She created the pieces and the audience activated them. She gave them away in the moment of performance, relinquishing them as she relinquished her clothing in "Cut Piece." They became the property of whoever took them, and the new owner could ascribe any meaning (or no meaning).

Still, over time Yoko would also characterize "Cut Piece" as a spiritual act about the power of giving that was inspired by a story about an incarnation of the Buddha who gave away his possessions and became enlightened. At other times she said it was about vulnerability, trust, and a call for peace. Of her experience while performing the piece, she wrote, "I felt kind of like I was praying. I also felt that I was willingly sacrificing myself." Once she said, "When I do the 'Cut Piece,' I get into a trance, and so I don't feel too frightened." But she admitted that despite her defiant stoicism, sometimes her body shook. The audience couldn't tell she was afraid; she was adept at internalizing fear and projecting confidence because she'd been doing it since she was a child, in bed, watching through the window as Tokyo burned.

INTRODUCTION

Ocean Child

THOUSANDS OF BOOKS AND ARTICLES have been written about John Lennon and the Beatles, and in most of them, Yoko Ono is a caricature, a curiosity, or even a villain—an inscrutable seductress, a manipulating con artist, and a caterwauling fraud who hypnotized Lennon and broke up the greatest band in history. The Lennon/Beatles saga is one of the greatest stories ever told, but Yoko's part has been hidden in the band's formidable shadow and further obscured by flagrant misogyny and racism.

When Yoko met John, he was at the height of his unprecedented fame. John once quipped that the Beatles were more popular than Jesus. It was only a slight exaggeration.

When John met Yoko, she had also attained a measure of fame, negligible compared to Lennon's but she was ascending in the international avant-garde art world. She became half of "John and Yoko," the world's most famous couple—musicians, artists, and peaceniks—the "wondrous mystic prince from the rock 'n' roll world dabbling . . . with this strange Oriental woman," as Lennon described the public's perception of "the missus" and himself.

Her vilification began immediately. Beatles fans stood vigil outside Apple, the Beatles headquarters in London, and, when Yoko appeared, they screamed at her to go back to her own country. She was called an "ugly Jap."

Racist and sexist comments came from the press, fans, the Beatles' circle, and the other Beatles. The musician and artist Klaus Voormann, a friend of and collaborator with the group, said, "*Bitch* was how Yoko was referred to by the men she threatened—and she threatened the lot of them." John had Yoko come with him to the recording studio when the Beatles worked, and in 2021, Paul McCartney admitted to interviewer Terry Gross, "We were not too keen on it at all because it was like, 'Who is this? And why is she sitting on my amp?'" By the early 1970s, Yoko was, according to TV talk-show host Dick Cavett, "one of the most controversial ladies since the Duchess of Windsor." More recently, journalist Ray Connolly updated the Buckingham Palace reference, saying, "Meghan Markle's treatment when she got together with Prince Harry was nothing compared to the hatred directed at Yoko when she got together with John."

Details of her independent life and work were mostly deemed unimportant; she was irrelevant except for the impact she had on Lennon and his band. As a result, most people's impressions of her come from the tired, sensational, and fictitious versions of the story that began when she met John and ended with his murder, a period of just fourteen of her ninety-plus years.

HER STORY BEGINS IN TOKYO. As a child, Yoko experienced material privilege but suffered from emotional poverty; her parents were distant and dismissive. Not only were they unavailable, they isolated her from other children. She was taught that she was too good for them and they'd take advantage of her. She craved love and connection, but those needs were never fulfilled in her youth, and in response she built walls between herself and others. As she grew older, her aloofness was often seen as arrogance, but it masked a deep longing and sadness.

Much of Yoko's personal and creative life was a direct response to her parents' neglect and a series of traumas she endured. When war broke out in 1941, she was eight. At twelve, she experienced the horror of the firebombing of Tokyo, and the trauma continued when the family was evacuated from the capital to a village where she had to beg and barter for food. When she returned to Tokyo, the city was in ruins.

Yoko was raised in Japan and America, bifurcated, feeling alienated in both the East and the West. Growing up, she attended exclusive junior and senior high schools. She excelled but was anxious, depressed, and lonely. She attempted suicide as a teenager. Ultimately, she found refuge in her imagination and in art.

She attended college in Tokyo and New York but dropped out of both. She then moved to Greenwich Village, where she helped foment a revolution in the way people thought about and made art. "She never wanted to be limited to a single art form," according to curator, critic, and art historian Hans Ulrich Obrist. "She is a painter, poet, sculptor, filmmaker, architect, writer so she wasn't accepted in any one of those worlds. There was even resistance in the avant-garde." As a singer, she divided even the avant-garde world by using her voice as a wailing instrument—dissonant, moaning, screaming, reaching the depths of agony and the heights of ecstasy, which won her some fans but more scorn.

After her initial failures to connect with audiences (and another suicide attempt), she was lauded for her art in New York and London, where she met John Lennon in 1966. And while it's true that when Yoko met John, he was already at the pinnacle of his fame, *she* was the artist whose work *he* came to see. "I'd been told about this 'event,' a Japanese avant-garde artist coming from America," he said. "She was red-hot. There was going to be something about black bags, and I thought it was all gonna be sex: artsy-fartsy orgies. Great! Well, it was far out, but it was not the way I thought it was going to be."

Yoko's work was intentionally provocative, which was exciting for Lennon and an audience that wanted to be provoked but enraging for the mainstream audience that came to her by way of the Beatles. The year Yoko met John, the Beatles were on the record charts with pop songs like "Paperback Writer" and "Yellow Submarine"; Yoko was wailing and moaning onstage and having people get in bags. She released a film called *No. 4 (Bottoms)* that consisted entirely of images of naked buttocks.

John, who was miserable at the time—he felt stifled and trapped as a Beatle and unhappy in his marriage—was enchanted by the lightness and humor in Yoko's work and moved by the pathos. He once said that he thought Yoko expressed herself so effectively—so *purely*—that many people couldn't bear it. "That's why they couldn't take Van Gogh," he said, "it's too real, it hurts."

They fell in love, and John became her greatest ally, friend, and collaborator. Yoko felt she'd found her other half. It gave her hope for a kind of happiness she hadn't believed was possible. She'd never experienced the type of love and connection she had with John. She felt safe with him; it was a reprieve from her pain and loneliness. However, she was blindsided when she was attacked by the press and public for being with him; she was blamed and reviled when the Beatles broke up.

Wounded by public condemnation, Yoko devoted herself to what was most important to her: art, music, activism—and her husband. More than a decade of solo and collaborative work followed. Yoko's concepts of wish fulfillment and positivity can be seen in her solo work and her collaborations with John. The songs "Imagine" and "Give Peace a Chance" sprang from her art and thinking. Her philosophies about art and activism were the bases of many of their campaigns for peace. Of the famous bed-ins, John said, "The actual peace event we staged came directly from Yoko."

They collaborated on irreverent, funny, profound, and inspiring events, music, art, and political action—often combinations of those—and Yoko and John became arguably the most famous couple in the world. They split up for a period John termed his "lost weekend," but they reunited and became more devoted to each other than ever. In 1975, they had a child, Sean Taro Ono Lennon, and through the late 1970s, Yoko was as content as she'd ever been in her life.

Then came the assassination heard around the world. The working-class hero was dead. Yoko had been at her beloved's side, and she was decimated.

The murder proved to her that she'd been right all along: The world was unsafe.

And that great trauma was just the beginning. In the aftermath of John's death, she was betrayed, robbed, and blackmailed, and her life was threatened. The journalist Barbara Graustark, who first interviewed Yoko and John for *Newsweek* in 1980 and later edited stories about her at the *New York Times*, said, "There was very much a sense of trying to go on as an artist, trying to go on with Sean, but constantly being reminded, 'Are you going to be next? Is someone coming for you?'"

Even amid the barrage, Yoko never stopped working. After the murder, she embarked on a remarkably successful effort to protect John's legacy and keep him relevant. And though her artistic endeavors would forever be eclipsed by her association with the fallen idol, she began a new phase of solo work. The myth of the girl who broke up the Beatles endured, but a parallel storyline began to emerge, a correction of the trite, sexist narrative.

A long and eclectic list of artists, musicians, critics, and historians came to recognize Yoko as a pioneer in their respective fields. The reassessment started in the art world. Since 2000, many of the world's major museums have staged retrospectives of her work. She was presented with the Golden Lion for Lifetime Achievement at the Venice Biennale in 2009. Writing about her 2014 Guggenheim Bilbao exhibition, art critic Jonathan Jones asked rhetorically, "Is there any contemporary art style that she did not pioneer?" The most comprehensive retrospective yet, *Yoko Ono: Music of the Mind,* opened at the Tate Modern in London in 2024—when she was ninety-one. The *Financial Times* review was headlined "The Conceptual Art Pioneer Gets Her Due."

Yoko's music was also reevaluated. Reissues of her early albums, which had mostly been ignored or panned, were lauded. A diverse array of musicians praised her. Kurt Cobain called her "the first female punk rocker." Pete Townshend observed, "She was one of the first art terrorists, combining deep morality with confrontation and shock." In 2020, the pop singer Miley Cyrus had a note from Yoko, including her signature, tattooed on her shoulder. Kim Gordon summed it up: "Yoko is still one of the most radical musicians today. She is so ahead of her time."

In the 2000s, remixes of Yoko's songs were played on rotation in clubs and bars around the world, and after twelve of her records hit number one on the

Billboard Dance Club chart, the *New York Times* crowned Yoko a "neo-disco queen." She went on to have thirteen number-one dance hits.

Meanwhile, she continually created new music, collaborating with cutting-edge artists. Her influence was acknowledged by musicians such as Gordon, Patti Smith, Thurston Moore, Laurie Anderson, Lady Gaga. and RZA. David Byrne said, "People were focusing on the Beatles, but out there on the edge of experimental music—with John Cage and people like that—Yoko was creating a new music: these beautiful, ethereal songs and also fierce songs that indicted war and inhumanity."

There was also a gradual shift in the way her lifetime of political action was viewed. She was an influential activist devoted to ending gun violence, combating hunger, eliminating nuclear weapons, and exposing and ending violence against women. She worked to raise awareness of and support treatment for AIDS and other diseases. She was an ardent environmentalist who celebrated nature. Mostly, she was recognized for her work for peace, more than half a century of performances, songs, poster and billboard campaigns, films, installations, protests, writings, and other advocacy. Rich Thomas wrote in *Magnetic* magazine, "Before there was Bono, there was Ono."

Yoko was also acknowledged as a pioneer of feminism. She made incendiary feminist art, including controversial works like "Cut Piece," the film *Fly*, and *Arising*, an interactive piece in which she asked women around the world to contribute stories about their suffering. Her songs "Woman Power," "Sisters, O Sisters," and "Angry Young Woman" became feminist anthems. Female liberation was the theme of her album *Feeling the Space*. Over decades, she inspired countless women. Cyndi Lauper said that when she was sixteen, Yoko opened her eyes to the way women were treated by society. "She broke the freakin' mold of what an artist could be and what a woman could be. She was sexy, expressed herself without restraint, and she was wild. She showed me how to leave the place where people told me, *Somebody has to come and fix you*. She told me it was okay to be who you were—who I was."

Finally, there was a shift in the way Yoko was perceived as a thinker. When I interviewed John in 1980, he told me, "She's the teacher and I'm the pupil.

I'm the famous one, the one who's supposed to know everything, but she's my teacher. She's taught me everything I fucking know." More people began to appreciate her for what John described as her "wisdom from another world." "Yoko's coming out of a hybrid Western and Eastern sense of postmysticism," DJ Spooky—Paul D. Miller—said. "She's a shaman. Shamans were transcendent figures who could guide you on an experience. That's how I view her."

Yoko suffered greatly but also experienced great joy. She offered her work with the intention of inspiring and healing. She combined art with activism, challenging individuals to take personal responsibility for global peace. Her message has been clear and consistent: Human suffering is universal but we're resilient. Together we can change the world.

IN 1980, WHEN I WAS twenty-four and a fledgling journalist, I landed a coveted assignment: to interview Yoko and John for *Playboy* magazine. I just had to get them to agree to it. In answer to my telegrammed request, Yoko's assistant called to ask when and where I had been born. The interview apparently depended on Yoko's readings of my astrological and numerological charts.

Evidently, the stars and numbers aligned. The next day, the assistant called to say that Yoko was considering my request and would meet me, so I flew to New York from Los Angeles. As instructed, I went to the Dakota apartment building on the Upper West Side.

The storied neogothic Dakota was so named because when it was constructed, in the early 1880s, its Upper West Side location was, within New York City, remote—like the Dakota Territory. In 1980, the building, which dominates the block from Seventy-Second to Seventy-Third Street on Central Park West, was known for a movie filmed there, Roman Polanski's *Rosemary's Baby*, and its celebrity residents, among them Lauren Bacall, Rudolf Nureyev, Leonard Bernstein, and, most famous of all, Yoko and John, who owned several apartments. They included the main residence, on the seventh floor, reached by a weary, groaning elevator with an ominous gargoyle that looked down on passengers. On the first floor was Studio One, Yoko's office, and there was an apartment that served mainly as a wardrobe closet. Elton John, a friend of Yoko and John's and godfather to their son, Sean, once sent the couple a teasing card with revised lyrics to the song "Imagine":

Imagine six apartments
It isn't hard to do
One is full of fur coats
Another's full of shoes.

After passing through the building's reception area, I found myself in Studio One. I walked through the outer office, past a wall of filing cabinets with cryptic labels—for example, APPLE, PALM BEACH, and HOLSTEIN COWS—reachable by a library ladder. There were bookshelves, framed posters, photographs, and a clock that was off by ten minutes. I removed my shoes as instructed before being escorted into Yoko's inner office.

Yoko is about five feet tall. "It is nice to keep oneself small," she once wrote, "like a grain of rice . . . make yourself dispensable, like paper." Her black hair was tied back. Even in the dim light, she wore dark wraparound sunglasses. She smoked a Nat Sherman cigarette. The first thing she said was "You have very strong numbers." She took a drag. "They're good with John's." An assistant brought us roasted twig tea.

I took in the room. Yoko's inner sanctum had a white carpet, a white couch, white chairs, and a sculpted white palm tree. There was a shoji screen and a piano. The walls were paneled wood and mirrored with glass cases that held Egyptian artifacts such as a grayed skull and a gold breastplate. A portrait of John and Sean, both with shoulder-length hair, hung on the wall. An ivory-and-jade-inlaid oak box rested on a glass coffee table cased in black iron; a gold snake slithered along a crossbar below the table. The trompe l'oeil ceiling was a painted sky.

Yoko told me about the project she and John were working on: an album—two, probably—"a dialogue between us, alternating songs, a couple talking to each other, telling a story."

I answered her questions about my concept of the interview. Trying to convince her to agree to participate, I brought her copies of previous *Playboy* interviews with, for example, Martin Luther King Jr., Albert Schweitzer, Bob Dylan, and President Jimmy Carter. After leafing through them, she responded, "People like Carter represent only their country. John and I represent the world."

Yoko told me that her reading of my astrological chart and my numbers had led her to conclude "This is a very important time for you," and she agreed to go forward, saying, "This interview will mean more than you can comprehend now." Then she dismissed me.

As I'd been instructed, I called her the next day, and she told me to come to the Dakota at noon. When I arrived, there was a message telling me to meet her and John at a nearby café.

THESE DAYS, JOURNALISTS ARE LUCKY to be allotted an hour or two with a movie or music star, but I spent almost three weeks with Yoko and John in September of 1980. I was with them most days from morning to night in their apartment, in Yoko's office, in coffee shops and restaurants, in the backs of limousines, and at recording studios. We took walks along Upper West Side streets and through Central Park. I interviewed them together and individually. They never once asked to go off the record. They were affectionate with each other. John lovingly teased her; in response, she rolled her eyes.

After I completed the interview and wrote the article, I returned to California. The magazine was scheduled to hit the stands in early December, but when my editor got an advance copy, he messengered it to the Dakota. Yoko called me in Los Angeles on the morning of Sunday, December 7. She left a message on my answering machine. When I returned the call, the phone was picked up but no one spoke. I was aware that John rarely answered the telephone, and when I heard a simple whistle on the other end of the line, I said I knew it was him. We talked for a while and then Yoko got on another extension. They were pleased with the interview. Yoko repeated that it was very important. We spoke for half an hour and discussed getting together when I returned to New York. The three of us had been going through their albums, one song at a time—John's Beatles songs, their collaborations, and their solo works, talking about their geneses and meanings—and I wanted to continue reviewing the songs we hadn't covered yet. Then we said goodbye.

The next night I was home watching *Monday Night Football*. The announcer Howard Cosell interrupted the game with the news that John had been shot and killed.

IT WAS INCONCEIVABLE. JOHN WAS dead. I tried to call Yoko, but I couldn't get through, so I packed a suitcase and caught a red-eye to New York. I took a cab to the Dakota, but it was impossible to get near the building. Thousands of people had been drawn there; the crowd spilled into Central Park. I got out and mourned with them.

I KNEW FROM OUR INTERVIEWS that Yoko and John had spent the previous five years, since Sean was born, living a quieter life than they ever had. John took on the rearing of Sean—he was the househusband—and Yoko managed the family business: their publishing companies, their stake in Apple, the Beatles record company, their legal cases, and their investments in art, antiquities, and property. At the time, their estate was rumored to be valued at one hundred and fifty million dollars. They had done some traveling, but by design, the Lennons were largely insulated. They had a handful of trusted friends but saw few others. As a result, when John died, Yoko was extremely isolated, and I became one of the people who circled the wagons around her as she struggled to survive a period she would later describe as the season of glass, when she was as fragile as glass and almost shattered.

In the years that followed, we became good friends, and I got close to Sean. I frequently visited them in New York and often stayed at the Dakota or at Yoko's Cold Spring Harbor estate. She was a night owl. Sometimes, in person or on the phone, we'd stay up talking through the night.

I interviewed Yoko for more articles and other projects, and I worked with her a few times. In 1983, I helped produce *Heart Play: Unfinished Dialogue*, a spoken-word record to promote the *Milk and Honey* album. The following year I helped assemble artists to cover her songs for the album *Every Man Has a Woman*. In 2000, she wrote the introduction to *All We Are Saying*, a book I published based on my interview with her and John. In 2008, I published a memoir about my family coping with the drug addiction of one of my children, and she readily granted me permission to quote lyrics from a song of John's and to borrow its title for the book: *Beautiful Boy*.

Over those years, I frequently traveled with Yoko. In 1987 I went with her to what was then the USSR for Mikhail Gorbachev's peace forum. I recall when Gorbachev quoted Lennon—*John* Lennon, not *Vladimir Ilyich* Lenin—to Yoko and the afternoon she and I were walking through the Arbat, Moscow's central thoroughfare, and Russian kids spotted her, gathered around, and sang "Imagine" in broken English. She was in tears.

I went with her and Sean to Japan. We traveled to Tokyo, Kyoto, and other cities, and I met members of her family, visited her ancestral and childhood homes, went to venues at which she'd performed before she knew John and to places they'd visited as a couple. Yoko and Sean also visited me in California. Sean came out on his own sometimes and stayed with my family. We went to Disneyland, and I took him surfing in Santa Cruz. I was often with Yoko and Sam Havadtoy, Yoko's boyfriend from 1981 to 2000 or so. I traveled with them to Japan, London, and LA, and to visit Sean at boarding school in Geneva. I was with her during some of the hardest years of her life, including when she was betrayed by people she trusted and when her life was threatened. For a short while, she, Sean, and Sam moved from New York to live near me in San Francisco because of threats on her and Sean's lives. I counseled her through some of those hard nights, but it was a two-way street. Yoko was a loyal friend who helped me and my family through our own turmoil. In *Beautiful Boy*, I tell the story of friends who helped save the life of my son, who was addicted to methamphetamine and living on the streets in San Francisco. These friends were Yoko and Sean. They brought him to stay with them in New York City and then to their upstate New York farm and got him into treatment for his addiction.

That was 2002. Yoko and I stayed in touch for more than a decade after that; I continued to see her in New York and San Francisco and we talked on the phone, but we slowly drifted apart.

I DECIDED TO WRITE HER biography in 2021. She had retired and had stopped granting interviews, but I'd interviewed her extensively over the years and knew her well. Still, I knew it would be hard to write Yoko's story because her life was complicated—and she was. Also, our friendship created a challenge. On one hand, my relationship with Yoko would allow me to write a book no one else could write. I had been present at events that no one else knew about and I had witnessed the impact of public events on her. Because I was there, I knew when certain press accounts and gossip were true and when they weren't. I saw sides of Yoko that others speculated about. I saw her at her worst, at her most paranoid and scared and despondent, but also at her best, when she was elated, creating, and inspired, exhibiting the kind of otherworldly wisdom John described.

But just as my friendship with Yoko allowed invaluable access and insights, it forced me to face a difficult and critical question: Can a journalist tell the truth about a friend? I wasn't interested in presenting a whitewashed version of Yoko's story—a friend's filtered idealization. Neither Yoko, nor Sean, nor their representatives read the manuscript of this book. Nonetheless, books written by friends of their subjects are inherently different from ones written by dispassionate biographers. There's a bias (I disclose mine at the outset), but many are uniquely insightful precisely because of the relationships between the authors and their subjects. I hope the reader finds that true here.

In this book, I didn't varnish the truth to depict Yoko as either a saint or a sinner. Instead, I did my best to strip the varnish away. I did my best to accurately reconstruct events and dialogue and report what actually happened. One thing I didn't have to do is surmise what Yoko is like. After decades of friendship, I know what she is like, and I did my best to show it.

In these pages, I expose Yoko's missteps and failures. I reveal the depth and sources of her pain and fear. I also show her profound wisdom, wit, humor, inspiration, talent, and joy; her resilience, compassion—her triumphs and genius.

Ultimately, this book is about more than a single person. To borrow from another Beatle, it's also a magical mystery tour through remarkable times and places. It's about how people are hurt and how they change. It's about survival. It's about those who see differently and think differently and suffer because of it. It's about art and creativity and the dream of peace.

When I look back on Yoko's ninety-plus years, I see one of the greatest stories of our time, a harrowing, exhilarating, and inspiring journey.

PART ONE

ABOVE US ONLY SKY

1933–1966

CHAPTER 1

"**M**Y PARENTS WERE CLOSE WITH each other but not with me," Yoko said once. "My father was very distant. When I was a child, if I wanted to see him, I would have to call his office and make an appointment. And my mother had her own life. She was beautiful and looked very young. She used to say, 'You should be happy that your mother looks so young.'"

Once Yoko said, "I adored my mother, but it wasn't reciprocated. She was too busy with her own life."

But though Yoko was profoundly hurt by her parents' neglect and resented them, she also expressed a kind of grudging respect for them. Of her mother, she once said, "I'm glad that my mother was that way rather than sitting around saying, 'My whole life was for you' . . . because that would have been a burden. I don't have that kind of sense of owing to her. . . . So in that sense, I admire her strength and intelligence. I had learned from my mother to be independent so I could survive as a person in the very high-pressure Yasuda-Ono family situation."

YOKO WAS NOT UNDERSTATING THE pressures imposed on her by the prominent family into which she was born. The Yasudas, her mother's side, were among the four most influential and wealthiest families in Japan from the late 1800s through World War II. The Yasuda *zaibatsu*—a family-owned conglomerate—included Yasuda Bank, once the largest in Japan (it became Fuji Bank). Yoko's father was a bank executive. "My mother used to say to me, 'Your father was only president of a bank, but my father *owned* one.'"

Isoko, Yoko's mother, was the granddaughter of Zenjiro Yasuda, who was once thought to be the richest man in Japan, according to the *New York Times*. "He was often referred to as 'the Japanese [J. P.] Morgan,' because, like his American counterpart, he was not only excessively wealthy but controlled the wealth of others through his banks." In addition to being a business leader, he dabbled in the arts, was devoted to Japanese traditions like the tea ceremony, and was a patron of Kabuki actors and sumo wrestlers. In his later years, Zenjiro became a philanthropist, donating the funds to build Yasuda Kōdō (Yasuda Auditorium) at the University of Tokyo and the Hibiya Open Air Concert Hall in Tokyo.

Isoko was the youngest child of Zenjiro's eldest daughter. (Zenjiro essentially adopted her husband so his son-in-law could take the family name.) Growing up, she had the run of an immense estate in Tokyo on which she rode horses and played in expansive gardens.

It was considered unacceptable for a woman in her family to have a career, but Isoko was allowed to pursue her passions. As she grew older, she was trained in painting, traditional singing, and musical instruments. Yoko described her mother as a *moga*—a "modern girl." There are photographs of Isoko wearing long, slinky dresses from Paris, strands of pearls, and bright lipstick. Her wavy hair was short and parted on the side like Greta Garbo's. Isoko attended lavish soirees, including one in the vacation resort of Karuizawa, where her family had a home in the woodsy outskirts of town. It was there she met Eisuke Ono, who was strikingly tall, cultured, handsome—and a musician.

THE FAMILY OF YOKO'S FATHER, Eisuke, traces its roots back to an impoverished samurai whose son, educated in the United States, was successful in business and eventually became president of the Industrial Bank of Japan.

From a young age, Eisuke was a gifted pianist and hoped to become a concert pianist. As a teenager, he performed concerts and recitals and was popular among the young set who summered with their families in Karuizawa. There, at a party at the vacation home of the Yasuda family, Eisuke met Isoko.

At the time, many marriages in Japan were arranged by matchmakers, but Isoko and Eisuke fell in love. "Grandmother told me many times that she chose my grandfather over countless other men who approached her family and herself in hopes to take her hand in marriage," Akiko Ono, Yoko's niece, recalled. Her family disapproved. The Onos were successful—Eisuke's father was also a bank executive—but the Yasuda fortune far surpassed the Onos'. Isoko's family was Buddhist; his was Christian. Also, a musician was unacceptable as a son-in-law. But that objection became moot when Eisuke acceded to his father's wish that he go into banking, reluctantly giving up his dream of being a musician. He attended Tokyo Imperial University, where he studied economics and mathematics. After graduating in 1927 at the age of twenty-five, he worked as a clerk in the Tokyo branch of Yokohama Specie Bank and rose through its ranks.

The Ono-Yasuda wedding, on November 3, 1931, was a glamorous affair attended by a who's who of Tokyo society.

The couple moved into a mansion among foreign embassies in one of Tokyo's most affluent neighborhoods. According to Yoko, Eisuke, rising at the bank, remained bitter that he had been pressured to abandon a career in music. Isoko tended the house, which mainly involved overseeing the more than thirty servants, and she continued to take painting and music lessons. She and Eisuke hosted glitzy parties. A member of the prestigious Sagami Country Club, Eisuke golfed three times a week.

In early February 1933, Eisuke moved to the United States to run the bank's operation in San Francisco. Isoko stayed in Tokyo. She was eight and a half months pregnant.

Isoko and Eisuke's daughter was born two weeks after he left, at eight thirty on the evening of February 18, 1933. She was named Yoko, which means "ocean child."

While Eisuke was abroad, Isoko lived with her parents on a Yasuda estate in Tokyo. Yoko knew her father only as a photograph. When she went to bed, her mother would show her a picture of Eisuke and tell her to "say good night to father."

There are family photographs and home movies that document Yoko's earliest years. In one snapshot, she's seated, holding a teddy bear, dressed in a onesie with a hood. In a movie, she crawls to her mother, who's asleep. Isoko wakes up and holds her daughter, gently snuggling and bouncing her.

Contradicting those images of a tender and attentive mother, as Yoko grew older, she became aware of Isoko's cold remove. She was glamorous, bigger than life, appearing and disappearing—out shopping, out to dinner. At parties Isoko threw, Yoko was brought out by a nanny so her mother's friends could ooh and aah, and then she was dismissed.

Yoko said Isoko pretended to be a doting mother for the home movies she sent to Eisuke: "She never spent so much time with me as she did when she was being filmed." Yoko said her mother "didn't really want to admit that she was a mother. She was always saying things like, 'Today I met so-and-so . . . they found out that I have children and they were so surprised! They couldn't believe it!' That kind of thing."

Although she was largely hands off herself, Isoko gave Yoko's nannies detailed instructions for her care. They were not to rock Yoko in their arms when they carried her because Isoko feared the motion would damage her brain. The staff was told not to help Yoko up if she fell. "I still remember vaguely several women in kimono staring at me without offering a hand while I was trying to get up from the ground," she wrote. She also recalled that the nannies were instructed to disinfect the seats of train cars with cotton balls soaked in alcohol when the family traveled. "My mother was germophobic," she continued. "As a result, I became a clean freak. Once I dropped a pencil I borrowed from a classmate sitting next to me because it was still warm from her body temperature. Even now I find it unpleasant to sit on a cushion or chair that still retains the temperature of somebody who had just been sitting there."

IN 1935, EISUKE SENT FOR Isoko and his daughter. Yoko was two and a half when she and her mother left Japan on the MS *Michuru*. Yoko would always remember the feeling of arriving in San Francisco—the bracing air, the light.

When Yoko and her mother disembarked, Eisuke was waiting on the dock wearing a long overcoat and a hat. He approached Isoko and kissed her. Then he noticed Yoko and gave her a perfunctory kiss. That was the first time she met her father.

As she grew older, she remembered Eisuke asking to see her hands. She held them out, and he responded curtly that they were too small for her to ever be a great pianist. "I think my hands actually shrunk when he said it," she said.

Yoko remarked on the disparity between the child in her family's home movies—tap dancing, playing—and her memories of loneliness and isolation. "I learned to show my parents what they wanted to see," she told me. "I wanted them to be proud of me, to like me. But I was very unhappy."

EISUKE SENT THE FAMILY BACK to Tokyo in 1937 when Japan went to war with China. Yoko was four and she now had a baby brother, Keisuke—Kei—who'd been born the year before.

For preschool, Isoko enrolled Yoko at Jiyū-Gakuen, the school Isoko had attended. It was a progressive school that focused on the arts, including singing and composing.

One of the teachers assigned the students to listen to sounds in the environment—the wind, birdsong—and translate them into musical notes. For

Yoko, translating sounds into musical notes came naturally. Of course, she didn't realize it at the time, but it was her introduction to conceptual art.

IN 1939, THE BANK TRANSFERRED Eisuke to its New York branch. A year later, on September 27, 1940, Japan signed the Tripartite Pact, officially allying itself with Germany and Italy. Isoko was afraid that the United States would soon stop allowing Japanese citizens to come to America, so she traveled to New York with Yoko and Kei to be with her husband.

The family lived in a suburb of New York City. Yoko, at seven, was sent to a public school. She experienced racism for the first time. "I would go to see a film and find that the baddies in the film were from Asia," she said. "People booing in the dark. Some people threw stones at us."

The family had to keep their house's windows closed because the neighbors complained about the smell of Japanese food. People yelled slurs as Yoko walked down the street with her parents. It was time to leave.

The Onos returned to Japan in February 1941, when Yoko turned eight. They left the United States just in time. The following year, over a hundred thousand Japanese Americans were forced from their homes and interned in "relocation centers."

Soon after the family returned to Tokyo, Eisuke was sent to Hanoi to be the assistant manager of the bank's branch there. Yoko was fatherless again.

YOKO BEGAN PIANO LESSONS WHEN she was three. As she grew older, she, like Isoko, was also tutored in traditional Japanese arts, including singing, calligraphy, and painting.

Few children were deemed suitable to play with her. "It didn't occur to me that I was supposed to play with people," she said. "My mother felt that the family would be taken advantage of if I had any friends."

Yoko was deeply lonely. She was alone so often that she'd ring for servants and ask for tea just so she could see another person.

Yoko survived her childhood by escaping into her imagination; her mind was her most reliable companion. She instinctively turned inward, spending hours sketching in a notebook and making up stories. She stared at the clouds and daydreamed. She found peace and safety in the constancy of the sky.

CHAPTER 2

O N DECEMBER 7, 1941, JAPAN attacked Pearl Harbor. The following day, December 8, the United States declared war on Japan. Eisuke was in Hanoi, where he'd become the bank's branch manager. Yoko was eight years old. She didn't understand what her father was doing; she knew only that he was gone. Eisuke had been absent for much of Yoko's life, but this was different. How could he have abandoned his wife and children—there was Yoko, Kei, and now a baby sister, Setsuko—during this dangerous time?

The war was confusing for a Japanese family with close ties to the United States. "Only a few months before that I was going to [an American] school pledging allegiance to the flag every morning," she said.

Initially, school in Japan continued uninterrupted, and Isoko did her best to carry on as if nothing had changed. However, by 1945 America was bombing Tokyo with impunity. There were nightly air raids. When sirens wailed, Isoko gathered her children and ran to the bomb shelter in their garden.

There was a radio in the shelter. Yoko listened to a program that broadcast the farewells of kamikaze pilots. "Before leaving, they were allowed to say something on the radio to their parents or family," Yoko told the BBC. "And they all said: 'Mummy, I'm going now, and I wish you a long life,' or something like that. It was just the most horrific thing that I've heard, and

I'll never forget that. . . . What an incredibly cruel thing to do to any human being. I think that changed my whole idea about war."

At school, there were drills in which the children would huddle under tables. At home, servants were conscripted or fled. There was chaos outside, and, always, Yoko's father was absent.

On March 9, 1945, wave after wave of bombers set Tokyo ablaze. Isoko hurried Kei and Setsuko into the bomb shelter, but because of Yoko's high fever, she was left in her bedroom. Through the window, she watched Tokyo burn.

Many of Yoko's classmates' families had fled to the mountains, but when Isoko decided to leave the city, she had a different plan. A friend had told her about a farming village in Nagano Prefecture, and Isoko pictured a bucolic rural community where her family could live until it was safe to return to Tokyo.

Isoko sent Yoko, now twelve, Kei, eight, and Setsuko, three, with the only remaining servant on a crowded train to the village in Nagano, where Isoko had bought a small home. When Yoko arrived, the roof was unfinished. With Isoko still in Tokyo, Yoko took on the role of adult, finding food for her brother and sister. She begged and bartered, trading kimonos, jewels, and antiques for rice.

When Isoko finally arrived, Yoko went with her to barter with more family possessions. Once, she and her mother had to pull their cart through a muddy rice paddy. She never forgot seeing her mother, who had always been impeccably dressed, covered with mud and looking "forlorn."

The local people "gave us a hard time," Yoko remembered. "They felt we were so spoiled [rich people from the city] and now it's our turn."

At the rural school Yoko and Kei attended, the other kids shunned and taunted them. She was called an American spy "for not singing the Japanese National Anthem fast enough." She recalled "being stoned by the village kids who hated people from the city."

Isoko often traveled back to Tokyo to retrieve more goods to trade. When she was gone, Yoko had to care for her brother and sister. "I found this farmhouse, and there was a pile of potatoes on the floor," she said. "I filled my knapsack with them—my knapsack was as large as I was—and it was so heavy I had to go two steps and rest, two steps and rest, all the way back to my village." Yoko and Kei foraged for mushrooms and mulberries.

The feeling of being afraid, ill, and starving—of wasting away—became a recurring theme in Yoko's art. The mental tricks she devised to survive also became central in her thinking and work. She continued to escape into the sky in her mind. She created imaginary feasts for her starving brother. Kei recalled her saying, "Eat this imaginary apple. It will fill you up." (He laughed. "It did fill her up—she was good at imagining—but those words didn't fill me up.")

Yoko was anemic and often sick due to malnutrition. At one point, she was diagnosed with pleurisy. She had to have her appendix removed, and because of a shortage of medications, the surgery was conducted without effective anesthetics. She was, as she would later reveal, abused by a doctor. In a future artwork, she described a doctor kissing her on the mouth.

These traumas shaped Yoko's life—she carried them with her. The lesson was clear: She could rely on no one but herself.

ON AUGUST 6, 1945, THE United States dropped an atomic bomb on Hiroshima. As many as 140,000 people died. Tens of thousands more died from injuries and radiation poisoning in the months and years to come. On August 9, a second atomic bomb was dropped on Nagasaki, where some seventy thousand more were killed. Japan surrendered on August 15.

Since they had no radio at their home in the countryside, Yoko's family didn't know the war had ended until Yoko went to school. She returned to Isoko and told her the news.

Four months later, Isoko decided to bring the family back to Tokyo, but according to her daughter-in-law Masako Ono, Isoko "was hopeless; she couldn't do anything," and it was left to Yoko, at twelve, to find a truck and hire a driver for the journey. They loaded their few remaining possessions into the truck, climbed in, and headed to the capital.

Yoko was stunned when they arrived. "Tokyo, this is Tokyo!" she would recall thinking. "It was a big field of nothing, people living in shacks."

ISOKO HAD NO CONTACT WITH Eisuke for over a year, but in early 1946, she received word from a relative, a diplomat, that her husband had been interned in Vietnam but was alive and would be coming home. Setsuko remembered Eisuke entering the gate in front of the house. "I saw this tall, handsome man approaching us. Everybody was so happy when he came home. My mother was joyous." Yoko saw him embrace her mother and remembered the pain she felt when she was two and a half and met her father the first time. Again, he was elated to see Isoko but hardly acknowledged Yoko or his other children. Although Yoko hadn't become inured to her father's physical and emotional absence (his remoteness would always be a factor in her life, feeding her self-doubt and influencing her relationships), for the first time, she was able to see inside him. He'd been a victim in the war. She realized his vulnerability, and her view of him shifted. Her resentment morphed into compassion. She saw that he suffered too.

AFTER THE WAR, JAPAN'S ECONOMY was in tatters, and the Ono and Yasuda family fortunes were greatly diminished. Yasuda and the other *zaibatsu* were dismantled. Eisuke's Yokohama Specie Bank was reorganized as the commercial Bank of Tokyo. Eisuke became an adviser to the new bank and then resumed his role as an executive.

Life for the Onos slowly returned to normal. Isoko did what was expected of her as a Japanese executive's wife: She entertained Eisuke's business associates and golf buddies. Yoko still had little contact with him. "My father had a huge desk in front of him that separated us permanently," she wrote. One meeting with Eisuke stuck out in Yoko's mind. "He was going somewhere, and we were all at the airport to see him off. About twenty people. And my father was like a politician. He just shook hands with everybody down the line with a half-smile that you put on when you shake hands. I was at the end of the line, and he did the same to me—stretched out his hand and said, 'Thank you very much for coming,' with that same smile. And I was crying, but my mother thought I was rather silly."

Eisuke played piano at parties and sometimes made Yoko perform too. Seated at the piano—the guests staring, Eisuke's eyes fixed on her—she could barely breathe; she was terrified she would make a mistake. She said she never once felt she had pleased him.

The self-doubt and shame caused by her father's criticism and her parents' neglect of her and always being the "other"—whether in the East or West, city or country—intertwined with the trauma of the war. Her nightmares became darker. She began having earaches so severe that she would lie in a dark room wearing sanitary pads like earmuffs to block out sound. She panicked sometimes without knowing why. She was afraid she would stop breathing. Sitting alone in her room, she counted her breaths, thinking: "My God, if I didn't count them, would I not breathe?"

At other times she held her breath. "And then I realized I hadn't taken a breath for minutes. I was afraid I'd die. I was afraid I'd disappear."

As she grew older, Yoko spent most of her time alone. She was plagued by self-doubt and mistrust. She felt that no one understood her. Her depression was unbearable sometimes. There seemed no way out. It led her to attempt suicide; later, she spoke about multiple attempts as a teenager. She survived by turning inward, daydreaming—once again staring at the sky—and writing, drawing, and composing. Art saved her.

AFTER JIYŪ-GAKUEN, YOKO WAS SENT to Keimei Gakuen, a Christian academy, and then Gakushūin junior and senior high schools, which she compared to Eton in England. She was mostly isolated from other children, but she was involved in the drama club, acting in and directing plays. The academics were rigorous, and the rigor continued at home, where she was tutored in languages and religion. She was forced to continue on piano. The pressure to play was suffocating.

When Eisuke was home in Tokyo, he sometimes had Yoko play duets with him. Rather than looking forward to those times as rare occasions to be with her father, she dreaded them. She craved his approval, but the only feedback he gave was to point out her mistakes.

Piano gave her little joy then, but Yoko loved writing. She filled notebooks with reflections, stories, drawings, and haiku and other poems. Indeed, she thought that someday she might like to become a writer, but her teachers were dismissive of her work. Because of their constant criticism, she thought she couldn't be a writer. She already knew she wouldn't be a pianist. She decided she wanted to become a composer—rather than play others' music, she'd write her own. She enjoyed composing in school, and Eisuke deified composers, so she hoped he'd be pleased. Nonetheless, she was nervous when she summoned the courage to tell him about her decision.

"My father was listening very carefully, very silently, and said, 'Hmmm—well I think that's a mistake' . . . He's one of those very classic persons, believes in the three big Bs—you know, Brahms, Bach and Beethoven, and all three of them happen to be men, as he politely mentioned. He thought that music composition . . . is a field that was too hard for women." He told Yoko that she had a good voice and suggested that she become an opera singer instead. She said he believed that "for women it's an easier thing to do—to sing somebody else's songs."

Complying with her father's wishes, Yoko continued with her singing lessons, focusing on German lieder and opera. When she was a high school senior, Eisuke advised her to take the entrance exam for the Tokyo College of Music.

Yoko had other plans. Eisuke was working at the Bank of Tokyo in New York City; she sent him a telegram in which she said she'd decided not to take the music exam. She asked for his permission to go to university and study philosophy instead. Her father agreed, in part because he respected his daughter's intelligence but, Kei said, "also because he knew she was stubborn."

CHAPTER 3

A S YOKO APPLIED TO COLLEGE, she received mixed messages from her parents about marriage. Isoko told Yoko that women and men were equal and that Yoko could have any career she wanted—she could even be prime minister of Japan. Isoko sometimes talked about marriage stifling a woman's ability to live a meaningful life. At the same time, marrying someone suitable—meaning someone with wealth and position—was the expected path for her. Her mother obsessed about Yoko marrying well and worried that she would not be able to find someone appropriate. Contradicting herself, Isoko chastised Yoko for her independence, saying, "Well, Yoko, you're too opinionated, you show your intelligence too much, and that's not going to work because nobody will want to marry you."

Once, her parents asked an uncle to introduce Yoko to candidates. He held a dance at his summer residence in the mountains, a kind of coming-out party for Yoko and her cousin. It was a glamorous event to which a dozen bachelors were invited. Infuriating her parents, Yoko hung out with the hired musicians, spending most of the time smoking and chatting with the piano player.

———

YOKO WAS ACCEPTED TO THE prestigious Gakushūin University to study philosophy, and she matriculated in the fall of 1952. It was an exhilarating time to be in college in Tokyo. Yoko's generation had been radically altered by the war and its aftermath. Many of Yoko's peers were emerging from the traumatic experience engaged, politicized, and hopeful about building a better future for Japan.

Yoko was the first female student in the philosophy department at Gakushūin. At first, she devoured books and participated eagerly in class discussions, but within months, she became disillusioned by what she viewed as the rigidity of academic thinking at the university and the sexism she experienced in the department. Yoko began to feel that philosophy, at least as it was taught at Gakushūin, "failed to consider emotion and the psychological side" of people, and as a result, "it was theoretical—cold and dead."

Her parents were disappointed and exasperated when she dropped out after only two semesters.

At the time, Eisuke was working at the Bank of Tokyo branch in New York City, and he and Isoko were living in Scarsdale. Yoko followed her family to New York and enrolled in a very different sort of college: Sarah Lawrence, in Bronxville.

Sarah Lawrence was founded as an all-women's college in 1926. The composer Meredith Monk wrote that Sarah Lawrence "teaches you that you have the right and duty to be what some people would call a troublemaker." For Yoko, it was a place where she could pursue composition, art, literature, and more.

Betty Rollin, a classmate of Yoko's who later became a renowned journalist, recalled a contingent of Sarah Lawrence girls "with framed photographs of their horses set carefully on their chests of drawers. It's safe to say that neither Yoko nor I were part of that group. . . . I was among another contingent, from liberal Jewish families, but Yoko was her own contingent."

Erica Abeel, also a classmate, was a dance student who went on to become a novelist. Abeel remembered Yoko fitting into one particular group of Sarah Lawrence girls: "[The school] attracted a certain artistic, high-strung nonconformist, which described Yoko perfectly. She was in tune with that segment of the student body. She was all about ideas. Creating work. Obsessed with creating."

Though Rollin said Yoko seemed aloof, Abeel said that "the aloofness seemed more of a function of shyness than snobbism. People don't think of Yoko as shy, but she was."

She was ambitious too. Rollin said, "She would roll over anyone she perceived as standing in the way of her artistic vision. If you didn't interest her, you didn't exist." Rollin brought Yoko home to spend a weekend with her family. "Yoko was shocked by my relationship with my parents," she said. "My Jewish mother was involved in our lives. We laughed and talked. Yoko marveled; she told me her mother was cold and formal and her father was like a foreign figure—she had to make an appointment to see him. I thought she must be exaggerating to make a point, but I asked her; she wasn't. You felt that weight on her—someone without mooring, drifting, lost, and striving. You felt [her] envy—not about anything material, but about my connection to my family."

Yoko had friendly acquaintances at Sarah Lawrence but no close friends. She did have boyfriends. One person she dated was Mel Woody, a Yale student who was friends with and had also dated Sylvia Plath (he was the inspiration for Cal in *The Bell Jar*). As Plath's biographer Heather Clark wrote, "Mel had started dating Yoko Ono, whom he met at a Sarah Lawrence mixer. ('She was clearly the most beautiful girl, but she was Japanese so no one was dancing with her.')"

In an interview, Woody recalled, "I danced with Yoko. Then, Yoko and I went up on a patio or balcony overlooking the woods and the campus, and we talked. And that was very pleasant. And then I got back on the bus and went back to New Haven."

That led to dates. She told Woody that she'd attempted suicide when she was a teenager. Eventually, he worried about Yoko "getting too attached" and ended the relationship.

———

AFTER THE RIGID ACADEMICS AT Gakushūin, Yoko was glad to study what she wanted to in this progressive environment, unconstrained by what she saw as irrational and artificial borders between academics and the arts. She painted, sculpted, and wrote poetry and short stories, but she had not let go of the dream dismissed by her father: She wanted to compose. Andre Singer, who taught music theory, composition, and piano, introduced her to twelve-tone music, a radical departure from traditional music, developed in the early twentieth century by Arnold Schoenberg and other composers. This fundamentally different sound (atonal, dissonant) excited her. She considered classical music her "family's bag," and she was finding something of her own in the work of these innovative composers.

As the months passed, Yoko spent less time in classes and more time in the music library, where she donned headphones, sat in a soundproof booth, and listened to the composers Singer and others introduced her to. Their work inspired her and, more important, validated her own explorations. Yoko began to experiment with twelve-tone compositions. She also began to incorporate words into some of her pieces. "I was writing in the style of atonal songs but with poetry on top of it," she said.

ONE DAY, YOKO, IN HER bedroom at her parents' Scarsdale home, became aware of birdsong. She recalled the whimsical lesson at Jiyū-Gakuen when the teacher had the students listen to sounds in nature and create a "score." That morning, she realized that the birdsong was far too complex to capture. Yoko first thought it was her own inadequacy—she didn't have the ability as a composer. Then she realized that it wasn't a lack of skill but the limitations of musical scoring. "If you wished to bring in the beauty of natural sounds into music, suddenly you noticed that the traditional way we scored music in the West was not the way," she told Hans Ulrich Obrist in an interview. "So I decided to combine notes with instructions."

She took out a sheet of paper and composed a score that would incorporate the true sound of birdsong. She titled it "Secret Piece" and wrote, "Decide on one note that you want to play. Play it with the following accompaniment: The woods from 5 a.m. to 8 a.m. in summer." Above a music staff, she wrote, "with the accompaniment of the birds singing at dawn."

She'd found a way to capture the sound of nature.

BESIDES COMPOSING, YOKO WROTE POEMS and stories, including some that were published in *The Campus*, Sarah Lawrence's school newspaper. A short story, "Of a Grapefruit in the World of Park," ran in its October 26, 1955, edition. It was about a group of friends on a picnic. A grapefruit is left uneaten, and the group considers what to do with it. A boy tosses the grapefruit, jabs it with a pencil, peels it, and then destroys it. The grapefruit would become a recurring theme in Yoko's writing and art.

Curator Christophe Cherix observed, "The grapefruit, a citrus hybrid, would soon become a metaphor of hybridity in Ono's work, conveying both a personal point of view—her crossing of the Eastern and Western worlds—and a new artistic approach able to combine existing disciplines."

Yoko initially thrived at Sarah Lawrence but became bored by the classes and annoyed by many of the teachers and students, especially because few people responded to what she was doing. The college was far more progressive than the university in Tokyo, but she still felt stifled.

In addition, living at home with her parents was oppressive—their reactions to her ranged from dismissal to exasperation, and their disappointment in the direction she was heading was infuriating. They talked about how women could do anything, but they still expected her to get married and settle down.

When she was younger, her anxiety had led her to hold her breath or count her breaths, fearing she'd stop breathing if she stopped counting. Now she sometimes sat in her room and lit matches one after another, watching them burn until they went out and left a plume of smoke.

"I was doing all that just to prevent myself from going mad, really," she later said.

YOKO FREQUENTLY ESCAPED TO NEW York City, especially Greenwich Village, where a cultural renaissance was under way. This was 1956, when the Beat Generation movement was at its height. Allen Ginsberg's epic poem "Howl" was released that year; Jack Kerouac's *On the Road* came out a year later. Miles Davis and John Coltrane were performing regularly at Café Bohemia. Yoko attended poetry readings, exhibitions, and concerts with Erica Abeel or others or on her own.

"We'd often go into the city to hang out in the Village at cafés like the Figaro and San Remo bar, which was then a Beat hangout. Gregory Corso would peddle poems at the San Remo in exchange for a plate of pasta," Abeel recalled.

"My crowd also knew people involved in starting up Off Broadway theater so we'd go see productions, say, of *The Balcony* by Jean Genet, and a whole raft of Beckett plays. . . . We were awfully arty."

As she gravitated toward the city, Yoko was increasingly disillusioned by college. One reason was frustration about the reception of her work. "Whenever I wrote a poem, they said it was too long, it was like a short story; a novel was like a short story, and a short story was like a poem. I felt that I was like a misfit in every medium."

She had slowly withdrawn mentally from school and officially dropped out at the end of her junior year in 1956. She described herself as feeling "asphyxiated by conservative teachers." In her view, even Sarah Lawrence was limited in comparison to the thrilling art and music scene she was discovering in New York City.

CHAPTER 4

I N EARLY 1956 AT A recital Yoko was attending, a man approached her and mentioned that they'd met a few years earlier in Japan at her uncle's party in Karuizawa. It was where she was supposed to meet her future banker or diplomat husband. He'd been the piano player. To her parents' chagrin, Yoko had spent the evening with him, smoking and talking. Yoko remembered him. They had a lot in common.

Toshi Ichiyanagi was born in Kobe. Like Yoko, he was twenty-three—their birthdays were two weeks apart. Also like her, Toshi had taken piano lessons since he was three. By his teens, he was identified as a prodigy and began to win competitions. At twenty-one, he moved to New York to attend Juilliard.

Toshi spoke softly but was articulate and thoughtful. Their backgrounds were similar—both of them educated in Western and Japanese art and music—and they were excited by the scene in New York.

At Juilliard, Toshi initially immersed himself in traditional classical music but discovered experimental music, including the work of the twelve-tone composers who had inspired Yoko. He studied the music of Schoenberg, Anton Webern, and others considered the fathers of electronic music, and he was enamored of John Cage, who was revered as a kind of guru in New York's avant-garde scene.

Toshi was a star student who was developing into a virtuoso pianist. He held recitals and performed concerts at the college and at other New York City halls.

They began a romance, Yoko's first serious one. Part of the attraction on Yoko's part may have been the fact that her parents would be horrified by the prospect of Toshi—the piano player at the Karuizawa party!—as a son-in-law. Indeed, when Yoko and Toshi became engaged, Isoko and Eisuke were mortified. They opposed the marriage because Toshi didn't have much money, didn't come from a prominent family, and was a musician. They weren't convinced even when Yoko pointed out their hypocrisy: Eisuke's family was less well off than the Yasudas, and he too had been a musician.

Yoko and Toshi married. Though they were unhappy about the marriage, Isoko and Eisuke nonetheless hosted a reception "because of social pressure," according to Beate Gordon, a friend of Yoko's who attended. The guests were a mix of Eisuke's business associates and Yoko and Toshi's friends from the music and art worlds. Yoko wore a "scandalous" (according to Gordon) short white dress.

From that point on, Eisuke and Isoko cut Yoko off financially. The couple lived frugally. Toshi earned a bit from playing concerts and copying musical scores. Yoko worked part-time as a typist. Both of them were employed by Gordon, who ran the performing arts department of the Japan Society. They were paid to demonstrate Japanese folk arts at universities and colleges. Yoko appeared in kimono, recited haiku, demonstrated calligraphy and origami, and interpreted for Gordon's tea-ceremony presentations. She was paid twenty-five dollars per demonstration.

THROUGH HER SARAH LAWRENCE CONNECTIONS and Toshi's at Juilliard, they met other artists who'd also been drawn to the Greenwich Village scene. They shared a desire to make art that was the antithesis of uptown art, which they saw as traditional and conservative. Many were influenced by Dada and Marcel Duchamp and inspired by Cage, who was at the center of the movement.

Galvanized by this community, Yoko continued to work on her compositions. They reflected her mental state, which was ever changing, swinging from elation to depression and sometimes mingling them.

Even a work that could be seen as pure Zen poetry—the single-word instruction "Breathe"—was born out of the trauma of war and Yoko's distress as a young child when she had to remind herself to breathe because she was afraid she'd forget and die. "Lighting Piece," also called "Match Piece" (the instruction: "Light a match and watch till it goes out"), was born of the time she was compulsively lighting matches, staring at the flames until they expired.

YOKO WAS MAKING ART NONSTOP but wasn't showing it publicly. "I couldn't figure out how to present my work, because I didn't know how to communicate with people," she said. "And I didn't know how to explain to people how shy I was."

The people who surrounded her didn't help. Toshi provided companionship, and she respected him, but though he was soft-spoken, he was domineering, as were the other men in "the scene," who would monopolize conversations and dominate collaborations. The men around Yoko continued to treat women as inferior, both intellectually and artistically. She'd get together with the male artists and talk ideas, and still she'd be asked to make tea.

THE ARTISTS IN YOKO'S CIRCLE were in awe of and inspired by the composer John Cage. They called him JC—as in Jesus Christ.

Cage's most famous work debuted on August 29, 1952, at a concert hall in Woodstock, New York. Called 4′33″, the piece had taken him five years to complete. Pianist David Tudor sat down before a Steinway on an otherwise empty stage. Tudor sat erect. Then it began. He closed the cover over the piano keys and commenced to play . . . nothing. At prescribed intervals between the piece's three movements, he opened and closed the lid of the keyboard. Tudor didn't play one note. After four minutes and thirty-three seconds, he walked off the stage. That was it. "It has been called 'the Silent Piece,' but its purpose is to make people listen," Alex Ross explained in his 2010 profile of Cage in the *New Yorker*. He quoted Cage: "There's no such thing as silence. You could hear the wind stirring outside during the first movement. During the second, raindrops began pattering the roof, and during the third people themselves made all kinds of interesting sounds as they talked or walked out."

Some people did walk out, and many were angered, but it was a seminal performance in the history of avant-garde music.

IN THE LATE 1950s, TOSHI enrolled in a course Cage taught, called Experimental Composition, at the New School for Social Research in Manhattan. Yoko wasn't enrolled but accompanied him to one of Cage's lectures. Many of those in that avant-garde crowd—including Yoko and Toshi—also attended talks by D. T. Suzuki, a Japanese scholar and writer, at Columbia University. Cage was there too. One night, a composer, Stefan Wolpe, introduced Yoko and Cage at the Russian Tea Room. They met again after a concert at Carnegie Recital Hall. She admired Cage's vision and work. Also, she said, "What Cage gave me was a confidence that the direction I was going in was not crazy. It was accepted in the world called 'the avant-garde.'"

With Cage at its heart, the New York avant-garde art scene was vibrant with nightly exhibitions, concerts, poetry readings, performances, and "happenings." Artists, writers, dancers, poets, composers, actors, and musicians created and collaborated on work that pushed the boundaries of art. Yoko met more composers in Cage's circle and other artists working independently and together.

———

YOKO AND HER ARTIST FRIENDS wanted to show their work, but it was challenging for them to find venues to stage their events. In late 1960, she went looking for space downtown, where rent was cheap. At 112 Chambers Street, a building a couple of blocks from the Hudson River, she saw a sign advertising a rental. The top floor was a two-thousand-square-foot rectangle. There was no hot water or electricity. Dim light came in through dirty windows. Yoko loved it and signed a lease in December. The rent was $50.50 a month.

One day, composer Richard Maxfield called and said that he and La Monte Young, also a renowned composer in the avant-garde scene, wanted to hold concerts and needed a space. Yoko and Young began coproducing what became an historic series of loft concerts at 112 Chambers Street. The first concert took place on Sunday, December 18, 1960, soon after she signed the lease. "I hadn't figured out how to wire it yet," Yoko explained. "But it was beautiful. We did it under candlelight."

It snowed that day and she worried that no one would come, but about twenty people, including Tudor, Cage, and Cage's partner, dancer and choreographer Merce Cunningham, did come. The event featured Terry Jennings, a composer, saxophonist, and pianist. Toshi and Young also performed that night. A flyer said it was informal and people should "come prepared to sit on the floor." A one-dollar donation was requested.

The second event in the loft series was a concert by Toshi. Yoko was one of nine performers who participated that night. The series continued for seven months and featured a wide range of artists, musicians, dancers, and poets.

Yoko never headlined a loft performance, but she showed her work at others' concerts. She displayed early iterations of instruction paintings, including "Painting to Be Stepped On," a piece of canvas on the floor waiting—as in its title—to be stepped on. The footprints that accumulated on the canvas completed the piece. The work was inspired by stepping paintings in fifteenth-century Japan. As Yoko explained, "A 'stepping painting' (*fumie*) was used to distinguish Christians from non-Christians. A person was asked to step on the portrait of Christ. Those who could not were immediately taken away to be crucified. Most Japanese Christians refused to step on the portrait, despite the consequences, which they were aware of. As a young child, I was terrified by the story, but I also promised myself that I would be a person who adhered to her principles just as the Japanese Christians did. Later, in New York, I felt the urge to release myself from that little girl in me and to step on a painting."

Yoko debuted other works at the loft. They included "Pea Piece," which had the score "Carry a bag of peas. Leave a pea wherever you go." The piece evolved over time, as her works often did. For the iteration in her loft, she threw peas at the audience while whipping her long hair in circles. (The sound of her moving hair was the "music.") "Pea Piece" evoked the rural Japanese ritual of throwing beans to ward off demons.

She also performed "Kitchen Piece," which had the instructions "Hang a canvas on the wall. Throw all the leftovers you have that day on the canvas. You may prepare special food for the piece." Yoko threw eggs and Jell-O at a huge piece of canvas attached to the wall, splashed sumi ink on the surface and wiped it around with her hands, then lit the canvas on fire.

"Kitchen Piece" was performed at a time when an American woman's place was still considered to be in the kitchen. Betty Friedan's seminal work *The Feminine Mystique*, which exposed the "problem that has no name"—that is, the depression and malaise suffered by American housewives—wasn't published until 1963. "Kitchen Piece" could be interpreted as a demonstration of the rage American women felt about the role they'd been saddled with, but like much of Yoko's work, it was playful and humorous. It poked fun at the status quo.

The late 1950s and early 1960s was a time of extreme conservatism in American culture. TV shows like *Leave It to Beaver* and *Father Knows Best* painted a portrait of idealized white American domesticity. Every mother was a homemaker. There was almost zero representation of people of color on American TV screens aside from grossly stereotypical portrayals. Couples could not be shown sleeping in the same bed. And it wasn't until *Psycho*, in

1960, that a flushing toilet was allowed to be seen in a feature film—and then only after director Alfred Hitchcock convinced the censors it was essential to the film's plot.

Against this backdrop of repression and intense moralizing, Yoko and her fellow artists created their irreverent works. Some of Yoko's conceptual pieces were pure whimsy, but in others she was illuminating the hypocrisy and cruelty of a system designed to keep women and those who didn't fit into society's rigid constraints in their place. Yoko was at the forefront of a movement that was challenging the old ways of thinking. She and her friends were making a revolution with art and ideas.

YOKO CONTINUALLY PRODUCED NEW WORK, but she never had a solo event or headlined a concert in the loft series. She was constantly upstaged by the male artists, including Toshi, and La Monte Young increasingly took sole credit for producing the series, pushing Yoko aside. Once he introduced Yoko to a reporter as the "chick who owns this loft."

"Women in art were only known for being 'lays,'" Yoko said. "'Oh, that girl' they would say, 'she's been with so-and-so, and with so-and-so. She's been around.' Though men sleep around just as much, they never get that! They are not going to be known as so-and-so's boyfriend." It's easy to forget how sexist the art world was then.

But Cage recognized her contribution. "Yoko became an important person in the New York avant-garde," he said. "People came from long distances to attend the performances. They were the most interesting things going on."

THOUGH YOKO NEVER HAD A solo concert at the loft, she showed her work there and elsewhere. She was part of "An Evening of Contemporary Japanese Music and Poetry," which took place on April 3, 1961, at the Village

Gate, a jazz nightclub. She was one of three composers on the bill—the others were Toshi and Toshiro Mayuzumi. She recited poems and narrated *A Grapefruit in the World of Park,* a performance sharing the title with the short story she'd published in the Sarah Lawrence college newspaper. Beate Gordon, who was in the audience, remembered an empty baby carriage being pulled across the stage by a wire as Yoko chanted:

let's count the hairs of the dead child
let's count the hairs of the dead child

Yoko read the text while performers, including Toshi, John Cage, La Monte Young and David Tudor, acted out her instructions, improvising, "for instance by laughing aloud or playing atonal music," according to MoMA curator Christophe Cherix. "At times, the work was irreverent—as when a toilet was heard flushing during the action—and at others somber and dark, but as a whole it was deeply personal and experimental in its attempt to bring together poetry, music, theater and performance."

YOKO CONTINUED TO EXPERIMENT WITH "instructionalizing" pieces. She created entire events from a line of text. There was "Laugh Piece" ("Keep laughing a week"), "Cough Piece" ("Keep coughing a year"), and "Wall Piece for Orchestra" ("Hit a wall with your head"). The instruction for "Hide and Seek Piece" read "Hide until everybody goes home. Hide until everybody forgets about you. Hide until everybody dies."

In a letter to Cage, Yoko explained, "My music is performed only to induce a situation in which people can listen to their own mind music."

An essential component of Yoko's instruction pieces was that they disrupted the relationship between the viewer or listener and the artist. Like many artists in the Greenwich Village scene, she considered the art world and art itself to be elitist and detached from the lives of most people. With her instruction paintings, the audience was drawn in as participants—indeed, cocreators. Rather than having a prescribed composition of notes and chords on a musical staff to guide, dictate, and limit the audience's experience, Yoko's scores released them, allowing them to follow their imaginations and instincts.

Yoko's score for "Water Piece" (1964) read, "Steal a moon on the water with a bucket. Keep stealing until no moon is seen on the water." If you watch people contemplate the instructions in this composition, you'll see how it accomplishes Yoko's goal. Their faces change as they engage with the piece. It inevitably makes them smile. That smile is the genius in Yoko's instruction pieces.

In 1965, she created "Self Portrait," which was a mirror in a manila envelope. You opened the envelope, pulled out a mirror, and saw—yourself. It wasn't the artist's self-portrait; it was *yours*. "Self Portrait" metamorphosed into "Box of Smile." In 1971, she created small plastic boxes inscribed A BOX OF SMILE Y.O. Open it and there was a mirror inside. When you saw yourself, you got it—your smile was in the box. You completed the piece.

CHAPTER 5

I N THE EARLY SPRING OF 1961, Yoko got a call from a friend who told her that a guy who had come to a loft performance was planning to open his own gallery to hold similar events. The friend told Yoko that all of her artists were moving to this new space.

George Maciunas, from Kaunas, Lithuania, had, like many artists in her circle, been profoundly influenced by Cage's Experimental Composition class at the New School. Also like them, he was interested in Dada and Eastern philosophy, especially Zen Buddhism. He met La Monte Young in the Cage class. Young introduced Maciunas to more people in that avant-garde crowd and told him about the loft series. Maciunas came to a performance.

After Maciunas attended the loft event, he was inspired to open his own exhibition and performance space. He rented one on the upper floor at 925 Madison Avenue and called it AG Gallery. He began producing exhibitions and events, including ones by artists who'd also shown at Yoko's loft.

Yoko was concerned about someone stealing her idea until Maciunas called her and invited her over. She liked him and was thrilled when he said he wanted to give her a solo show.

She worked feverishly. She planned to show two types of work. For the rear of the gallery, she created abstract calligraphy paintings in sumi ink. The rest of the gallery was filled with instruction paintings. Pieces included "Water-drop Painting," which consisted of a bottle of water hanging upside down. The water dripped through a pinhole and fell on a piece of canvas. The AG Gallery space had no electricity (it was cut off when the bill wasn't paid), but as Yoko later said, that "actually worked to my advantage" for another piece, "Shadow Painting." Pieces of canvas were hung beside a window. "Sunlight streaming through the gallery windows cast shadows on the canvases, making beautiful natural changes to them throughout the day," Yoko explained.

Yoko and Maciunas made a flyer for the show, and word spread through their network of artists. The exhibition opened on July 16, 1961, for a two-week run.

The exhibition was important in Yoko's career, although few people came. Cage came. Artist Isamu Noguchi did too. He stepped on "Painting to Be Stepped On" "with a pair of elegant Zohri slippers."

The sparse attendance was disappointing, but it didn't stop Yoko and Maciunas from judging the exhibition a success. Her show was the final exhibition at AG Gallery. Maciunas ran out of money and closed the gallery, but he was undiscouraged. He immediately moved on to a new obsession.

MACIUNAS HAD IDENTIFIED CAGE AND other artists in that circle, including Yoko and Toshi, as part of an art movement. They were united by their unconventional approaches to art and their resistance to working in a single art form—like Yoko, many mixed and matched painting, music, performance, dance, poetry, film, sculpture, and photography. Rather than discrete objects, they made events designed to engage the audience in unexpected ways.

Maciunas believed these artists should be united as a community modeled after artists' collectives in Europe. He decided to give the movement a name, and he consulted Yoko, but she bristled. A "movement" was, for her, antithetical to art that had broken free of the past—of movements.

But Maciunas was determined. He showed up one day lugging a huge dictionary. He opened it and excitedly pointed to a word: *fluxus*. "It had many meanings, but he pointed to 'flushing,'" Yoko recalled. "'Like toilet flushing!' he said laughing, thinking it was a good name for the movement. 'This is the name,' he said. I just shrugged my shoulders in my mind."

INSPIRED BY THE DADA MANIFESTO by Tristin Tzara, Maciunas wrote a manifesto for Fluxus. The movement's mission: "Purge the world of bourgeois sickness, 'intellectual,' professional, & commercialized culture. PURGE the world of dead art, imitation, artificial art, illusionist art, mathematical art. PURGE THE WORLD OF "EUROPANISM!" Fluxus would "PROMOTE A REVOLUTIONARY FLOOD AND TIDE IN ART. Promote living art, anti-art, promote NON ART REALITY to be grasped by all peoples, not only critics, dilettantes and professionals."

Yoko wasn't the only one who resisted joining Maciunas's movement. No artists signed the manifesto. But regardless of her ambivalence about being part of a movement, Yoko was immersed in the world of Fluxus artists, who were reinventing art. Alexandra Munroe, a curator and art scholar, said, "You have no idea how bold it was to make [this] art. . . . You're dealing in the 1960s with a framework of what art is, and it is a painting on the wall at Leo Castelli. Everything Fluxus was about was scrappy, ephemeral, gesture. It was a performance—it wasn't meant to last."

Yoko and other artists who were part of or on the periphery of Fluxus attended one another's events, collaborated, and supported each other. They were creating a kind of found family of artists and intellectuals. But even here, among them, Yoko felt separate. She also felt increasingly distant from Toshi—she concluded they shouldn't have gotten married. As usual, to combat her feelings of loneliness and depression, she immersed herself in work.

YOKO HELD HER FIRST MAJOR solo concert, *Works by Yoko Ono,* at Carnegie Recital Hall, a 299-seat auditorium attached to Carnegie Hall, on November 24, 1961, and she enlisted many of her friends—La Monte Young, Jonas Mekas, George Brecht, Jackson Mac Low, and others—to perform in her pieces. She included an iteration of *A Grapefruit in the World of Park* that had performers laugh, read nursery rhymes, and play atonal music while Yoko read her evolving text. At one point, two men were tied together. Empty cans and bottles hung off them, and they were instructed to move across the stage without making a sound. Yoko had a performer lurk in the bathroom all evening. She explained, "Whenever I go to a toilet in a film theater, I always feel very scared. If nobody's there I'm scared, but if somebody is there it's even more scary. So I wanted people to have this experience of fear."

The Carnegie Recital Hall performance was "a big moment for me," Yoko said. It was reviewed in the *New York Times.*

> One thing you can surely say about today's new music: the farther out it gets, the harder it is to describe. . . .
>
> Here are some of the things that happened in almost total darkness at Carnegie Recital Hall late yesterday afternoon, all in the name of music:
>
> Against a taped background of mumbled words and wild laughter a girl spoke earnestly about peeling a grapefruit, squeezing lemons and counting the hairs on a dead child. Musicians in the corner made their instruments go squeep and squawk.
>
> Two dancers stood up and sat down alternately for some ten minutes in silence. Then they sat down to a laden table and ended by breaking all the dishes.

The Carnegie concert was also notable as it was the first time Yoko used her vocalizations in a major performance, though she'd been developing for years the singing and vocalizing techniques that would become famous, or infamous, including when she jammed with Toshi, Young, Cage, and other musicians and performed a cappella at others' concerts.

Her style drew on her formal training in Japanese singing but was wholly her own. In the December 7, 1961, issue of the *Village Voice*, critic Jill John-ston wrote about the Carnegie performance: "Yoko Ono, I assume it was Ono, concluded the work with amplified sighs, breathing, gasping, retch-ing, screaming—many tones of pain and pleasure mixed with a gibberish of foreign-sounding language that was no language at all."

In 2017 Yoko said, "When I performed at Carnegie Recital Hall in 1961 . . . I took and morphed my vocalization, consciously, from kabuki and noh."

She would explain it further in an interview with *Rolling Stone*. "There's one particular kabuki singing style called *hetai*, a kind of storytelling form that's almost like chanting and requires you to strain your voice a bit. I also listened to tapes of my voice playing backward and tried to make sounds like that. And I listened to Indian singing, Tibetan singing . . . all that mixed."

Yoko's vocalizing emphasized breath, guttural singing, and throat sing-ing. She moved from faint whispers to gut-wrenching wails. She keened and howled. Taking a page from Cage, she incorporated silence in her performances. John Lennon later spoke about what he described as her "sixteen-track voice" in an interview. It was the sound of childbirth, of rage, of terror—but also ecstasy. "Hers was a voice from another world," Laurie Anderson said. "There was the screaming and sometimes it's like a ghost moaning in another language—an animal language." Anderson added that Yoko's vocalizations expressed "not only her pain but humanity's pain."

TOSHI AND YOKO'S MARRIAGE WAS over all but legally when he returned to Japan to explore the flourishing avant-garde scene there. In Tokyo, his career took off. He went on to become one of the nation's most lauded composers.

Yoko had moved out of the loft. With Toshi gone, she was living in various friends' apartments and then with Abeel for several months. Abeel needed a roommate to help pay the rent on her apartment in a brownstone at Eightieth and Riverside Drive. Yoko set up in the back bedroom, Abeel in the leaky front room.

When Yoko moved out, she left Abeel with a several-hundred-dollar phone bill for calls to Japan; Yoko often called Toshi, and sometimes talked to him for hours. To collect the money for the bill, Abeel tracked Yoko down at an apartment on the Upper West Side, where she was living with the actor Warren Finnerty. Abeel pounded on the door; Yoko answered, naked except for a bedsheet, and handed Abeel a wad of cash.

IN LETTERS AND ON THE phone (those expensive international calls), Toshi encouraged Yoko to return to Japan to show her work in what he described as an exciting scene that was even more far out than New York.

Yoko was nervous about returning, but things had stalled in Manhattan, and she traveled to Tokyo in March 1962. The city seemed to have been remade. As Toshi promised, the avant-garde scene was exploding. Fluxus itself gained a foothold in Japan, but there was an existing avant-garde art movement called Gutai. "Like Fluxus, Gutai was a performative, low-tech, everyday-materials kind of art," critic and essayist Louis Menand explained. "One of the earliest Gutai works was 'Challenging Mud,' in which the artist throws himself into an outdoor pit filled with wet clay and thrashes around for half an hour. When he emerges, the shape of the clay is presented as a work of art."

Tadanori Yokoo, an artist friend of Yoko's who would become famous as "Japan's Andy Warhol," was part of the Tokyo avant-garde. There was a large network of performers and artists "working out their dissatisfaction somewhere between the sane and insane," Yokoo said.

Yoko and Toshi stayed together in an apartment her parents owned in a high-rise. Toshi introduced her to artists and musicians. He arranged for her to present her work at the Sogetsu Kaikan (Sogetsu Art Center), the center of the avant-garde music and performance-art world in Tokyo.

She spent two months preparing for the opening on May 24, 1962.

In the lobby of Sogetsu Kaikan, Yoko mounted an exhibition, *Instructions for Paintings,* which consisted of twenty-two instruction poems handwritten on pieces of paper and tacked on the wall. The exhibited pieces were purely text-based—"to be realized in the mind of the viewer." Audiences would go through the exhibition before and during the performances that took place in the hall.

With Toshi's help, Yoko rallied some thirty artists, writers, critics, and musicians to participate in her pieces. "Since the event I had put on was inspired by 'Buddha's half-eyed posture,' and I wanted to make it look as though everything happened from evening to night, the hall was dimmed almost to the extent of total darkness," she wrote. "By doing so, people would be able to . . . sense a kind of *kehai* (vibration) that is not visible to the naked eye. That was what I had intended."

The venue was packed. She staged pieces from New York along with new compositions.

One was "Sweep Piece." A musician friend of Toshi's used a broom to sweep the stage and hall. That was it. He swept throughout the program.

Other works included "A Piano Piece to See the Sky." Decades later, in the *New York Times,* Jason Farago described it: "She gently, almost imperceptibly, touched the keys. Soon she started breathing heavily, as if the all-but-inaudible playing had exhausted her. [Then] she smoked a cigarette in slow motion."

She also performed "Audience Piece," in which two dozen people stood at the edge of the stage and stared into the audience for hours. In this piece, the line between the audience and the performers was blurred. The piece continued until after 1 a.m.

Yoko wrote, "The audience became exhausted being in the dark for four to five hours. So, in short, it received a bad reputation."

"Bad reputation" summed it up, though a few reviewers were intrigued. An influential critic, Takiguchi Shuzo, wrote, "What a strange artist has come. What she is doing, however, is natural and logical. I consider it as a natural 'action' against contemporary art, which has corrupted and has been standardized and confused." But other reviews were brutal. American academic and critic Donald Richie, writing in the magazine *Geijutsu Shincho,* said, "In terms of Yoko Ono's work, I don't see any originality at all."

Yoko was confused by the critiques, and she was angry—especially because many reviewers focused on her, not the work, commenting on her association with America and her gender. Yoko recalled a reviewer—"a Norman Mailer of Japan"—who attacked "women wearing pants coming back from abroad thinking they know something."

She hadn't been prepared for such overt misogyny. And it became even more glaring when Toshi helped organize a major Japanese tour for John Cage and David Tudor, and Yoko was among the musicians who performed with them.

On the 1962 tour, Yoko sang Cage's "Aria." According to *Slate*, she offered "vocal lines that pirouette between postures of sensuality and aggression, depending on what else she's hearing in the piece. At points, there are also hints of Ono's early-in-life classical vocal training, most traces of which she would later gleefully discard as a solo artist."

Yoko also performed in Cage's "Piano Walk," lying down on the strings of an open grand piano with her hair draped over the edge. Cage, Tudor, and a third musician hit the strings with random objects.

In contrast to Yoko's mainly negative reception, Cage and Tudor's concerts earned ecstatic reviews. Cage's impact on the Japanese music world was described as "*Jon Keji shokku*"—"John Cage Shock." The Cage events "turned the country on its ear," according to the *Los Angeles Times*.

The positive reaction to Cage compared to the criticism she'd received was demoralizing. She summed up how she felt in an interview with Munroe: "Who was I beyond Toshi's wife and John Cage's friend?" It only served to reinforce her feelings of rejection and isolation. She was trying to connect through her work, but she'd never felt more alone.

After the Cage tour ended, Yoko fell into a deep depression. It was exacerbated by her parents' reaction: When Eisuke and Isoko heard about their daughter's concert, they were horrified.

She'd vocalized her turmoil onstage—screaming, crying out—but no one was listening. Once again, she felt alone and unloved. Her depression got worse and led to a number of suicide attempts. In the middle of the night, "almost unconsciously," she would get out of bed and go to the window of the eleventh-story apartment. "I would try to jump out," she wrote. Toshi stopped her. Then one night she took a handful of pills. When she regained consciousness, she was in a mental hospital.

She remained there until a stranger entered her life.

CHAPTER 6

BORN IN GREENWICH VILLAGE, ANTHONY Cox was a New York–based painter and sculptor. He also acted and made films. For money, he worked at an advertising agency. He became immersed in the counterculture. "I grew up with the whole scene—I was a beat, then I was a beatnik, then I was a hippie," he once explained. "I went through the whole drug trip. I was taking acid when you could get acid for free."

Tony knew La Monte Young and first saw a piece of Yoko's in a book by Young and poet and performer Jackson Mac Low that included Fluxus and other artists' work. He was intrigued.

Tony traveled to Japan in 1962 to study calligraphy and its relationship to Zen Buddhism. While there, he wanted to meet Yoko. Attempting to find her, he tracked down Toshi and called him. Toshi told Tony that Yoko was in the mental hospital.

She refused several attempts he made to visit but finally relented. Tony found Yoko heavily sedated. He spoke to her doctors and learned that she was on a high dose of Valium. "He was dedicated and very concerned about me," Yoko wrote. "He said, 'I will help you get out of here.'"

Jeffrey Perkins, a friend, said that Tony told the director of the hospital that Yoko was a famous artist in New York. "He could convince anyone of anything." He threatened to call the newspapers and say that she was being held against her will. She was released.

Yoko returned to the apartment she shared with Toshi. She was confused, anxious, still depressed, and extremely vulnerable when she and Tony became romantically involved. In November 1962, she became pregnant with his child.

Yoko and Toshi divorced, and she married Tony on June 6, 1963. "We were treated badly by many Japanese who hated that she was in an interracial relationship with a '*gaijin*,'" Tony said. This included her family; they had opposed the marriage to Toshi, but at least he was Japanese. Isoko and Eisuke were aghast that she married a foreigner. Also, Tony had no serious career, which worried her parents. Yoko and Tony moved into an apartment in Gaijin Mura (Foreigners' Village). "The forerunners of what we now call hippies had gathered in this Gaijin Mura," Yoko wrote. She and Tony taught English and worked as voice actors dubbing Japanese films for overseas markets.

YOKO'S DAUGHTER, KYOKO ONO COX, was born in Tokyo on August 3, 1963. Yoko was thirty years old and had recently attempted suicide, been institutionalized, gotten divorced, and then remarried, and she in no way felt ready for a child. "I was still struggling to get my own space in the world," she said. "I felt that if I didn't have room for myself, how could I give room to another human being?"

Yoko knew from her own experience how much a self-centered mother could hurt a child, and she wasn't completely hands-off. She said, "I wasn't particularly taking care of her, but she was always with me—onstage or at gallery shows, whatever. When she was not even a year old, I took her on stage as an instrument—an uncontrollable instrument, you know. My communication with her was on the level of sharing conversation and doing things."

Yoko also said that being a mother changed her in a significant way: "The time that I decided I never [again] wanted to commit suicide was right after

I had my first child, Kyoko," she said in 2009. "Her birth freed me from that desire."

THOUGH THEY WERE IN THE same city, Yoko and her family had almost no contact; her parents had all but written her off. She made several attempts to connect. Yoko and Tony brought Jeffrey Perkins with them when they visited Isoko and Eisuke in Karuizawa. Perkins recounted, "We took a drive out to the country, went through an elegant bamboo grove to a very modern house. In the living room, a tall, elegant man came in—quiet, slowly walking with a cane." They stayed only briefly. "Basically, Yoko was proving to her parents that she had a retinue with her; she always had to prove herself to her mother and father, but she never could. She was sad when we left."

Her state of mind can be seen in "Line Piece III," composed in 1964, which reads, "Draw a line with yourself. Go on drawing until you disappear."

AROUND THIS TIME, TONY PUSHED Yoko to publish her instruction pieces in a book. "Yoko was a purist, in that she valued the ideas (concepts) *as* the art works, and felt it was a form of compromise to objectify . . . or publicize them," Tony wrote to me. "While I understood this, I was more pragmatic: I wanted to create objects we could sell to support our family."

Yoko resisted the idea for a while, but eventually she agreed. Tony had five hundred copies of *Grapefruit* printed and bound in July 1964. If ordered in advance, the small square book cost three dollars; after publication it went for six dollars. The collection was a culmination and summation of the work Yoko had developed to date, a look inside her mind and a validation that she was doing something significant.

Many of the instruction poems in *Grapefruit* had been presented at the loft events, Village Gate, AG Gallery, and the Japanese concerts and exhibitions.

The book included "Secret Piece," the one she'd written in 1953 when she was twenty—it was the original instruction poem inspired by Yoko's attempt to score birdsong. There was the score to "Painting to Be Stepped On." Some of the pieces were whimsical, such as "Tunafish Sandwich Piece":

Imagine one thousand suns in the
sky at the same time.
Let them shine for one hour.
Then, let them gradually melt
into the sky.
Make one tunafish sandwich and eat.

Some instruction pieces reflected Yoko's desire to connect with others as a remedy for loneliness—her own and other people's. One, from 1963, was "Touch Poem for a Group of People," which she performed in many forms over the years (the instruction: "Touch each other"). There were a half dozen other "Touch" poems. Another piece about connecting was "Pulse Piece" ("Listen to each other's pulse by putting your ear on the other's stomach").

Many of the pieces reflected her inner turmoil. "Voice Piece for Soprano," from 1961, read:

Scream.
1. against the wind
2. against the wall
3. against the sky

"Blood Piece," from 1960, read:

Use your blood to paint.
Keep painting until you faint. (a)
Keep painting until you die. (b)

The publication of the book was important to Yoko, and not merely because she and Tony had a product to sell. Later, she recognized that "*Grapefruit* was like a cure for myself without knowing it. It was like saying, 'Please accept me, I am mad.' . . . Those instructions are like that—a real need to do something to act out your madness."

"People didn't know what to make of *Grapefruit* then," said Erica Abeel. "Now it's a revered artifact." In the Museum of Modern Art catalog for a 2015 exhibition of Yoko's work, Christophe Cherix wrote that the book "served as a kind of portable museum of her artwork to date" and that it was "a book of prophetic importance to the art of the 1960s." Cyndi Lauper said, "When I left home at 17, I took 3 things with me in a paper bag: an art pad, a pair of socks, and Yoko Ono's book *Grapefruit*. I also took my dog Sparkle, but she wasn't in the bag. Sparkle died, but *Grapefruit* is still with me."

AFTER THE PUBLICATION OF *GRAPEFRUIT*, Tony organized concerts in Kyoto and Tokyo. The book was sold in the lobbies of the halls. Tony served as presenter and promoter of the events. He had fallen into the role of assistant, often a grudging one. Sometimes they argued. Or, as Dan Richter, a friend of the couple, said, "*He* argued. She just took it."

Yoko went forward with ambitious programs, beginning with a performance on July 20, 1964, at Yamaichi Concert Hall in Kyoto, billed as "Contemporary American Avant-Garde Music Concert: Insound and Instructure." In the lobby of the hall was an exhibition of Yoko's Instructure works. *Instructure* was a word Yoko coined, a combination of *instruction* and *structure*. The works were examples of Yoko's paintings "to construct in your head." Like the home she lived in when her family evacuated to Nagano, the pieces were waiting for someone to come along and complete them. Instructions were written in Japanese and English on cards displayed on white pedestals. They prescribed mental actions to be performed with materials on the pedestals, which included pubic hair, toothpicks, and fingernail clippings.

While the Instructure pieces were on exhibit in the lobby, Yoko's Insound concert took place in the hall.

The concert included "Fly Piece"—a humorous interactive work in which ladders were placed on the stage and people climbed the rungs and "flew" off. There was "Bag Piece," a work she'd debuted in New York. For that night's iteration, Yoko and Tony got in a muslin bag. They could see out, but all spectators could see was an amorphous moving form "like a living stone." Yoko explained, "By being in a bag, you show the other side of you, which is nothing to do with race, nothing to do with sex, nothing to do with, you know, age. Then you become just a spirit or soul." Her concept of bagism was partly inspired by Antoine de Saint-Exupéry's *The Little Prince*—as de Saint-Exupéry wrote: "It is only with the heart that one can see rightly; what is essential is invisible to the eye."

Her concert at Yamaichi Hall featured other performance pieces, but the main event was the finale, "Cut Piece." Yoko was nervous when she sat in *seiza* posture on the stage and, one by one, audience members came up and cut off pieces of her sweater and skirt with scissors. From the wings, Tony protectively watched those who came up. It was at this performance of "Cut Piece" that a man mimed stabbing her. It was the debut of a work that became one of her most famous and influential.

NEWS ABOUT YOKO'S CONCERT—PARTICULARLY "Cut Piece"— reached Eisuke and Isoko. All they grasped about the piece was that their daughter had been stripped nude onstage, and they were once again angry and ashamed. It would be a long time before they were willing to have any contact with Yoko again.

CHAPTER 7

STUNG BY HER FAMILY'S REACTION and more negative responses to her work, Yoko returned to New York in the fall of 1964. She left Tony and Kyoko behind. "I just had to rescue myself," she said.

"When I was alone, New York life was sort of okay," Yoko recalled. But Tony soon followed her back to Manhattan, bringing Kyoko.

They lived in a cramped third-floor walk-up on 1 West One Hundredth Street, shared with their friend Jeffrey Perkins, who had also returned from Japan. Perkins slept in the small second bedroom while Tony, Yoko, and Kyoko slept in the larger one. Perkins was witness to turmoil. "Tony yelled," he said. "Yoko was mostly silent and sad."

The couple had little money. Yoko worked as an interpreter and translator. She also returned to work at The Paradox, the macrobiotic restaurant, in exchange for permission to use the space to hold events after hours.

Her relationship with Tony was becoming untenable. Perkins didn't put all the blame on him. Yoko was exacting in the way she envisioned her art should be presented, and she was demanding of Tony, treating him as an assistant. "She would drive him nuts," Perkins said. "She was a prima donna, wanting to be the Elizabeth Taylor of the art world, which she became."

—————

GEORGE MACIUNAS WAS HAPPY TO have Yoko back in New York. Since AG Gallery closed, he'd been spreading the Fluxus word in New York and Europe. Fluxus caused a sensation in Europe, beginning in West Germany, where Maciunas staged events that included works by Yoko. Back in the States, he staged more Fluxus concerts. Yoko participated in some of the events.

Despite the building tension between them, Yoko and Tony worked together. Promoted and assisted by Tony, Yoko created new events, some under the auspices of Fluxus and some independent.

In 1965, Tony mimeographed copies of what Yoko called "Ono's Sales List," which appeared in a later edition of *Grapefruit*. It included, for example, an offer of a "soundtape of the snow falling at dawn" for twenty-five cents per inch of tape. "Touch" poems were for sale for $150 to $10,000. Also available for purchase were a "disappearing machine: machine that allows an object to disappear when button is pressed, 1,600 dollars" and a "sky machine: machine produces nothing when coin is deposited, 1,500 dollars."

The "Ono's Sales List" was conceptual and therefore didn't solve one of their real-life challenges: paying the rent. That was the problem with art that existed in the mind—it couldn't be sold. It's why Tony had pushed Yoko to publish *Grapefruit*, so they'd have something tangible to sell. They tried other ways to make money. At an event in 1965, she offered two hundred shares in herself at $250 each. Tony manufactured a version of one of the items on "Ono's Sales List," the "Sky Machine." If you put twenty-five cents into a slot in the machine, a card with the word *sky* popped out.

ON MARCH 21, 1965, YOKO had her second concert at Carnegie Recital Hall, which Tony organized and promoted. It was when she performed "Cut Piece" for an American audience. As opposed to the mostly negative response to the piece that audiences in Kyoto and Tokyo had, the New York audience was riveted. It was a major turning point.

In September, she performed in a Fluxus concert, also held at Carnegie Recital Hall. One piece she presented was "Sky Piece to Jesus Christ." Jesus Christ was John Cage. As the Fluxorchestra—an orchestra of Fluxus members—performed a piece of music, Yoko and others came onto the stage and wrapped the orchestra members with gauze. They continued wrapping the musicians until they could no longer play their instruments. The music stopped; the musicians had been silenced.

IN JANUARY 1966, GEORGE MACIUNAS called Yoko and asked her to participate in a Fluxus film festival he was organizing.

Back in 1964 in Tokyo, she had written scripts for movies, but they were concepts; she hadn't shot them. The scripts were instruction pieces. For the festival, she and Tony quickly shot three short films. One was *Eyeblink (Fluxfilm No. 9)*. This was a film of Yoko blinking in slow motion. There was also *Match*, or *One (Fluxfilm No. 14)*, a film of her "Lighting Piece" from 1955. In slow motion, she lights a match. "As the flame burns down, we become aware of the passing of time, the ephemerality of the physical object, and the transience of human existence," wrote Chrissie Iles in "Erotic Conceptualism: The Films of Yoko Ono."

The third film, *Fluxfilm16* or *No. 4 (Bottoms)*, became known simply as *Bottoms* because it was about bottoms—that is, human buttocks. "What initially inspired me to make such a film was our maid, whom I saw polishing the floor. . . .The movement of her bottom was indescribably humorous."

With Tony's and Jeff Perkins's help, Yoko filmed the naked bottoms of some of the Fluxus artists and other friends. The five-and-a-half-minute film was a succession of close-ups of these rear ends. *Bottoms* and a longer remake took their places in the pantheon of classic art films from that period. They were funny but also poignant in the way they stripped away our outer facade of self-seriousness and self-importance.

IN THE SUMMER OF 1966, Yoko was contacted by Gustav Metzger, a German artist and "socialist revolutionary," according to her description. He was organizing an event called the Destruction in Art Symposium (DIAS), a monthlong program of lectures and events in London. He invited Yoko to participate. Initially, she was reluctant to accept. She thought of New York as the mecca of art; London was provincial. But she accepted the invitation, in part to get away from Tony, as she later admitted.

Yoko headed to London the first week in September. As she had when she left Japan, she left Kyoko with Tony. Soon, though, Tony, with Kyoko in tow, followed his wife to London. The family rented a flat in Hanover Gate Mansions. Two of their neighbors were Dan Richter, a friend who'd moved to London from Japan, and his wife, Jill. Dan, a mime and actor, was hired by Stanley Kubrick to choreograph the opening scene of the movie *2001: A Space Odyssey*, in which he also played the lead ape.

The adjacent apartments on Regent's Park were in a building with a wrought-iron birdcage elevator. They climbed to each other's apartments by way of the living room balconies. The rent was fourteen pounds a week. Tony and Yoko's apartment was furnished with a table and chairs and rollout futons and little else. "Except," Jill said, "there were four pyramids in the main room. There were special forces in them. You'd go in them to absorb the energy." Dan said, "The apartments were rapidly becoming a gathering spot for artists, poets, film people as well as numerous hip types." Kyoko was there "like a mascot."

For the Destruction in Art Symposium, Metzger wrote a manifesto that was angrier than the one Maciunas had written for Fluxus. Destruction in Art was, he wrote, a response to the "scented fashionable cows who deal in works of art," and he called for the destruction of art galleries, which he termed "boxes of deceit."

DIAS, held at the Africa Centre in September 1966, included a three-day symposium and a month of events, including poetry readings, concerts, happenings, and exhibitions. Yoko was the only woman artist chosen to perform solo events. Over two nights, she presented a variety of new and old pieces.

For "Shadow Piece," she traced the bodies of twenty participants on a large strip of cloth at a playground that had been bombed during World War II. Art historian Kristine Stiles wrote that the piece "could not have been more poignant in its evocation of genocide and violence . . . her event offered a mute analogue to the imprints of bodies left on the sidewalks of Hiroshima after the bomb."

Yoko performed "Whisper Piece," which she'd debuted in Japan. Engaging the audience in the child's game, she whispered a word into a spectator's ear and asked them to pass it on. The word was whispered from one person to another until it reached the last audience member, who spoke it aloud. It had inevitably morphed into something completely different. After she performed it, she recalled, "Four or five very hot-blooded Destruction in Art Symposium–type male artists protested that my work was not destructive. But I was not interested in just smashing a piano or a car or something.

"I was interested in the delicate way that things change—in that kind of destruction which, in a way, is more dangerous. I whispered a word and the word went around and got destroyed."

Over two days at DIAS, Yoko also presented other works, including two performances of "Cut Piece." The second had the most aggressive response from an audience yet—she was almost immediately stripped naked. When it ended, she held up a sign that said MY BODY IS THE SCAR OF MY MIND.

She received the same positive response in London that she had in New York. In the *Financial Times*, Cornelius Cardew wrote, "She gave what can only be described as a highly polished recital of her work, conveniently broken down into 'pieces,' which were received by the majority of the audience with the kind of reverence usually given to concert pianists."

———

YOKO HAD PLANNED TO RETURN to New York when the symposium ended, but Swinging London was *happening*. Barry Miles, a writer who was a member of the organizing committee of DIAS, and Yoko had become friends, and through Miles, Yoko was dropped into the middle of the London scene. At art openings, concerts, and parties, artists like Claes Oldenburg and rock stars like Mick Jagger—and members of the Beatles—hung out.

LONDON WAS EXCITING, BUT THINGS with Tony were tense. He was pushing her more and more to collaborate with him. Yoko said, "He wanted it to be *both of us*. . . . All I wanted was someone who would be interested in my work. I needed a producer."

Yoko was caught between her frustrations with Tony and her fears of being alone. And she worried about Kyoko. "If parents don't stay together, the child will be miserable," she said. "But sometimes I could no longer control myself."

She left Tony once. "I held Kyoko in my arms, and I [ran] away from home. However, I didn't have any specific destinations. I became hesitant of going to my friends' places with a child. Yet I couldn't imagine myself sleeping on a station bench. . . . I couldn't make up my mind and stayed overnight at the place of a couple I knew. But Kyoko started crying in the middle of the night and didn't stop. Next morning, that friend said, 'Tony must be worried. You should go home.'" She did.

ONE AFTERNOON, YOKO WAS BROUGHT to visit Indica, a hip art gallery and bookstore co-owned by Miles. William Burroughs lived nearby. There was a club in the courtyard frequented by Paul McCartney, Eric Clapton, Mick Jagger, and others in the music scene. One of Miles's partners was John Dunbar, who was married to the pop singer Marianne Faithfull. He was friends with McCartney, who had introduced him to John Lennon. Apple Records, the Beatles label, was conceived in Dunbar's flat one "very acidy afternoon." Dunbar said, "Other galleries . . . it was dull: oil paintings of ships. We showed work no one else wanted to show."

At Indica, Yoko perused the books. *Grapefruit* was being sold there. Miles introduced her to Dunbar, who'd also attended DIAS. He asked her to perform at a benefit for London's first underground newspaper, the *International Times*. On October 15, Yoko performed a version of "Touch Piece" at the benefit. According to Dunbar, Tony Cox approached him and asked if he'd consider giving Yoko a one-person show at Indica. "He was a very persistent bloke," Dunbar said. "He twisted my arm." The exhibition that resulted would change her life.

PART TWO

THE BALLAD OF YOKO AND JOHN

1966–1980

CHAPTER 8

O N SEPTEMBER 14, 1966, THERE was an announcement in the *International Times* of an exhibition of "Instruction Paintings" by the "Japanese-born American artist Yoko Ono" at Indica Gallery, 6 Mason's Yard, St. James, London.

The exhibition, *Unfinished Paintings and Objects by Yoko Ono*, included pieces that Yoko had shown in the past as well as new work. There was a "Painting to Be Stepped On" and an "Add Colour Painting," which consisted of white wood panels meant to be painted on by visitors (brushes and cans of paint were nearby on a white chair).

"Eternal Time," set on a pedestal, was a version of "Clock Piece" that had a ticking second hand but no minute or hour hands. "Sky TV" was a closed-circuit TV that "brought the sky" into the gallery (a skyward-facing camera was set up on the roof). "Painting to Shake Hands (Painting for Cowards)" was built from the instructions "Drill a hole in a canvas and put your hand out from behind. Receive your guests in that position. Shake hands and converse with your hands."

Yoko created a chess set with a completely white board—that is, all the squares were white—and all white pieces. It was displayed on a white table with a pair of white chairs. (She later changed its title, "White Chess Set," to an instruction: "Play It by Trust," and in 1987, Yoko sent a "Play It by Trust" set to US president Ronald Reagan and to Mikhail Gorbachev, general secretary of the Communist Party of the Soviet Union. The meaning of the piece was less whimsical at the time of the Cold War with its message: War is futile; we're all the same, and we have to trust each other to achieve peace.)

A piece called "Forget It" was a sewing needle. It was realized through the instruction in the title. "Once I give the instruction 'Forget it,' you can never forget it," Yoko explained.

"Mending Piece 1" was a broken teacup "to be mended in your mind," one of many mending pieces she created that were inspired by the Japanese art of *kintsugi*, repairing broken ceramics with gold or other metals to celebrate rather than hide imperfections. This version was a broken porcelain teacup displayed alongside a tube of glue. The instructions for a later version of "Mend Piece" explained the work: "You are supposed to mend the cup. You might think you're just mending a cup, but you're actually mending something within you." Helped by Tony, art students, and gallery assistants Dunbar had recruited, Yoko worked on these and other pieces until, on November 7, 1966, she was putting finishing touches on the show, readying for the opening the following day.

A FEW DAYS EARLIER, DUNBAR had run into John Lennon and told him about an exhibition he was staging at Indica. He mentioned Yoko's "Bag Piece"—people would be getting into a huge bag and doing . . . whatever they wanted.

John was already one of the most famous and recognized humans who had ever lived. Lennon was born in Liverpool, England, on October 9, 1940. His father, Alfred, was a merchant seaman who was absent for most of his life. His mother, Julia, left him to be raised by her older sister, Mimi. He visited his mother sometimes; Julia taught him to play the banjo and introduced him to the music of Elvis Presley. When John was seventeen, she was killed by a drunk driver. "I lost her twice," he told me when I interviewed him in 1980.

"And that was very traumatic for me. . . . It just absolutely made me very, very bitter. The underlying chip on my shoulder that I had as a youth was *really* big then. . . . My mother was killed just when I was reestablishing a relationship with her." And he didn't see his father for decades—Alfred turned up again when John was wealthy and famous.

In 1956, when he was sixteen, John formed a band. By early 1958, both Paul McCartney and George Harrison had become members. Drummer Ringo Starr joined in 1962. That quartet—which John christened the Beatles—would go on to be the bestselling musicians of all time. "Beatlemania" swept the world. Besides their bestselling records, they produced and starred in blockbuster films, and their concerts were riotous spectacles.

By 1966, however, John was becoming overwhelmed, exhausted, and depressed. The Beatles had just completed what would be their last world tour after years of nonstop touring, recording, and filmmaking. There was pressure to keep churning out hit songs. John was miserable. The previous year the Beatles had released the album *Help!* The title song was John's. "I was crying for help," he said.

In spite of his mood, John took Dunbar up on the invitation to visit the gallery and showed up at Indica the night before the opening of Yoko's show. She wasn't happy that Dunbar had let someone in early. *What's he doing?* she thought.

"The place wasn't really opened, but John Dunbar, the owner, was all nervous, like, 'The millionaire's come to buy something,'" John recounted. "He's flittering around like crazy. Now I'm looking at this stuff. There's a couple of nails on a plastic box. Then I look over and see an apple on a stand—a fresh apple on a stand with a note saying 'Apple.' I thought, you know, *This is a joke, this is pretty funny.* I was beginning to see the humor of it."

John asked Dunbar, "How much is the apple?"

"Two hundred pounds."

"Really? Oh, I see. So how much are the bent nails?"

Then Dunbar brought Yoko over and introduced her to John.

John was waiting for something to happen—an event, the bags he'd been told about. "Where's the people in the *bag*, you know? All the time I was thinking about whether I'd have the nerve to get in the bag with whoever. You know, you don't know who's gonna be in the bag."

He finally asked, "Well, what's the event?"

In reply, Yoko handed him a card that said "Breathe" on it.

John said, "You mean—" and he panted.

Yoko said, "That's it, you've got it."

I've got it! John thought.

John turned his attention back to the apple on a stand. He grabbed it and took a bite.

Yoko was shocked and upset. The piece was about the cycle of life—the apple would rot and eventually disintegrate. It hadn't occurred to her that someone might take a bite out of her sculpture.

Though she was miffed, she was also impressed by his audacity.

John wanted to *do* something. He saw a ladder leading up to the ceiling where there was a spyglass hanging down. "I went up the ladder and I got the spyglass and there was tiny little writing there [on the ceiling]." When you balanced precariously at the top of the ladder and looked at the ceiling through the magnifying glass, you could read, in tiny script, the word *yes*.

That tiny *yes* impressed John. "Well, all the so-called avant-garde art at the time and everything that was supposedly interesting was all negative, this smash-the-piano-with-a-hammer, break-the-sculpture boring, negative crap. It was all anti-, anti-, anti-. Anti-art, anti-establishment. And just that 'yes' made me stay in a gallery full of apples and nails instead of just walking out saying, 'I'm not gonna buy any of this crap.'"

The nails John was referring to were part of another piece on display, "Painting to Hammer a Nail." This version of a piece Yoko had first conceived five years earlier was a white wooden panel hanging on the wall. A hammer dangled on a chain and there was a can of nails on a chair below the board.

John asked if he could hammer a nail into the piece of wood, but Yoko said no. Yoko would joke about it later: "It's so symbolic, you see—the virginal board—for a man to hammer a nail in."

Dunbar gave Yoko a pointed look and said, "Let him hammer a nail in."

John later observed that Dunbar was probably thinking, *He's a millionaire, he might buy it.* But Yoko cared more about how it looked than selling it.

Yoko and Dunbar conferred, and finally she turned to John and said, "Okay, you can hammer a nail in for five shillings."

"Well, I'll give you an imaginary five shillings and hammer an imaginary nail in," John shot back.

"And that's when we really *met*," he said. "That's when we locked eyes and she got it and I got it."

LATER, SOME PEOPLE ACCUSED YOKO of having pursued John—essentially stalking him. This angered Dunbar. "It's absolutely not true," he said. "Who knows what was going on in their heads, but Yoko was preoccupied with the exhibit. He was just some guy who I made a big deal about. She didn't stalk him or pursue him. She was too cool for that. They wanted her to be the evil witch, but she wasn't one. She was just this girl John fell in love with." He referred to a book written later by Miles, his partner in Indica. "[His] book talks about her chasing John in a taxi, but she did not. I was right there."

It is just one of the untruths that have dogged Yoko throughout her life. It didn't matter how many times she and John told the story of what happened or how often Dunbar confirmed it.

That night when Yoko got home, she saw the Richters. Yoko mentioned that everyone was excited about someone who had visited the gallery.

"She didn't understand the Beatles were a big deal," Dan said. When Yoko said Lennon's name, Dan said, "Yeah, he's famous."

When Tony joined them, Richter told him about Yoko's day at the gallery. "Yoko even met a Beatle," he said.

"It was Tony who was excited about Lennon," Richter continued. "After that, he emphatically encouraged Yoko to pursue John as a patron."

Yoko wasn't oblivious to the Fab Four. She said, "I had heard about the Beatles, and I knew the name Ringo, and nobody's going to believe me but still that's exactly how it was. Ringo hit me because '*ringo*' is 'apple' in Japanese. . . . Rock and roll had passed me by. But I met him and felt he was an incredibly interesting man."

What struck her was John's sense of humor; that and something harder to define. She said, "[In] the crowd I was in, in the avant-garde, there were a lot of guys who were extremely interesting as composers, but I didn't feel anything coming from them. No kind of *guy* thing. He had a charge, a force. And I felt that." But she had no intention of doing anything about it. It wasn't just because she was still married to Tony. "By the time I met John in Indica I was telling myself I was too busy to think about men," she said. "I was so cynical that when I saw John and noticed how nice he looked, I thought, 'Oh, there it is.' But I wasn't going to pursue it."

THE INDICA EXHIBITION OPENED AS planned, with a fresh apple to replace the one John had bitten into. A glittery crowd of beautiful people flowed through the gallery, inspecting the works and following Yoko's instructions. Outside, there was a party in Mason's Yard.

The Indica show stayed up for two weeks, over the course of which Yoko visited the gallery most days and often staged events, including "Bag Piece," in which she and Tony and others got in bags. (John missed his chance, but he would get in the bag later.) "[The show] was a lot of fun but made no money," Dunbar said. "Not one piece sold."

WHILE YOKO CONTINUED TO MAKE new work, John's band made more hits. In February, they released a double-A-sided single with Paul McCartney's "Penny Lane" backed by John's "Strawberry Fields Forever." The latter was the first Beatles song Yoko heard. "It was pretty good," she said. "For a pop song."

After Indica, Yoko ran into John at an art opening. John told Jann Wenner of *Rolling Stone*, "I sort of looked away because I'm very shy with people, especially chicks. We just sort of smiled and stood frozen together in this cocktail-party thing."

After the opening, months passed before they saw each other again. During this period Yoko sent John a copy of *Grapefruit*, an action that's been described as part of her efforts to ensnare him. But she had an orange crate filled with copies of the book, and she often gave them to critics and others she met.

John kept *Grapefruit* by his bed. "I used to read it, and sometimes I'd get very annoyed by it," he said. "It would say things like 'paint until you drop dead' or 'bleed.' Then sometimes I'd be very enlightened by it. I went through all the changes that people go through with her work." He would say of *Grapefruit*: "If you do some of the things in it, you stop going crazy in a way."

LATER THAT YEAR, YOKO SET out to make a new version of *No. 4 (Bottoms)*. She wanted to create a longer version based on the same script ("String bottoms together in place of signatures for petition for peace"). She said, "Nothing about bottoms is aggressive. The front part of a human being is capable of hammering back when attacked, but bottoms are incapable of retaliating. . . . Bottoms must be the true pacifists."

Yoko and Tony filmed it at the town house of a friend. Tony built a tread-mill on which people walked while they were being filmed. Yoko filmed hundreds of bottoms and devoted hours to editing the film. "It wasn't just put together," she said. "The sequence [of the bottoms] was important."

Yoko believed *No. 4 (Bottoms)* was groundbreaking. She wrote, "In 50 years or so, which is like ten centuries from now, people will look at the films of the 60's. They will probably comment on Ingmar Bergman as a meaningfully meaningful filmmaker, Jean-Luc Godard as the meaningfully meaningless, Antonioni as meaninglessly meaningful, etc., etc. Then they would come to the *No. 4* film and see a sudden swarm of exposed bottoms—that these bottoms, in fact, belonged to people who represented the London scene. And I hope that they would see that the 60's was not only the age of achievements, but of laughter."

The movie was to debut in April at London's prestigious Albert Hall, but first it had to be approved by the British Board of Film Censors. On March 10, 1967, Yoko, Tony (carrying Kyoko on his shoulders), friends, and supporters delivered hundreds of daffodils to the board's office and outside on the street handed flowers to passersby. But the flowers didn't help their cause. Yoko was devastated when the board failed to approve the showing of the film. The *Evening Standard* reported, "Miss Yoko Ono's bottom [*sic*] film will not, after all, be shown in the Albert Hall. . . . This latest blow seems to have utterly demoralized Miss Ono and her American husband, Tony Cox. 'We are so depressed we can't function right,' says Mr. Cox. Miss Ono, her head in her hands, nods in agreement."

THAT SPRING, AS THE BEATLES released *Sgt. Pepper's Lonely Hearts Club Band* and, a month later, the single "All You Need Is Love," Yoko was holding an event. According to the poster, it was a "Be-In with Yoko Ono on a Kite-Flying Hill During the Day" at Hampstead Heath, London.

No. 4 (*Bottoms*)—a film of "many happy endings," as Lennon would quip—was finally shown, though not at Albert Hall (that would come fifty years later). The writer and zoologist Desmond Morris was in the theater. "When the audience discovered that 'Yoko Ono No. 4' [*sic*] consisted solely of extreme close-ups of 365 pairs of naked buttocks, each pair being given fifteen seconds screen time, there was a near riot. . . . ," he wrote. "The effect of staring at a long succession of these wobbling, undulating buttocks was strangely mesmeric. . . .

"By the time the thirty-sixth pair of buttocks appeared on the huge screen, one man could control himself no longer, leapt on the stage, and started caressing the giant buttock cleft that loomed above him."

"In London, everybody was talking about the *Bottoms* film," Yoko said. "Everyday I'd see in the newspapers some joke about the *Bottoms* film."

John's wife, Cynthia Lennon, later claimed that he made fun of the movie when he read about it in the paper. "One morning at breakfast he pointed out an article in the newspaper to me. It was about a Japanese artist, Yoko Ono, who had made a film that consisted of close-up shots of people's bottoms. 'Cyn, you've got to look at this. It must be a joke. Christ, what next? She can't be serious!' We laughed and shook our heads. 'Mad,' John said. 'She must be off her rocker.'" But later John said that *Bottoms* was "as important as *Sgt. Pepper*."

YOKO AND JOHN'S CONNECTION GREW around their work. She accompanied him to a Beatles recording session for the first time on September 25, 1967 (the band was recording "The Fool on the Hill"). Two days later, she launched the "13 Days Do-It-Yourself Dance Festival." People who sent a pound or "a pound's worth of flowers" to "Yoko Ono Dance Company" at 25 Hanover Gate Mansions could join the conceptual festival. They received instructional postcards from Yoko every day for thirteen days. She sent John the instructions too.

At the end of August, the Beatles manager and John's friend Brian Epstein had overdosed and died. John was devastated. There was the loss of Epstein and the continuing stress of the obligation to record and pop out hits. Meanwhile, according to his biographer Philip Norman, John said, "Cards kept coming through the door, saying 'Breathe' or 'Dance' or 'Watch the lights until dawn,' and they'd upset me or make me happy, depending how I felt."

Yoko didn't want a new relationship, but she and John talked on the phone and flirted. "There were times when he would call me," Yoko recalled. "He wasn't chatty—'Hi.' Then silence," she said. "I wasn't chatty either. There [were] a lot of silences in the phone call." They were becoming friends.

CHAPTER 9

YOKO WAS INTRIGUED BY JOHN. She was still uncertain, though—and nervous. Her relationship with Tony was deteriorating, but by then she had realized how famous John was and she worried it could affect her life if she became involved with him. But when John invited her to his house in Kenwood, she went. He sent a car for her. She didn't know what he wanted.

When Yoko arrived at John's house, he told her he'd read her "Ono's Sales List." Listed among the objects for sale was "Light House," which was "a house constructed of light from prisms, which exists in accordance with the changes of the day." John wanted one built in his garden. "I said, 'It's very sweet . . . but it's conceptual,'" Yoko explained.

After that meeting, Yoko and John talked on the phone more. They spoke about music, philosophy, books, religion (John was interested in Zen), politics, and art. He was fascinated by the avant-garde scene, and she told him about Fluxus. He knew about Cage, had been turned on to twelve-tone music and experimented with electronics, but he was eager to hear more. He opened up about his frustrations with being a Beatle, and she about her work being so often misunderstood.

They also talked about their families and the ways they'd been hurt as children. On the surface, their childhoods couldn't have been more different.

Yoko's wealthy, elite family in Tokyo contrasted sharply with John's lower-middle-class upbringing in Liverpool. But in spite of the differences in their circumstances, they both suffered because of their parents' absence and neglect. As children, they both felt misunderstood and lonely; they'd wondered if something was wrong with them—if they were crazy or if the world was. And they both still suffered. They were lonely and sometimes depressed.

THEY WERE ALSO BOTH FRUSTRATED in their marriages.

Things were getting worse with Tony. One morning, Yoko woke up and he wasn't home; he'd been gone all night. Tony's half of the bed hadn't been slept in. "I realized that there was a half-empty space in my life," Yoko said. She imagined a room in which everything—the bed, table, chair, cup and saucer—was sliced in half.

"Half-A-Room" became an art piece when Yoko was offered an exhibition at Lisson Gallery. She wanted to create an installation but needed a backer. Tony had handled fundraising in the past, but given how poorly she and Tony were getting along, she realized this time she had to do the fundraising herself, which she found embarrassing. She grudgingly asked John. "There was something sad about making John Lennon be an art patron when he was such a brilliant artist himself," she said. So she said to him, "Well, why don't you put a piece in there, too?"

She explained the concept of her "Half-A-Room" installation, and he immediately suggested putting the other half of the room in bottles. That would be his contribution to the exhibition.

"I just thought that was an incredible idea, and I just stood there," Yoko said. "It was beautiful." It wasn't only that he understood her work. "That's when I knew we were totally on the same wavelength."

And just as Yoko was shocked to find someone on her wavelength, John was excited to find someone who "got" him, encouraging ideas of his that most people would denigrate. "Half-A-Room" was the first of many collaborations that would redefine their lives.

Yoko's exhibition, called *Half-A-Wind* (it was also called *Yoko Plus Me*), opened October 11, 1967. It included other works, among them "Glass Hammer," which was exactly that: a shimmering, fragile glass hammer that would shatter if it was used—another call for peace. But the main piece was an installation, the realization of her "Half-A-Room" idea: the interior of an apartment in which everything in it—the chairs, bookshelf, a vase with flowers—was painted white and cut in half. The other halves were conceptually held in John's "Air Bottles," as they were called, empty glass containers with hand-lettered labels indicating what was inside; "Half a Chair," for example.

John didn't attend the opening; he claimed he was "too uptight." In 2014, Jonathan Jones interviewed Yoko and wrote about the Lisson show in the *Guardian*: "Like the half-destroyed room at its heart, the title spoke of loss, absence, incompleteness." Yoko told Jones, "We are all just half a person." But Jones chose to see not what was lost, but what was to come. He continued, "In fact, at that moment she was in the process of finding her other half: Lennon helped with the exhibition."

A COUPLE OF MONTHS LATER, Yoko was invited to show *Bottoms* and other works at an arts festival in Belgium. She traveled there for the screenings. From Belgium, she accompanied other artists to Paris, where she performed her voice experiments at a café. Someone in the audience came up and told her that Ornette Coleman, the legendary jazz saxophonist, bandleader, and composer, was in the audience and wanted to meet her.

"Ornette told me, 'I dig what you do with your voice,'" Yoko said. "'Would you like to do a piece with me? I'm playing at the Albert Hall [in London].'"

"Listen, if your band is willing to play my composition, then I'll do it," Yoko said, although she didn't intend to return to London yet.

"When I said the piece had to be mine, Ornette was laughing, but he said OK."

Yoko thought, "Okay. I'll go back and do that because it sounds very special," she said. "So I went back to London just to do that . . . and also to see my daughter."

Yoko wrote a score for Coleman's band, but his musicians weren't all that happy with performing a piece by "some sort of kooky girl," as Yoko remembered it. "They had some objections, but they respected Ornette, and he said, 'Just play it like what she says.'"

"Like what she says" meant they should ignore the fact that there was no musical notation in Yoko's score. It was a set of written instructions. For example:

"Think of the days when you had to suffer in silence for 10 days of eternity before you could give, and yet you were afraid of giving because what you were giving was so true and so total, you knew that you would suffer a death after that."

And the instruction for section two: "Total silence—let's see how long we can hold it, or how long it is necessary. It is the most tenderest of silences—of making love."

The rehearsals and the concert, which took place in the center of the Albert Hall arena, were recorded. Yoko performed a piece called "AOS"—a combination of the Japanese word for *blue* and the last three letters of the English word *chaos*, referring to the "blue chaos of war"—with the Coleman Quartet. The version recorded during the rehearsal lasted seven minutes and was released later on the album *Yoko Ono/Plastic Ono Band*. Critic S. Victor Aaron wrote, "Now, I'm not a fan of Ono's caterwauling but somewhat surprisingly, she combines with Coleman's crew pretty naturally on 'AOS.' While Coleman plays trumpet, Ono uses her wordless voice for much of the song like a saxophone."

The Coleman concert was important for Yoko's reputation—Coleman was hugely respected, and he had embraced her.

WHILE YOKO WAS READYING FOR the Ornette Coleman perfor- mance, John, accompanied by Cynthia, traveled to the ashram of Mahari- shi Mahesh Yogi in Rishikesh, India, to study transcendental meditation at the behest of fellow Beatle George Harrison. Harrison had found spiritual answers in the teachings of the maharishi. He hoped John, Paul, and Ringo would too. Cynthia Lennon, for her part, hoped her and John's marriage would be improved by the trip. However, as she later wrote, "[In India] John was becoming increasingly cold and aloof toward me. He would get up early and leave our room. He spoke to me very little, and after a week or two he announced that he wanted to move into a separate room to give himself more space. From then on, he virtually ignored me, both in private and in public."

Later John told me that in India, he was "trying to reach God and feeling suicidal." The teachings of the maharishi didn't help. He took refuge in his correspondence with Yoko. They exchanged postcards and letters. A typical postcard from Yoko was like an instruction from one of her events: "I'm a cloud. Watch for me in the sky."

John said, "And I'd be looking up trying to see her, and then rushing down to the post office the next morning to get another message. It was driving me mad." He couldn't stop thinking about her.

John told me, "I came home from India and realized that I'd been thinking about her because I was in love with her."

MEANWHILE, YOKO'S HUSBAND, TONY, CAME and went. Some- times he'd try to connect with her. Once he suggested that he, Yoko, and Kyoko take a vacation in the South of France, but Yoko said no. Tony and Kyoko went to France on their own in May 1968.

Cynthia was also away—on holiday in Greece—when John asked Yoko to come over to his house. Their platonic friendship had grown in intensity over the year and a half they had known each other. When Yoko arrived, it was awkward at first. They went upstairs to his recording studio and he played her tapes he'd made—"all this far-out stuff, some comedy stuff, and some electronic music," John said. Yoko suggested they make a tape together. They took acid and began recording. "She was doing her funny voices and I was pushing all different buttons on my tape recorder and getting sound effects," he said. "And then as the sun rose, we made love."

Yoko and John told the story many times. "Yoko and I were on the same wavelength right from the start, from that first night," John told journalist Ray Coleman, another Lennon biographer. "That first night convinced me I'd have to end my marriage to Cyn."

The next year, when an interviewer asked Yoko how meeting John changed her life, she said, "He's changed everything in a sense that I was a very lonely person before I met him. . . . When I met John I started to open up a little, through love, you know, and that's the greatest thing that happened to me yet."

CHAPTER 10

THE STORY CONTINUES WITH CYNTHIA returning from Greece and finding Yoko and John at the house, drinking tea. (Some accounts have Yoko wearing Cynthia's bathrobe, but Yoko said that wasn't true.) John seemed unconcerned about the impact of his affair on his wife and son, Julian, but Yoko worried about hurting her daughter. Still, she said, "We both knew this was it."

THREE WEEKS AFTER THAT FIRST night together, Yoko and John went, as a couple, to the launch of the Beatles' tailoring business in Chelsea. They were mobbed by the media. The next day, the press reported that John had been with someone other than his wife—and the public outrage began. Yoko was a homewrecker. Addressing the sexism inherent in that charge, she said, "They never thought about the other side of it: that John might have broken up *my* home too."

———

THEY WERE EXCITED ABOUT WORKING together and almost immediately staged a two-person exhibition of their work, *John Lennon and Yoko
Ono: Four Thoughts,* at London's Arts Lab. It included an unfinished wooden
sculpture; visitors were left to add to the piece. A collaboration of artists had
begun.

John asked Yoko to come with him to the recording studio, where the
Beatles were beginning to work on their next record; it was officially called
The Beatles but, because of its solid white sleeve, it became known as the
White Album.

She'd been to the studio before, but this was the start of her regular visits
to Beatles' recording sessions, which were dissected and harshly criticized.
She was attacked as an intruder interfering with the magic of the Beatles, but
she went because John wanted her with him.

"The other Beatles were pissed off, because John had always been the one
who said no girlfriends were allowed into the sessions," Barry Miles recalled.
Beatles producer George Martin said, "When John hitched up with Yoko, he
said, 'Yoko is now a part of me. . . . As I have a right and left hand, so I have
Yoko. That's me. And wherever I am, she is.' And that was a bit difficult to
deal with. . . . And her influence would be felt. To begin with, everyone was
irritated by it."

"The Beatles had developed a way of working over several years," according to journalist Ray Connolly. "Any intrusion into this tightly knit team
had to be disturbing. . . . Paul would say he found it inhibiting to have
Yoko around."

Yoko's experience was different. "I was just living my own world inside,"
she told journalist Paul Zollo. "Dream world. I was sitting there just thinking
about all the stuff I'm doing in my head. So I was there and in a way I wasn't
there."

But she *was* there, always, and the resentment grew, but how the others
felt about Yoko's presence didn't matter to John.

Most of the songs for the *White Album* had been written in India. John
had written "Julia" about his mother, but he referred to Yoko in the song:

"Ocean child calls me." In the studio in London, he had Yoko sing a line on "The Continuing Story of Bungalow Bill." She also sang backup on "Birthday."

The Beatles began recording a new song for the *White Album*, John's "Revolution." One version that appeared on the record, "Revolution 1," was a thrilling but traditionally structured song. Another version, "Revolution 9," was described by Beatles scholar Mark Lewisohn in *The Beatles Recording Sessions*. He explained that the Beatles recorded seventeen takes of "Revolution." Then, as he wrote, "Take 18 was different. . . . The last six minutes were pure chaos—the sound of a 'revolution,' if you like—with discordant instrumental jamming, plenty of feedback, John Lennon repeatedly screaming 'alright' and then, simply, repeatedly screaming, with lots of on-microphone moaning by John and his new girlfriend Yoko Ono."

After the studio session, John, working with Yoko, added sound effects and tape loops.

Paul McCartney told Connolly privately that a Beatles album wasn't the place for "Revolution 9," but John "was unbending."

AS AN ARTIST, JOHN WAS very clear that this was a direction he was interested in going. "Once I heard her stuff—not just the screeching and howling but her sort of word pieces and talking and breathing and all this strange stuff . . . I got intrigued, so I wanted to do one," he said.

John often emphasized that Yoko had been an artist in her own right before he met her and that she was the one who inspired *him*. "She's a musician who worked in experimental music for years before she inspired and aided in the creation of 'Revolution 9,' the most avant-garde track ever included on a Beatles' album," according to Zollo.

By the time Yoko and John held another joint event—at St. Michael's Cathedral in Coventry—their collaborative work was already reflecting the nature of their relationship. They created a piece to celebrate their connection, planting two acorns in pots, symbols of fresh starts and potential and maybe even the fortitude of an oak tree. They placed a bench nearby. A program for the event read, "This is what happens when two clouds meet." "Our sculpture is two acorns planted in the ground, one facing to the East, the other to the West," Yoko explained. "The acorns symbolize our meeting and love for each other, and also the uniting and growth of our two cultures." Time would nurture their love and reveal how it fostered a meeting of worlds and grew. But fans later dug up and stole the acorns.

ON JUNE 18, 1968, YOKO and John attended the opening of *In His Own Write,* a play based on John's book, at the Old Vic Theatre, and the public was outraged. Yoko and John sat in the front row. Hecklers yelled out, "Where's your wife?" and "Where's Cynthia?"

The press upped its attacks, and fans outside Abbey Road Studios, mostly female fans, taunted Yoko and John when they came and went.

Yoko had become one of the world's most hated women.

IN OCTOBER 1968, CONNOLLY, ON the staff of the *Evening Standard,* called Apple to request an interview with Yoko. He had interviewed McCartney and had met John. "At that time Yoko was on the scene, but nobody really knew her," he explained. She agreed to her first major interview for a mainstream publication. They met one night at the recording studio. Connolly admitted he had a preconceived idea about the article. "The idea was 'This mad girl is stealing our Beatle.'" However, Connolly said, "She didn't come across like that. She was good to talk to. She was very bright. What amazed me was how little she knew about the Beatles. You couldn't discuss what was on the flip side of a record or anything like that—she had no idea. That wasn't her interest. She made no attempt. What she would say is 'Well, I don't know many of John's things and he doesn't know many of mine either.'"

Connolly had profiled Cynthia Lennon and compared her to Yoko. Cynthia "was the wrong one for him. She wasn't zany, she wasn't kooky, she wasn't any of those things. He'd been with lots of girls; it was impossible not to. Suddenly Yoko turns up and she was different. She was totally different from anyone he'd ever met before. He just fell for her hook, line, and sinker."

The profile was extremely positive, but according to Connolly, "no one cared. They were far more interested in the sensational story: Yoko as home-wrecker, Yoko hypnotizing John."

In late June, newspapers reported that Cynthia was suing John for divorce, and the outrage escalated, but the vicious attacks didn't stop the two of them from creating new work. John had attended art school and made art privately—he drew and experimented with an eight-millimeter film camera—but Yoko inspired him to show his work with her and on his own. On July 1, 1968, he opened a solo exhibition called *You Are Here,* which he dedicated to her.

To open the event, he released 365 white helium balloons stamped YOU ARE HERE. Each balloon had a tag asking the finder to write John, care of the gallery. John was saddened by the response; he recalled people writing, "'You and your Jap bastard' and all that."

The reactions of the public, the press, and the other Beatles stung, but it also drew Yoko and John closer together. As she told journalist Barbara Graustark, interviewing her for *Rolling Stone*: "[It was the] two of us against the world."

John later said that Yoko was the "girl with kaleidoscope eyes" he'd longed for, and he credited her with saving him when he was "the nowhere man," unhappy and lost.

He described her as "the fulfillment of my whole life." He appreciated her purity, naïveté, and sophistication, a combination of confidence and shyness. She was exuberant—excited about ideas. She truly believed, as he did, in love and peace. She also had a sadness and was open and vulnerable. They shared this feeling of alienation. "We saw each other's loneliness," she said.

A couple of years later, John would tell an interviewer: "I always had this dream of meeting an artist woman I would fall in love with. Even from art school. And when we met and were talking I just realized that she knew everything I knew—and more probably. And it was coming out of a woman's head. It just sort of bowled me over. It was like finding gold or something."

And it was a two-way street.

Yoko had never allowed a man to impinge on her time or career. She had collaborated with both Toshi and Tony, but she did what she wanted. She had never subsumed her life under a man's the way she did with John, agreeing, for example, to sit in the recording studio for hours while John worked—in spite of the palpable resentment from John's bandmates and others around the Beatles. But she was in love.

YOKO AND JOHN MOVED INTO Ringo's flat on Montagu Square. On October 18, 1968, the police showed up at the front door. The couple wasn't taken completely by surprise. A journalist tipped John off that the drugs squad was planning a raid. "I was thinking that Jimi Hendrix had lived there, so God knows what we might find in the carpets," John said. They scoured the house to make sure there were no drugs or paraphernalia.

Yoko and John were in bed when the police pounded on the door. John let them in, and the police searched the flat and discovered—or claimed they discovered—a stash of cannabis.

They were arrested, charged, and released. Later, in court, John pleaded guilty to a possession charge to spare Yoko the stress of a trial—primarily because, as they announced in late October, she was pregnant.

BOTH YOKO AND JOHN ALREADY had children, but this pregnancy felt different. They were excited about having a child together.

In the meantime, they focused on a new album.

Even before he and Yoko were a couple, John had wanted to produce a record of Yoko's experimental music. Now that they were together, John wanted to release an album of the music they had made the night they consummated their relationship. It combined loops, sound effects, Yoko's vocalizations, and their banter. They called the resulting album *Unfinished Music No. 1: Two Virgins.*

The title connected the album to Yoko's body of "unfinished" artworks. She told curator and critic Hans Ulrich Obrist, "I did not give any instructions to follow. I just titled it 'unfinished music.' I thought that the hip ones will understand by then. It was, after all, a decade or so after I presented the idea [of unfinished art and compositions] to the world. But I don't think anybody was able to make head or tail of it."

When the album was released, many of those who actually listened to the music were confused, and some, especially those expecting anything resembling Beatles music, were horrified.

The cover of *Two Virgins* caused far more stir than the music did. Yoko and John were nude. They'd had an employee set up a camera on a tripod in their flat. Everyone else left the room, Yoko and John disrobed, and John posed with Yoko after pressing a shutter with a time delay.

The resulting photographs were the front and back album covers (their fronts and backsides, respectively).

Yoko explained, "When we shot the picture for that jacket, I was four months pregnant. So, my belly had already become bigger. I wanted to focus on the beauty of a woman with a baby bump. I didn't try to photograph a woman from a particular angle that would make her look beautiful."

THE *TWO VIRGINS* COVER MADE a profound statement about Yoko and John's relationship. If anyone hadn't gotten it yet, they were together. As a romantic couple. As artists working together. The furor escalated; people went from attacking Yoko as a homewrecker to accusing her of destroying Lennon as an artist. Talk of John being under Yoko's spell percolated; she was forcing him to do outrageous—nutty, abhorrent—things. And he was shoving her down the public's throat.

The next medium they chose for collaboration was film. They made two films. One was also called *Two Virgins*; in it, they superimposed their faces over each others'. The other was *No. 5 (Smile)*, fifty-two minutes of John in close-up. In slow motion, he sticks out his tongue, raises his eyebrows, and smiles.

Yoko later said about those two films, "We were mainly concerned about the vibrations the films sent out—the kind that was between us."

The films were screened at the Chicago International Film Festival. The audience was asked to bring musical instruments. Half the audience walked out, but the rest remained, playing flutes and banging on tambourines.

When the *Two Virgins* LP was released in the States, the distributor insisted on wrapping the record in brown paper. Apple Records' distributor EMI worried that negative publicity about John might hurt sales of the *White Album*, but it immediately shot to number one. There was some consternation about that album too, much of it, predictably, about "Revolution 9," the Yoko and John collaboration.

ON NOVEMBER 4, YOKO GOT sick—there were complications with her pregnancy. She was rushed to Queen Charlotte's Hospital. John refused to leave her side, camping out in the room. One day he made a recording of the baby's heartbeat.

Yoko had a misscarriage on November 21, and Yoko and John were devastated. John blamed the miscarriage on the drug bust and the press and public's attacks on her.

The miscarriage didn't stop Yoko from working. At that time, she made one of her most powerful and controversial films. Still in the hospital, she began directing a film of one of her *Thirteen Film Scores*, concepts she had published the previous year. The title was *Film No. 6 (Rape)*. The written instructions:

"The cameraman will chase a girl on a street with a camera persistently until he corners her in an alley, and, if possible, until she is in a falling position."

Following Yoko's direction, a camera crew followed a girl as she went along the street, into a cemetery, and back to her apartment. "The girl in the film did not know what was happening," Yoko explained. She was terrified.

Yoko told the *New York Times*' Michael Kimmelman, "The cameraman doesn't say anything and just keeps on following. Suddenly it becomes a very violent film, not in a physical sense but in a mental sense."

When it was screened, the ethics of making the controversial film were questioned; the subject was genuinely terrorized. However, the film received stunning reviews. At a screening Yoko attended, women broke down sobbing. It was a profound expression of the pain and violation Yoko was experiencing—but it was also about the victimization of all women.

ON NOVEMBER 28, 1968, YOKO and John appeared at Marylebone Magistrates' Court. John plead guilty to the charge of possessing cannabis; the court fined him one hundred fifty pounds plus court costs of twenty-one pounds. It was merely a slap on the wrist, but the drug conviction would come back to haunt them.

Outside the court, Yoko was confronted by jeering Beatles fans. One pulled her hair.

CHAPTER 11

A FTER BEING INITIALLY REJECTED IN New York and Japan, Yoko's art had finally been lauded in New York and London. She'd offered herself to her audience, and the public had finally embraced her. She had been *seen*. She started to taste the satisfaction that connecting to people through her art brought her. Then Indica opened, and she met John. He saw her too, instinctively understanding her and her work. Their relationship evolved. For the first time in her life, she experienced real love, "total communication." She felt that she had finally overcome the pain of her childhood. But she paid a price. She wanted to be accepted, but now she was reviled. She and John turned to work to cope—and, as they admitted, they also turned to drugs.

IT HAS BEEN REPORTED THAT Yoko and John began to use heroin after the miscarriage. One account has her trying the drug earlier, when a musician in Ornette Coleman's band gave it to her in Paris. The musician James Taylor said he might have introduced John to opiates; he didn't specify heroin. Whoever gave them the drug first, they began using it together. They said they never injected heroin, only snorted it. They went through periods of heavy use, withdrew from the drug, and frequently relapsed.

John told *Rolling Stone*'s Jann Wenner about when Peter Brown, a Beatles assistant, walked into the office, shook John's hand, and said nothing to Yoko. "He doesn't even say hello to her. That's going on all the time. And we get into so much pain that we have to do something about it. And that's what happened to us. We took 'h' because of what the Beatles and others were doing to us."

When Yoko and John retreated to their bedroom for extended periods, Dan Richter left packets outside their door. "Sometimes they seemed fine," Richter said. "Sometimes they appeared to be stoned. They'd go off it and then get back on. But it did take a toll on one hand. On the other, they used it to get through a very hard period."

IN THE BEGINNING OF 1969, the Beatles gathered at Twickenham, a soundstage in London where they'd shot scenes for the movies *Hard Day's Night* and *Help!*, to rehearse songs for a new album, *Get Back*. The title would be changed to *Let It Be*. The story of the making of that record has been told, retold, revised, argued about, edited, and reedited over decades. The sessions were filmed for a documentary. In fact, two documentaries were released, one in 1970, also called *Let It Be*, and one in 2021, *The Beatles: Get Back*. (A restored version of *Let It Be* was released in 2024.)

The director who oversaw the filming was Michael Lindsay-Hogg, who'd made films for the Beatles and knew Yoko and John from a TV special he filmed, *The Rolling Stones Rock and Roll Circus*, which featured them. *Let It Be* has been called the band's "breakup film." David Remnick, writing in the *New Yorker* in 2021, said *Let It Be* is a "dimly lit portrayal of bitter resentments and collapsing relationships."

For at least three of the four Beatles, making that record and film was a sometimes onerous obligation. According to Lindsay-Hogg, "They were all in different stages of ennui, but Paul was the only one who wanted to be there . . .

John definitely didn't want to be there." When John did show up, Yoko was with him. Always. "So for the first time there were five people sitting within the creative circle," according to Lindsay-Hogg.

At different times, each of the four Beatles was unhappy. There was tension. "They loved playing together—that was obvious—but Paul was the only one who was still committed to the group above all else," Lindsay-Hogg said. "He tried to keep it together. The others were moving on."

At one point in the sessions, Yoko did wield a microphone and jam with the band and there was a touching interlude when she and John waltzed while George played for the others a new song he'd written, "I Me Mine." Mostly, at least according to the edited footage of the sessions, she was the well-behaved girlfriend. Yoko painted, thumbed through a Beatles fan magazine, scribbled in a notebook, sewed, ate toast, offered John gum, and occasionally whispered in his ear.

There was sneering and snarkiness and resentment when Yoko and John were out of the room.

Once Paul said, "We probably do need a central daddy figure to say, you know, 'Nine o'clock, leave your girls at home, lads.'"

At another point he admitted it was "difficult [writing songs] with Yoko there. I start writing songs about white walls because then John and Yoko would like that."

"THE ONLY THING ABOUT BEING in love . . . it takes so much time," Yoko told journalist Betty Rollin, whom she knew from Sarah Lawrence, when Rollin interviewed her for *Look* magazine. "The work suffers." But she didn't stop working. Following the *Let It Be* sessions and as the Beatles worked on *Abbey Road* (*Abbey Road* would be released first), Yoko made films, including *Self Portrait,* which was forty-two minutes of John's semi-erect penis. The finished movie was shown only one time, at the Institute of Contemporary Arts in London in 1969.

Yoko also put on an experimental jazz concert at Cambridge University. John had suggested that she announce she was coming with a band, and the audience was surprised when the band was *him*. It was a far-out performance of Yoko vocalizing—warbling, screaming, yelling—while he crouched at her feet, his back to the audience, aiming the guitar at an amp, sending out screeching feedback.

YOKO'S AND JOHN'S DIVORCES HAD been finalized during the *Let It Be* sessions, and they'd talked about getting married. On March 12, 1969, they heard that Paul had married Linda Eastman. John was eager to move forward with their own wedding, but Yoko was ambivalent. "I'd never really wanted to be married the other two times," she told Philip Norman. "It was just something I'd fallen into."

But John insisted. When I asked him why, he responded, "Because we're romantic. . . . Intellectually we know it's all bullshit and all that but getting married was at least as important as getting divorced. . . . And rituals are important, no matter what we thought as kids."

Yoko came around. "We knew that we shouldn't need a marriage license or anything, but I did feel sentimental about our relationship. I wanted to be able to commit myself ritually to John."

They made a modest plan to be married by the captain of a ferry going across the English Channel. On a boat, they'd avoid the press. They went to the ferry terminal in Southampton, but they weren't allowed on the boat because Yoko didn't have the required passport. They flew to Paris to regroup. The couple went from there to Gibraltar, where a registrar performed the ceremony. The official marriage certificate records the wedding of Yoko Ono Cox and John Winston Lennon on March 20, 1969. The couple were both dressed in white. Yoko wore a white top and tiered miniskirt, white knee socks, white sneakers, and a floppy white sun hat, and John wore a white corduroy suit, a white turtleneck sweater, and white sneakers.

———————

IMMEDIATELY AFTER THE WEDDING, YOKO and John focused their attention outward. In March 1969, the war in Vietnam was raging. In America and England, massive anti-war protests were being held. Along with marches, protesters held sit-ins. Yoko came up with a twist on the sit-in: She and John would stage a bed-in—a "Bed-In for Peace."

They knew that their marriage was big news, so they decided to use their honeymoon to protest the war in Vietnam. It was performance art that "came directly from Yoko," John said, with the purpose of "getting people talking about peace on the front pages of the newspapers."

"For us, it was the only way," Yoko said. "We can't go out in Trafalgar Square because it would create a riot. We can't lead a parade or a march because of all the autograph hunters. We had to find our own way of doing it, and for now bed-ins seem to be the most logical way. We think the bed-in can be effective."

Four days after the wedding, Yoko and John headed to Amsterdam and checked into the Hilton. They made signs and taped them on the windows and walls of the presidential suite: HAIR PEACE, BED PEACE. John wrote, I LOVE YOKO, and she wrote, I LOVE JOHN.

"We're going to stay in bed for seven days instead of having a private honeymoon," John announced. "It's a private protest."

Yoko continued, "For the violence that's going in the world. Instead of making war, let's stay in bed."

"And grow your hair!" said John. "Let it grow until peace comes!"

On March 25, 1969, they put on their pajamas and got in the king-size bed.

After the scandal caused by the nudity on the *Two Virgins* album cover, perhaps it shouldn't have been surprising that people assumed the bed-in had something to do with sex. But, John said, "There we were, like two angels in bed, with flowers all around us, and peace and love on our heads. We were fully clothed. The bed was just an accessory."

They gave a hundred or so interviews during the week. There was cynicism among some in the press, but Yoko and John were sincere in their hope for and belief in love and peace and their conviction that the bed-in could help. "It's the best idea we've had yet," John said. Later, at a press conference, he said, "Yoko and I are quite willing to be the world's clowns if by so doing it will do some good."

The press conference after the bed-in was held at the Hotel Sacher in Vienna. Yoko and John held the press conference from inside a white bag, from which they addressed the press and answered questions. They talked about the bag and Yoko's concept of bagism allowing for "total communication without prejudice."

Yoko later explained that she spent much of her life wanting to disappear into a box from which she could see outside but where she could remain safely hidden. The bag allowed it. The same was true for John in a different way—in the bag, he could, at least in theory, stop being the famous John Lennon.

On *The David Frost Show*, when asked about bagism, John said, "If people did interviews for jobs in a bag they wouldn't get turned away because they were black or green or [had] long hair, you know."

Frost responded, "They'd get turned away because they were in a bag."

IN MAY YOKO AND JOHN released their second experimental album, *Unfinished Music No. 2: Life with the Lions*, the follow-up to *Unfinished Music No. 1: Two Virgins*. The title was a play on *Life with the Lyons*, a popular show on BBC Radio. It was another intensely personal record, even more than *Two Virgins*. The most powerful "song"—or statement—was a five-minute, nine-second track that included the beating heart of their unborn baby, which John had recorded at the hospital before the miscarriage. It was followed by two minutes of silence.

The album was met by the press and public with, at best, bafflement and, more commonly, derision.

———

YOKO AND JOHN DECIDED TO flee the constant harassment in London. They looked at properties on the outskirts of the city and were drawn to Tittenhurst Park, ninety minutes from London near Ascot, a massive property that included a grand Georgian mansion and seventy-two acres of gardens. As a child Yoko had felt lonely and isolated in her family's estates, but she now felt the need for an oasis where they would be protected from the press and public. John paid one hundred and forty-five thousand pounds for the property, and Yoko began attending to its restoration and remodeling. An outbuilding temporarily became a Hindu temple and the residence of friends of George's, Hare Krishnas. Yoko and John built a recording studio—Ascot Sound Studios—and a lake.

Even as they settled into Tittenhurst Park, Yoko and John wanted to hold another bed-in, this time in New York City. It was a tumultuous time in America. Martin Luther King Jr. and Robert F. Kennedy had been killed the year before, and the war in Vietnam continued, as did massive demonstrations against the war. This time Yoko and John wanted to hold their protest in the country that was actually waging the war. However, John's drug conviction prevented them from entering the States, so instead, they held the bed-in in Montreal. They set up in the Queen Elizabeth Hotel for another seven-day event, and this time, Kyoko was with them.

Like the first, their second commercial for peace was widely covered around the world. Some of the coverage was positive, but, like last time, some of it was critical. One visitor to the hotel room was cartoonist Al Capp, whose *Li'l Abner* comic strip appeared in thousands of newspapers. He attacked the bed-in, *Two Virgins,* and—viciously—Yoko.

Sarcasm dripping, he said of *Two Virgins,* "I think that everybody owes it to the world to prove they have pubic hair. And you've done it, and I tell you that I applaud you for it." Capp accused John of staging the bed-in for money, to which John responded, "Do you think I could earn money by some other way, sitting in bed for seven days, taking shit from people like you? I could write a song in an hour."

At one point Capp eyed Yoko and said to John, "Good God, you've gotta live with *that*?" He called her Madame Nhu. John was enraged, but he controlled himself.

DURING THE BED-IN, IN RESPONSE to a reporter's question about the purpose of the event, John answered, "All we are saying is give peace a chance." Yoko told him the line should be a song. He wrote the lyrics with her help. (She later said, "'Give Peace a Chance' is basically John's idea. I might have thrown some words in.") When they recorded the song, the hotel room was packed with random celebrities, guests, reporters, and members of their staff. John played guitar, and those in the room—the group included Timothy Leary and his wife Rosemary and the comedian and musician Tommy Smothers—chanted the chorus.

John had said he wanted to write a song that would replace Pete Seeger's "We Shall Overcome," and in fact his and Yoko's song was often sung at peace demonstrations, civil rights rallies, and other protests. Later that year, "Give Peace a Chance" was sung by Seeger himself and half a million protesters at the Moratorium to End the War in Vietnam march in Washington, DC, on November 15, 1969.

The song was the first single John wrote without the involvement of any of the Beatles, but it was nonetheless credited as a Lennon-McCartney composition. Later John said he regretted giving coauthor credit to McCartney. "I didn't write it with Paul," he said. "It should have been Lennon-Ono."

———

"GIVE PEACE A CHANCE" WAS released the first week of July 1969 as a song performed by the Plastic Ono Band. The Plastic Ono Band was what Yoko and John thought of as a conceptual band that included anyone and everyone. Yoko had conceived of a conceptual band two years earlier when she was asked to do a concert in Berlin. She thought of sending a band made of plastic boxes that contained automated instruments and tape recorders that played her compositions. When she told John the idea, he made a model of the band with a piece of wood as a base. "He put a few plastic objects together," Yoko recalled, "a cassette box, a paperweight, the tube from a record cleaning cylinder brush, and created a little plastic model and said, 'well, we should call our band Plastic Ono Band.'"

They released "Give Peace a Chance" as a Plastic Ono Band single because, Yoko wrote, "It wasn't just John and Yoko on the record, it was all the people with us in Montreal and the audience—we wanted everyone in the world to join us and sing the song to create world peace. . . . So everyone on the recording is in it, everyone listening to the recording is in it, everyone who sings the song is in it, you're in it and everyone in the world is in it."

CHAPTER 12

AFTER THE SECOND BED-IN, YOKO and John returned to Tittenhurst Park. Having allowed Kyoko to attend the bed-in in Montreal, Tony now let her visit them at their home. And though Yoko and John weren't exactly friendly with Cynthia, she allowed John's son, Julian, to visit his father.

Kyoko looked forward to the time at Tittenhurst Park with her mother and John, though she didn't always get the attention she hoped for. Like her mother and grandmother before her, she remembered having the run of the sprawling estate but often being stuck with babysitters—"Actually, they weren't babysitters, they were just whoever happened to be around." Kyoko said she was put in the care of people who didn't know what was child-appropriate. Once Yoko and John asked her to pose for PR photos—"They thought cute photos of her daughter might help humanize my mom," Kyoko said. The photographer wanted her to pose naked on a horse—this was the sixties, after all. "I told Mom and John, 'I don't want to be naked.' They said I didn't have to, but I could tell they were disappointed."

Kyoko enjoyed it when Julian was there. "It was good to have someone to play with." Indeed, there were good times with Kyoko and Julian and Yoko and John at Tittenhurst Park.

————

ON JULY 1, 1969, KYOKO, five, and Julian, six, went with Yoko and John for a holiday in Durness, Scotland. John was driving the family in an Austin Maxi. He drove the car into a ditch.

They were taken to a nearby hospital, where Julian was treated for shock and Yoko, John, and Kyoko received stitches for cuts on their faces. Yoko also injured her back. Julian was taken to stay with John's aunt until Cynthia came for him. The others remained in the hospital for five days.

The car crash delayed John's return to London, so he didn't show up on July 1 when the other Beatles went back to the studio to work on the *Abbey Road* record. Yoko, who sustained worse injuries than John and the kids, was advised to rest in bed; when John finally returned to London, he arranged for a bed to be delivered to the studio for her.

Yoko's presence was still resented. Dan Richter said, "So sitting at the [mixing] board all you're looking at is Yoko in a bed. The rest of the band were just appalled."

Later he wrote, "It felt weird to be sitting on the bed talking to Yoko while the Beatles were working across the studio. I couldn't help thinking that those guys were making rock and roll history, while I was sitting on this bed in the middle of the Abbey Road studio, handing Yoko a small white packet."

The white packet was heroin.

Yoko recovered, and the bed was removed from the studio, but she and John continued using the drug. An interviewer once asked how it affected their relationship. "When we were on it, we were both on it, so it wasn't like we alienated each other. But it was self-destructive and unhealthy," said Yoko.

By August 1969, they were determined to get off heroin, and they suffered thirty-six hours of hell when they stopped. Yoko said, "We just went straight cold turkey."

John wrote the song "Cold Turkey" and communicated how withdrawal felt through the lyrics—"My feet are so heavy / so is my head / I wish I was a baby / I wish I was dead"—and through his anguished screams, which were, he said, inspired by Yoko's.

ON AUGUST 8, 1969, JOHN joined the other Beatles for a photo session that resulted in the famous cover image of *Abbey Road*. In September, he and Yoko flew to Toronto to perform at a rock-and-roll peace festival. It starred Chuck Berry, Little Richard, and Bo Diddley. John was asked to emcee, but he said he and Yoko wanted to perform instead. He put together a band that included Eric Clapton on guitar, Klaus Voormann on bass, and Alan White on drums.

Yoko, John, and the musicians rehearsed on the flight for the September 13, 1969, concert. During the flight, John told Voormann he was leaving the Beatles. John had already broken the news to Allen Klein, the band's manager, but Klein had convinced him to keep it from the others and the public for business reasons. No one else knew. The Canada show became legendary. It was the show that, Voormann said, introduced Yoko's singing to the world—"enraging people who already hated her, but for those who got it, it was thrilling; we *got* her."

John debuted "Cold Turkey." While he sang the song, Yoko performed her vocalizations, "which emphasized and punctuated the pain John expressed," according to Voormann. "Yoko chortled, whooped, screamed, and moaned, her voice an instrument dueling with John's guitar and voice." The group then played a song Yoko wrote for her daughter, "Don't Worry Kyoko (Mummy's Only Looking for Her Hand in the Snow)," followed by her "John, John (Let's Hope for Peace)." Introducing her, John announced, "Now Yoko is going to do her thing all over you." And she did.

"Don't Worry Kyoko" is important not only for its personal significance to Yoko but also for showcasing Yoko's vocalizations as they blended with the rock riff. (*Rolling Stone* called it a "mournful caterwaul of despair.") "John,

John (Let's Hope for Peace)" is also Yoko vocalizing but this time over an eerie, spacey, formless improvised track.

Voormann remembered, "People were just open-mouthed. They are at a rock'n'roll festival with Chuck Berry, and then suddenly this avant-garde thing is presented," he said. "I was up on stage, standing behind Yoko, she's screaming and shouting and croaking like a dying bird, and I felt 'this is about the Vietnam war'—I really saw tanks next to me and bombs falling and dead people, that was the thing she was expressing. But I thought: 'My God, John must be mad to do this.' I mean, we were lucky people didn't throw tomatoes at him."

Later Lennon would call "Don't Worry Kyoko" "one of the fuckin' best rock and roll records ever made."

More emotion—anguish—was expressed when the band played "John, John (Let's Hope for Peace)." Yoko began singing softly. Then she began crying out and screaming. Once again, John came in with his searing guitar.

Voormann recalled, "The audience was just . . . they didn't get it. What no one understood is that John and Yoko wanted to do it because it's for peace, and that's what they were there for." Voormann said that Yoko expressed her feelings about the war in the most visceral way, "trying to yell out, 'Don't do this war.'" He said, "The sad thing was, at a rock-and-roll festival with Little Richard, Bo Diddley, [it was] completely the wrong place. That was a piece of art she was doing, but people didn't know."

When they got back to London, they were still excited about the concert. "The buzz," John said, "was incredible. I never felt so good in my life." Given his experience of the evening, he was baffled by reports in the papers that he and Yoko had been booed throughout the performance.

"I'm sure some people booed but I didn't hear it," Voormann continued. "Her screaming was so loud and our instruments on full throttle, feedback like crazy—that's all we could hear, her screaming for peace."

JOHN WAS ALL IN ON his partnership with Yoko, and he made this clear on September 20 in a business meeting at Apple with the other Beatles and Klein, who was negotiating a new deal with their distributor, Capitol Records. Philip Norman reported that John finally told them what he'd already made clear to Klein and Voormann: "You don't seem to understand, do you? The group is over. I'm leaving."

There. John, not Yoko, broke up the Beatles. George had been ready to quit a few times, but John ultimately broke up the group. Yoko *was* a catalyst; John often said that she gave him the strength to do what he wanted to do—and she gave him somewhere to go, personally and with his art.

Voormann recalled John's state of mind at the time. "Before he was with Yoko, John was really in bad shape. One time we were sitting outside, and he sat gazing at this bush, and he ripped off the leaves, saying, 'I'm so unhappy,' and he started crying. . . . When Yoko came that changed one hundred percent. She gave him what he needed. Of course that was the end of the band. It was natural. John moved on."

John himself saw meeting Yoko and moving on from the Beatles as part of growing up. In the interview I conducted in 1980, he said, "You know the song: 'Those wedding bells are breaking up that old gang of mine' . . . the old gang was over the moment I met her—I didn't consciously know it at the time, but that's what was going on."

Although John did break up the Beatles, it's possible that the band stayed together longer than they would have because of Yoko. She accompanied John—literally holding his hand sometimes—to the sessions that resulted in the final Beatles albums. As Voormann said and as John often repeated, John was miserable then. If Yoko hadn't agreed to stay by his side, he might have left earlier. There's a version of the Beatles story in which there'd be no *Let It Be* or *Abbey Road* without Yoko. During the writing and recording of those albums, John had a foot out the door. If he hadn't had Yoko, the other foot might have followed sooner than it did.

Instead of being blamed and pilloried for breaking up the group, maybe Yoko should be thanked for keeping the band together during that fertile period.

————

AS FAR AS THE REST of the world was concerned, John was still a Beatle, but as an artist, he had moved on. Yoko and John set up in an office at Apple headquarters and, on September 25, went to Abbey Road Studios to mix the Toronto Rock and Roll Revival festival tapes for an album. The first half of the album *Live Peace in Toronto* included rock standards they'd performed at the festival, as well as "Cold Turkey" and "Give Peace a Chance." The second half included Yoko's songs. When *Live Peace* was released, criticism was directed at the side on which Yoko's compositions and performances were featured. The *All Music Guide to Rock* said, "Side two, alas, was devoted entirely to Ono's wailing, pitchless, brainless, banshee vocalizing."

On October 20, 1969, a month after *Abbey Road* came out, Yoko and John released their third experimental album, *Wedding Album*. Side one of the record included Yoko and John whispering, calling out, yelling out, screaming out each other's names with, as backdrop, their beating hearts. "Amsterdam," the second side, consisted of recordings from the bed-in in Amsterdam. The album came in a box and included photos, drawings, and a picture of a piece of wedding cake. The album did poorly, but John said he didn't care. "It was like our sharing our wedding with whoever wanted to share it with us. We didn't expect a hit record out of it. . . . That's why we called it *Wedding Album*. You know, people make a wedding album, show it to the relatives when they come round."

They also released a studio version of "Cold Turkey" as a single backed by Yoko's "Don't Worry Kyoko." The song "Cold Turkey" peaked at number fourteen in the United Kingdom and thirty in the United States, and John made more headlines with his response to the limited success of the record. Back in 1965, the Beatles had been honored by Queen Elizabeth at a ceremony at Buckingham Palace, during which they were awarded MBE (member of the Most Excellent Order of the British Empire) medals. John had given his medal to his aunt Mimi, who kept it on the mantel in her home. On November 25, 1969, he retrieved the MBE and sent it back to the queen with a note: "I am returning this MBE in protest against Britain's involvement in the Nigeria-Biafra thing, against our support of America in Vietnam and against 'Cold Turkey' slipping down the charts. With love. John Lennon of Bag."

AS THE YEAR WOUND DOWN, Yoko and John announced that they'd dubbed 1970 "Year 1 AP (After Peace)." The statement they issued read, in part, "We believe that the last decade was the end of the old machine crumbling to pieces   And we think we can get it together, with your help. We have great hopes for the new year."

Tony had remarried. With his wife, Melinda Kendall, he was staying at a farm in Aalborg, Denmark. Everyone was getting along for the moment, and Tony invited Yoko and John to spend New Year's 1970 with them. Kyoko has mixed memories of the three weeks in Aalborg. "That was actually one of the better times," she said. "My mom and dad and stepmother got along. John was great. They all played mah-jongg for hours, made food together—did some kind of juice diet they'd been put on by Dick Gregory. There were no assistants. There were moments we'd all be getting along." But, she continued, "then there'd be a falling-out about something. Just this up-and-down situation."

They remained in Demark and didn't attend the January 15, 1970, opening of *Bag One*, an exhibition of John's lithographs. Encouraged by Yoko, John had produced thirty-six lithographs from drawings he'd made of them at the wedding and at the bed-in—and in bed; some of the drawings were sexually explicit.

Fourteen of the lithographs were put on display at a London gallery. The day after the opening, the gallery was raided by the police. Eight drawings were seized on the grounds that they were "indecent." A detective said of the drawings, "Many toilet walls depict works of similar merit. It is perhaps charitable to suggest that they are the work of a sick mind."

Yoko said, "I was only thinking about . . . the artistic merits of the drawings when I encouraged him to release them. I totally forgot about the subject matter . . . I mean, that angle . . . how it would be taken. There was a tremendous furor when they were released. So now we were terribly embarrassed."

Yoko and John remained in Denmark through the controversy. When they finally left, at the end of January, for Yoko, saying goodbye to Kyoko was harder than ever.

BACK AT TITTENHURST, YOKO AND John mainly stayed in their upstairs bedroom. The melancholia hit again. Denmark had been a welcome break, and it had gone relatively well, but the dark moods returned, engulfing them sometimes. The seized lithographs and absurd anger about them felt like a fresh wound. They bickered. John expressed his frustration in flares of anger. When they were directed at her, Yoko shut down. After an argument, John would apologize.

There was some good news when the Marlborough Street Magistrates' Court threw out the case of John's erotic lithographs. Then came the bigger news: In April, Paul announced his solo album, *McCartney*, and said he was leaving the Beatles. For once, Paul took the brunt of the ire. A newspaper appeared with the front-page headline "Paul Quits Beatles," and, as John's biographer Ray Connolly wrote, "Within hours he became the most hated man in the world." John was angry; he'd kept his vow of silence about the breakup, but Paul announced it to promote his new record.

Later that month, Jann Wenner, who wanted to conduct a major interview with John for *Rolling Stone*, traveled from San Francisco to Tittenhurst, but Yoko said John was too depressed and paranoid to meet him. She was struggling too. Adding to her malaise, she was pregnant again and worried about another miscarriage.

GIVEN HIS MOOD, JOHN WAS particularly receptive when he was given *The Primal Scream,* a book written by an American psychologist, Arthur Janov. He became excited about the therapy's promise of a liberating "primal scream," billed as "the cure for neurosis." It made him think of Yoko's vocalizing.

John passed the book along to Yoko, who was also intrigued. She called Janov and asked him to come from LA to treat them. Therapists usually didn't travel to treat patients, but Yoko and John weren't typical patients. With his wife and co-therapist, Vivian, and their children, Janov flew to England. The plan was for him to work with John while Vivian treated Yoko.

Later Janov broke the therapists' ethics code and spoke in depth about John. He said that when he arrived at Tittenhurst Park, John was "in bad shape. He couldn't leave his room." Janov said, "John had about as much pain as I've ever seen in my life." Janov never spoke about Yoko, but she was depressed too, though at the time she was functioning better than John was.

Yoko and John began the therapy and continued it for a month until Janov informed them that he had to get back to his clinic in LA. He advised them to come to LA and continue therapy with him and Vivian there.

Yoko and John traveled to Los Angeles and rented a house in Bel Air. Every day they went to Janov's offices in West Hollywood to talk and scream and cry. For John, the therapy was revelatory, for Yoko, not as much, though she did tell the BBC, "I think in fact Primal Therapy did a lot of good for us." However, they became disenchanted when Janov wanted to film them during their sessions. They refused, and he became angry. Regardless, John had spent four months in LA, which was longer than he was legally allowed to be in the States. Janov later said, "They cut the therapy off just as it started, really. We were just getting going."

Before they returned to England and Tittenhurst Park, in late July Yoko was rushed to the hospital, where she had another miscarriage.

Yoko and John were devastated and, as usual, poured their grief into their art.

CHAPTER 13

I N LA, WHEN THEY WEREN'T in primal-therapy sessions or sunning at the pool in Bel Air, Yoko and John were working on songs, including some they'd started in London. The depression that had driven them to therapy and the pain that erupted during the sessions came out when they returned to the studio in England to make a pair of albums, *Yoko Ono/Plastic Ono Band* and *John Lennon/Plastic Ono Band* with a version of the Plastic Ono Band made up of John on guitar, Klaus Voormann on bass, and Ringo on drums. Yoko said the musicians were brilliant on her record. She said that in the past "Klaus and Ringo were pretty silent about what I was doing, but this time they got really turned on."

Ringo said, "Her record was fun because it was like a jam, and then she'd go off on her crazy singing."

Yoko explained why her vocalizations were so raw and animalistic on the record. "If you were drowning you wouldn't say: 'I'd like to be helped because I have just a moment to live.' You'd say, 'Help!' But if you were more desperate, you'd say, 'Eiough-hhhhh.'"

The song "Why?," in which she screams "Why" over and over again, could be seen as a protest against the war, or wailing despair about her miscarriages or the onslaught of hate she'd received, or a combination of everything.

The next song on the album, "Why Not?," could be seen as the ironic answer to the question—the universe's response.

Yoko edited, manipulated, sped up, slowed down, and augmented her tracks, adding sound effects to create her album. "I never will forget the dawn in the Abbey Road Studio when John and I hugged each other after completing the *Yoko Ono/Plastic Ono Band* album," she said. "When I was a little girl, I read of Monsieur and Madame Curie discovering radium, with, naturally, the Madame sitting in the driver's seat. That was how I felt. . . . At the time, I was a composer who was stretching her ears to the edge of the boundless universe. We were there and nothing else seemed to matter."

Whereas Yoko's record was a collection of improvisations, John's was a collection of crafted songs, raw and searingly honest ones. In "Mother," John screamed out for his parents: "Mommy, don't go, Daddy, come home."

John screamed more on "Well Well Well" (about Yoko). His other songs included "Love," "Working Class Hero," and "God." In "God," John said he summed up everything he'd learned to that point. To the fans who looked to him as a beacon or leader, he said, "The dream is over." He explained that the lesson was "Well, you make your own dream. That's the Beatles' story, isn't it? That's Yoko's story. That's what I'm saying now. Produce your own dream." John ends the song with "I don't believe in Beatles. I just believe in me—Yoko and me. That's reality."

Like their albums' titles, the covers they created were almost identical. You have to look closely to see that the photos on the jackets are reverses of each other—John leaning back on Yoko, Yoko leaning back on John, posed in the same spot in the yard at Tittenhurst Park.

The albums were released on the same day in December 1970. Predictably, John's received widespread attention. Yoko's album eventually got its due, and both records became classics in their respective genres, John's at the edge of rock and Yoko's at the edge of the edge. *John Lennon/Plastic Ono Band* is arguably Lennon's best record ever and one of the best rock-and-roll albums ever made. Yoko's album was groundbreaking in the field of experimental music. It would be cited as inspiration by Lady Gaga, Kim Gordon, David

Byrne, Laurie Anderson, RZA, and others. "Wide swaths of avant-garde rock, postpunk, sound art, and experimental electronic music simply wouldn't exist without the fearless curiosity of *Yoko Ono/Plastic Ono Band*," according to critic Marissa Lorusso.

YOKO AND JOHN WERE BOLSTERED by the experience of making the albums, but they were stung by the continued attacks from the press and public. When the two went out, fans yelled for Yoko to go back to her own country. John received racist letters, including ones warning him Yoko would slit his throat as he slept. They called her a "Jap," "Dragon Lady," and other slurs.

The racism and misogyny behind Yoko's denigration over the years can't be overstated. Artist and writer Kate Millett, Yoko's friend from the 1960s Greenwich Village scene and author of *Sexual Politics*, told me, "Outside Japan, Yoko is the most famous Japanese person who ever lived, but being a strong feminist, she never fit the stereotype of the obedient, passive Asian wife or the seductive geisha. She got in people's faces and screamed. People didn't like a person from Japan screaming, and they didn't like a woman screaming. A screaming Japanese woman enraged them."

Indeed, one reason Yoko was attacked with such vitriol from the start was that she didn't look like other rock-and-roll girlfriends or wives, the Bond girls, supermodels, and *Playboy* Playmates. Nor did she act like them. The *New York Times*' Amanda Hess wrote, "Her image stands in contrast to that of other Beatles partners—modelesque white women in chic outfits who occasionally swoop in with kisses, nod encouragingly and slip unobtrusively away."

Racist and sexist comments on Yoko's looks and work continued to appear in the press. One of the most blatant examples came in December 1970 in *Esquire* magazine. To publicize the *Plastic Ono* records—and, as John was wont to do, to steer attention from himself toward Yoko—they had granted interviews, including an in-depth one for *Esquire* for a feature on Yoko. The article became famous not for journalist Charles McCarry's comprehensive interview but for the blatantly racist title and illustration. The title:

"John Rennon's Excrusive Gloupie."

The subtitle extended the slur: "On the load to briss with the Yoko nobody Onos." The illustration was a full-page caricature of Yoko, wild-haired and domineering, holding a miniature beetle—or Beatle—on a leash. It had John's face.

THAT YEAR, YOKO MADE AN astonishing film that reflected how she was feeling then—and in some ways, how she'd always felt: attacked, a victim.

Film No. 11 (Fly), unrelated to the "Fly Piece" she performed in Kyoto in 1964, began as one of Yoko's concepts in her 1968 *Thirteen Film Scores* with the instruction "About a fly going from the toe to the head of a lying naked body, crawling very slowly. The whole film should take about an hour."

Yoko said the idea for the film came "when I thought about that joke where someone says to a man: 'Did you notice that woman's hat?' and he's looking at her bosom instead. I wondered how many people would look at the fly or at the body."

Yoko filmed *Fly* in a friend's apartment over two days. An actress lay nude on a bed. Yoko painted sugar water on her so flies would stay on her body.

The camera follows in close-up as one fly and then several flies crawl across the woman's breasts, lips, thighs, stomach, and eyelids. She remains passive, allowing herself to be trod on.

Critics and historians identified some of the same themes in *Fly* as in "Cut Piece." It was discussed as a film about a woman's vulnerability and victimization. It was called a "manifesto . . . where bodily reparation and self-reclamation prevail as major themes." It was also described as a response to Yoko's experience as a child during the Second World War—being a victim—and, like "Cut Piece," as a work about letting go of ego.

The movie reflected how Yoko felt about the harsh judgments that came because of her race and sex as well as her art and all she'd been saddled with—the purported breaking up of the Beatles and hypnotizing of John. But it was also about all women.

Yoko explained, "There's all sorts of levels of understanding [of *Fly*], I'm sure, but it has something to do with the life of a woman. . . . The fly is crawling over you and [you're] just taking it."

ONE MORNING, YOKO AND JOHN sat together at a piano in Tittenhurst Park and worked on a song. Yoko received no credit for inspiring and cowriting that song, which became one of the most important records ever made, an international anthem. The song, "Imagine," was a synthesis of Yoko's philosophy and her conceptual art.

Though John wrote the melody, the idea, title, and lyrics were inspired by Yoko's concept of wish fulfillment; indeed, the song is a series of wish and instruction pieces: "Imagine there's no countries," "Imagine no possessions," "Imagine all the people sharing all the world." It was specifically inspired, John said, by *Grapefruit*. Many pieces in *Grapefruit* asked the reader to imagine:

"Imagine letting a goldfish swim across the sky."

"Imagine one thousand suns in the sky at the same time."

"Imagine your head filled with pencil leads."

"Imagine the clouds dripping."

But Yoko did more than inspire "Imagine." As John told me in 1980, she was cowriter, writing the lyrics with him. "I wasn't man enough to let her have credit for it," he admitted. "I was still selfish enough and unaware enough to sort of take her contribution without acknowledging it."

In an interview with the BBC, he said, "If it had been Bowie [I'd written it with], I would have put 'Lennon-Bowie,' you see. If it had been a male—Harry Nilsson—'Old Dirt Road' is 'Lennon-Nilsson.' But when we did ['Imagine'], I just put 'Lennon' because, you know, she's just the wife and you don't put her name on, right?"

"The song 'Imagine' could never have been written without her," John would declare.

John recorded "Imagine" at Tittenhurst Park in May. Strings were added in July at a studio in New York. The single, released October 11, 1971, became a standard. Interviewed in 2006, former US president Jimmy Carter said, "In many countries around the world—my wife and I have visited about 125 countries—you hear John Lennon's song 'Imagine' used almost equally with national anthems." Carter didn't mention Yoko. Bono told *Rolling Stone*'s David Fricke that what he liked best about "Imagine" "is the Buddhist core of the song, the idea that imagination precedes action, that you imagine something before you make it true." That's all Yoko.

John believed he and Yoko had written something politically relevant and, at the same time, commercial: "Anti-religious, anti-nationalistic, anti-conventional, anti-capitalistic, but because it is sugarcoated it is accepted."

It became the most acclaimed song of John's solo career. At one time it was number three in *Rolling Stone*'s list of the best songs of all time. The magazine described it as Lennon's "greatest musical gift to the world." It wasn't just John's gift.

Yoko said, "I feel in the big picture the fact that John and I met was to do this song."

CHAPTER 14

WHILE YOKO AND JOHN WERE building their utopian vision, the fragile peace that Yoko had with her ex-husband was collapsing. Kyoko was almost eight, and a lot had changed since they had been Tony's guests in Denmark.

Tony made Yoko's access to Kyoko more difficult until finally he took off with Melinda and Kyoko without warning. Through their lawyers, Yoko and John learned that Tony had taken Kyoko around Europe and settled in Majorca, Spain, where he'd enrolled her in a transcendental meditation preschool. Yoko and John flew there and went to the school. They picked up Kyoko and brought her to their hotel. Preschool staffers called the police to report that Kyoko had been kidnapped.

More than fifty years later, Kyoko recalled that day. It was confusing and scary. She said she was happy to see her mother and John, shocked at being snatched, afraid of what her father would say, and scared because she anticipated what was coming: another of her parents' fights. What transpired was even worse than that. Yoko and John were arrested in their suite at the hotel and taken to police headquarters, and Kyoko was returned to Tony.

Yoko and John were released but ordered to return to Majorca to face further questions about the incident. (They left but sent Dan Richter to Majorca; the case was later dropped.)

Yoko and John were far from dependable parents, but Tony was also erratic and unpredictable. He was charismatic but also paranoid, and the kidnapping in Majorca added to Tony's fear that Yoko and John wanted to take Kyoko away from him. At first he allowed Kyoko to visit them again in Tittenhurst Park, but then he disappeared with her again. And once more, Yoko was distraught. John instructed his lawyers to find Kyoko, but months went by and there was no sign of her.

Yoko and John turned to work. They both planned records to follow the *Plastic Ono Band* albums. They served as each other's sounding boards as they wrote and rewrote tracks, and they sat together in the studio when they recorded them. They were used to working together in the studio by then. Yoko admitted, "We would argue, of course. We were two very temperamental, very emotional, people. . . . That was part of our communication."

On John's record *Imagine*, he included the love songs "Oh My Love" and "Oh Yoko!" Commenting on "Oh My Love," John said the song was "a joy to write and a joy to sing and record! Written with Yoko—based on her original lyric—we finished it very quickly one late night together, the beginning of the melody being started last year." Some of the other songs on the *Imagine* album sprang from John's continuing self-examination. "How can I go forward if I don't know which way I'm facing?" he sang in "How?" The lyrics to "Jealous Guy": "I didn't mean to hurt you / I'm sorry that I made you cry / I didn't want to hurt you / I'm just a jealous guy." John called the album *Plastic Ono* "with chocolate coating," and indeed, the songs were less raw than the earlier album.

Yoko's *Fly* was a double album that included the soundtrack to the *Fly* film, which featured vocal improvisations by Yoko played forward and backward, accompanied by John's guitar. "Midsummer New York" was straight and fierce rock and roll reminiscent of Elvis's "Heartbreak Hotel." "Mindtrain" was a seventeen-minute jam built around Yoko's vocalizations ("a masterpiece of avant-garde rock," according to the *Guardian*). "Mrs. Lennon" was dirge-like, centered on piano and guitar with Yoko singing "Husband John extended his hand / extended his hand to his wife / And he finds / and suddenly he finds that he has no hands / They've lost their bodies!" In that song, she "fearlessly confronts a selfhood fragmented by inequity and circumstance," according to *Pop Matters*.

Among the other songs on the *Fly* album was "Hirake," also a jam centered on Yoko's vocalizing. It's a revolutionary track. In it, "you'll hear not only the B-52's but Patti Smith, Talking Heads, Lene Lovich, that whole popular art rock school of which Yoko was the major source," wrote Peter Occhiogrosso in the *Soho News*. The lyrics to "Hirake": "Open your box, open your trousers, open your thighs, open your legs, open open open open oh." An executive at EMI, the record label that distributed the album, called the lyrics to "Hirake" "distasteful" and said Yoko had to redo her vocals. Instead, John overdubbed more guitar and blasts of feedback to obscure the words.

On *Fly* there were also versions of "Telephone Piece" (a phone ringing; Yoko answers it) and "Toilet Piece" (a flushing toilet).

Yoko and John also made the publication of a new, expanded edition of *Grapefruit* a joint project. This time she had a legitimate publisher, and the book included a very brief introduction by John. ("Hi! My name is John Lennon. I'd like you to meet Yoko Ono.") There were book signings at which fans lined up, and Yoko and John chatted with them and gave autographs.

To promote the book in England, Yoko and John gave interviews at Tittenhurst. A film crew helped them realize their vision of a full-length movie to accompany the *Imagine* and *Fly* albums.

THE *IMAGINE* MOVIE SHOWCASED THEIR estate, but Yoko and John's time at Tittenhurst was almost up. They moved to New York later that summer. John explained their move bluntly at the press conference for *Grapefruit* at Apple headquarters: "In England I'm regarded as the guy who won the pools.

She's regarded as the lucky Jap who married the guy who won the pools. In America, we are both treated as artists."

Another reason for the move was Kyoko. Since Tony had fled with Kyoko, there had been no word from him and no news about his whereabouts for months. Eventually, Yoko learned that Tony, Melinda, and Kyoko were in America. A lawyer said Yoko would have a stronger chance of getting Kyoko back if she and John were in the States too.

In New York City, they took over a wing of the St. Regis on Fifth Avenue and Fifty-Fifth Street while they looked at apartments and buildings to rent or buy. In the hotel, they had three adjoining seventeenth-floor suites. In one they wrote and conducted business, mostly from bed, as usual. The other suites became offices where their assistants worked on Yoko's and John's projects, including the *Imagine* film.

The movie they made was a string of what were later called music videos for the songs on *Imagine* and *Fly*. Yoko said, "We wanted to make a surrealistic film in the tradition of Buñuel and Cocteau. . . . I think that now it's more or less known as a forefather of MTV." The film began with the song "Imagine." John played a white piano and sang the song as Yoko, dressed in white, opened the white shutters in the all-white drawing room at Tittenhurst Park, letting the light flood in. It was followed by a succession of short films also shot at Tittenhurst Park and at locations in New York and London. In New York, they recruited other St. Regis guests for cameos. Fred Astaire happened to be staying at the hotel and readily signed on. Jack Palance, also a hotel guest, was enlisted. George Harrison visited, and he was filmed too. Dick Cavett and Palance participated in Yoko's "Whisper Piece," and Yoko and John performed other works, like "Bag Piece."

They listen to the ground and objects through a stethoscope as Yoko's "Don't Count the Waves" plays. John rows Yoko across the Tittenhurst Park lake to the island in the center, where they play her "Play It by Trust" chess set. While John sings "How Do You Sleep?," they play pool—blindfolded. They're on a beach while "Mrs. Lennon" plays, and they write in the sand "John loves Yoko" and "Yoko loves John," and the messages are washed away by the rising tide. In the final scene, Yoko and John run to each other, calling each other's names. They run past each other.

TO YOKO AND JOHN, NEW York City felt open and free—freer, at least. For the most part, they could walk down the street without being stopped; passersby who recognized them left them alone. Autograph seekers were polite. People flashed peace signs. Even paparazzi were relatively respectful. Unlike in London, there was little racist heckling directed toward Yoko and fewer admonishments about her breaking up the Beatles. By fall 1971, they considered New York City their home.

They spent time hanging out with Yoko's artist friends, including many of the Fluxus crowd, who seemed less interested in John's fame than in his art.

They also spent time with Andy Warhol and his crowd. Warhol was captivated by celebrity and hence was obsessed with Yoko and John. According to Blake Gopnik's biography of Warhol, the artist wanted to photograph Yoko and John, and they played "a hilarious game of cat and mouse where the three paranoid celebrities tried to figure out who was using who and who had the most to gain from a portrait of the couple."

In New York, Jim Harithas, director of the Everson Museum of Art in Syracuse, ran into Yoko at a Madison Avenue gallery and told her he wanted to show her work. In a follow-up meeting at the St. Regis, he said, "Look, the whole museum is yours. You can expand the show in any direction, and we'll accommodate it." Reflecting on that moment, Harithas said that with the growing strength of the women's movement, he was eager for Everson to be the first museum to have an exhibition entirely dedicated to a woman's work. "Some of my male colleagues in the museum profession were really irritated about it. The mainstream then was Pop Art—commercial-looking art made by white men."

The show Yoko prepared was ambitious. She recruited George Maciunas to help design the exhibition, including the graphics. Yoko designed and

Maciunas executed a poster of the event that became iconic: a photomontage of Yoko's and John's faces forming the letters in the words *This Is Not Here*, which became the name of the exhibit. The first time Yoko used the *This Is Not Here* concept was ten years earlier, in 1961. She staged a show at a gallery that had what she considered an ugly cabinet. She put the sign THIS IS NOT HERE on the cabinet. In 1992, Yoko explained, "The idea came to me when I was living in a small room where there was a big, heavy cabinet I could not move and it was really boring me. So I put a sign on it that said THIS IS NOT HERE to erase the cabinet from my mind."

The exhibit filled the Everson's galleries and hallways. Some of the pieces had previously been shown in New York, Japan, and London. Many were based on instruction poems from *Grapefruit*.

"Amaze" was a Plexiglas maze with a toilet in the center. Harithas said, "I think it was the same expression of taking a common everyday object that you use in a certain way and, like Duchamp, raising it to a work of art. He did the urinal, she did the toilet. It was the first answer to the Duchamp that I'd ever seen."

There was "Apple"—an apple on a stand—the same piece John took a bite of at Indica.

For "Water Event," Yoko invited over one hundred artists and others to collaborate with her by supplying an object to which she could add water. An artist contributed a Volkswagen convertible to be filled with water. Andy Warhol had a videotaped piece of a watercooler with audio of people chatting around it. Dick Cavett sent a top hat, artist David Bourdon contributed an ice tray, and George Harrison sent a milk bottle. Bob Dylan sent an album, *Nashville Skyline*, and it was placed on a pedestal upon which Yoko could pour water.

There was a window in the gallery. Rather than cover it to create a solid wall, she put a sign on it that made it an artwork: "Painting to See the Sky By."

In an introduction to the Everson exhibition, Yoko said, "In this show here I'd like to prove the fact that you don't need talent to be an artist. 'Artist' is just a frame of mind. Anybody can be an artist, and anybody can communicate if they're desperate enough. There's no such thing as the imagination of artists. Imagination would come out of necessity."

About Yoko's idea that everyone can be an artist, Harithas said, "It's important to consider how radical that was, not just on an individual level but in a much broader sense. With the exception of what we were doing at the Everson, in those days you never saw exhibitions by women or non-white people. Opening up these possibilities to everyone and being so inclusive was revolutionary. That was the power of that show."

THE DAY BEFORE THE EXHIBITION opened, a line of several thousand people formed outside the museum. Word had leaked out that Yoko and John were having an art opening, which morphed into a rumor that the Beatles were reuniting in—of all places—Syracuse, New York.

The Beatles reunion rumor started because Yoko had a plan for a concert/jam session as a birthday gift for John. Klaus Voormann, Ringo, producer Phil Spector, and other musicians would be there. Soon thousands of people were camped outside the museum to witness the Beatles reunite. Fans literally broke down a door. "Then when word started filtering out that this wasn't going to happen, the mood started turning really dark," according to David Ross, who was Harithas's assistant at the time. Some artworks got broken. Responding to the chaos, Allen Ginsberg began playing a harmonium and chanting, and the chanting spread throughout the museum. "He completely turned the mood into something transcendent," said Ross.

YOKO'S EXHIBITION RECEIVED LITTLE CRITICAL attention ("Of course it was news, but it was celebrity news," Ross said). She received more attention two months later when an ad announced another show. This one was to be at New York's prestigious Museum of Modern Art. The only hitch was that the museum hadn't actually invited her to stage an exhibition. Nonetheless, Yoko placed an ad in the *Village Voice* that showed a photo of a stretched-out car parked in front of the MoMA emblazoned with the exhibition's title: *Yoko Ono—one woman show.* In the photo, she walked behind the car carrying a shopping bag on which a large *F* had been printed. She was passing just below the MoMA sign, so the *F* was lined up between the words *modern* and *art*, successfully rechristening the institution "the Museum of Modern (F)Art."

Those who came expecting to see the show encountered a man wearing a sandwich board out front. Yoko had typed a description of the exhibition in which she explained that she'd released flies in the museum and instructed viewers to go around the city to find them. The flies would be identifiable because Yoko had blasted them with her perfume ("the flies are distinguishable by the odour which is equivalent to yoko's").

As people exited the museum, they were asked how they liked the Yoko show. Though there'd been no show, some people said they'd enjoyed it. The exhibition was partly a protest against the museum's sparse attention to women and Asian artists.

Years later, on MoMA's blog *Inside/Out,* Whitney Graham wrote, "Perplexing, thought provoking, and amusing, Ono infiltrated the Museum's walls and the consciousness of its visitors without having any work on display." In the *New Yorker,* Andrea Scott wrote that the exhibition was "a feminist critique disguised as a whoopee cushion."

CHAPTER 15

THE WAR IN VIETNAM CONTINUED at a time when Yoko and John were increasingly associated with the peace movement. Since the late 1960s, Abbie Hoffman and Jerry Rubin, two of the cofounders of the Youth International Party (Yippies), were among those on the forefront of the anti-war movement, organizing and leading mass demonstrations across the United States. When Rubin read that Yoko and John had moved to New York, he tracked them down to enlist them in the cause.

After an initial meeting, newly allied with Rubin, Hoffman, and other leaders of the radical left, Yoko and John participated in concerts and protests. In addition to protesting the war, the group fought for other causes. One was the case of John Sinclair, who cofounded the White Panthers in solidarity with the Black Panthers and had been convicted of distributing marijuana after selling pot to an undercover cop. Yoko and John performed at a benefit concert called the John Sinclair Freedom Rally (later released as a film, *Ten for Two*; Sinclair had been sentenced to ten years for selling two joints) in Ann Arbor, Michigan, on December 10, 1971. Three days later, Sinclair was freed.

What wasn't known at the time was that the audience didn't include only those who were sympathetic to Yoko and John's causes. It also included informants for the FBI.

YOKO AND JOHN HAD ALREADY been flagged as subversives by the Nixon administration. They had been public about their loathing of the war and the US president—"Tricky Dicky," as John called Nixon in "Gimme Some Truth" on the *Imagine* album. The apparent result of the concert—Sinclair's freedom—emphasized the power they had to stir up support and put pressure on the establishment. This is when the Nixon administration set its sights on them, according to historian and journalist Jon Wiener.

The administration focused its efforts on deporting John—he was vulnerable to deportation because of his drug conviction in England—and he was a Beatle. Before Nixon was done, the attorney general, the Immigration and Naturalization Service, and the FBI had all been marshaled. Yoko and John were followed, their phones were tapped, and several times, John was ordered to leave the country.

Initially unaware that John had been targeted by the administration, Yoko and John moved out of the St. Regis into an apartment at 105 Bank Street in New York's West Village. John Cage was their next-door neighbor. The apartment became a gathering place for revolutionaries.

On December 17, 1971, Yoko and John performed at another benefit, this one to aid the relatives of prisoners and hostages killed during a riot at the state prison in Attica. Yoko and John mounted the stage. They played a set that included John's "Attica State." Yoko sang a new song, "Sisters, O Sisters" ("Oh, sisters, oh, sisters, let's give up no more / It's never too late to build a new world"). Then they sang "Imagine."

The year was winding down. Before it did, though, Yoko and John released one more song—a Christmas carol.

After the bed-ins, Yoko had thought of more advertisements for peace, launching them in December 1969. She and John placed billboards in major cities around the world that read "War Is Over! If You Want It—Happy Christmas from John & Yoko."

That message became a song, "Happy Xmas (War Is Over)," which they wrote at the St. Regis and released in December 1971. "We were having our morning coffee in a hotel room facing the park," Yoko later recalled. "Then, still in the middle of our breakfast, we got this idea to write a Christmas song. We were fast workers, so the song was born by the time we finished our last morning coffee." John said, "This is going to be bigger than 'White Christmas,' you'll see."

Decades later, the *New York Times* wrote about the song: "It was, perhaps, an early example of a guerrilla media campaign, using celebrity power to transmit a subversive message."

As John hoped, the song took its place among Christmas classics. It has been covered by hundreds of artists —Andy Williams, Céline Dion, and Neil Diamond among them—sung by choirs, and played in shopping malls. It was another way for Yoko and John to tell the world *You can end the war*, this time wrapped in a Christmas song. And the song also included a message for Julian and Kyoko. It began with Yoko and John wishing their children a happy Christmas. For Yoko, it was heartbreaking because her daughter was still missing.

THE SEARCH FOR KYOKO CONTINUED. Yoko and John's lawyers had advised her to file for custody in the US Virgin Islands. She did, and on September 24, 1971, after a hearing in St. Thomas, Yoko was granted custody. This victory had no practical effect, given that there was no sign of Tony or Kyoko.

Three months later, in mid-December 1971, Tony resurfaced. He was with Melinda and Kyoko in Melinda's hometown of Houston, Texas. He went to court there with the aim of reversing the St. Thomas order.

The day after they performed at the Attica concert, Yoko and John, accompanied by a friend, the curator Jon Hendricks, flew to Houston for a hearing.

In Houston, a judge reversed the decision of the court in the Virgin Islands and awarded temporary custody of Kyoko to Tony. But he also awarded visiting rights to Yoko and ordered that Kyoko be allowed to spend Christmas with her mother. However, Tony failed to produce Kyoko, and he was arrested.

"My dad was in jail," Kyoko told me. "My dad wouldn't produce me, so her lawyers got him put in jail for contempt of court. And it was Christmas Eve. I remember seeing my dad on the news on TV. Sitting in the jail cell. My dad's lawyer got him out on bail, and he came and got me."

Kyoko said, "We jumped bail and went underground. So then my dad was a felon wanted by the FBI for kidnapping."

After Tony fled, Yoko's lawyers asked the court to give her temporary custody of Kyoko. Yoko won, and Tony was ordered to surrender Kyoko. "The bottom line is that she won Kyoko," Hendricks explained. "She got full custody again. But winning was one thing; getting Kyoko back was different."

Tony and Melinda had taken Kyoko and disappeared. Yoko and John's lawyers and Allen Klein were tasked with finding them. They hired detectives. Yoko consulted psychics. Finding her daughter consumed her. Though she didn't want Tony arrested and wouldn't force Kyoko to see her if she didn't want to, she didn't stop pursuing her.

People called Yoko and offered information about Kyoko in exchange for cash. Even the people who were supposed to be helping them took advantage of the situation. "And there was one private detective in particular," Yoko said. "I said, 'Look, I don't want you to do anything anymore about it. You are frightening them,' you know? So he goes to Chicago and did a big press interview saying, 'Yoko is not interested in the child.'" She also spoke of one instance where a detective claimed he'd chased Kyoko and Tony in his car and told her, "It was great. We almost had them because we were speeding up and their car went off the pavement."

Yoko was horrified. "You're talking about my child in that car."

Yoko blamed John and Tony for separating her from Kyoko. John said he was guilty as charged.

"It was a classic case of men being macho," John said. "It turned into me and Allen Klein trying to dominate Tony Cox. Tony's attitude was, 'You got my wife but you won't get my child.' In this battle, Yoko and the child were absolutely forgotten. . . . It became a case of the shootout at the OK Corral. Cox fled to the hills and hid out, and the sheriff and I tracked him down."

Yoko said, "Allen called me up one day saying I won the court case. He gave me a piece of paper. I said, 'What is this piece of paper? Is this what I won? I don't have my child.'"

Yoko disagreed with the decision to go to court, but she'd listened to Klein, the lawyers, and John. "I knew that taking them to court would frighten them and, of course, it did frighten them." As a result, Tony went underground with Kyoko.

IN FEBRUARY 1972, YOKO AND John were invited to cohost a week of *The Mike Douglas Show*, an American talk show seen by forty million people a week. "It's become a cliche that Woodstock was the defining moment of the counterculture, [but] when I watched these broadcasts in their entirety, I realized that, in reality, this week in 1972, when John Lennon and Yoko Ono essentially hijacked the airwaves and presented the best minds and dreams of their generation to the widest possible mass audience of what was then called 'Middle America,' was as far as the counterculture would ever get," according to Erik Nelson, who made a documentary about the event.

Yoko and John brought on their radical friends as guests, including Jerry Rubin and Black Panther Bobby Seale. During the broadcasts, Yoko performed art pieces, including "Mend Piece" and "Touch Poem for a Group of People." ("The audience's boisterous bewilderment to Yoko's performance-art pieces makes her seem like the wacky substitute teacher you always wished for," according to the *Phoenix New Times*.) On one show, Yoko, John, and

Chuck Berry, another guest, demonstrated macrobiotic cooking (they made hijiki pockets).

With Berry, Yoko and John performed Berry's "Memphis, Tennessee." It was a performance that made history because John Lennon and Chuck Berry performed together and because of Yoko's participation, which led to a new barrage of attacks on her. Berry seemed dumbfounded by Yoko's vocalizations.

The Chuck Berry spot was just one of many that drew fire. Still, Yoko and John enjoyed the experience and believed it accomplished their goal. She explained, "We wanted to do the shows to show that we are working for peace and love and also to change the world, not with violence, but with love."

Millions of Americans watched *The Mike Douglas Show*. And so did the FBI.

IRONICALLY, YOKO AND JOHN BECAME targets of the government at a time when they were becoming less enamored of the leaders of the radical left. They were still fully committed to the anti-war movement but had qualms about the organizers. The revolutionaries were bent on bringing down the system, but they couldn't articulate, at least to Yoko and John's satisfaction, what should replace it. As John sang in "Revolution," "We'd all love to see the plan."

Yoko and John were also angered by the sexism they observed among the anti-war radicals. John pointed out that Yoko was the only woman around: "We used to ask, 'Are there women in this movement? Where is Mrs. Hoffman? Or your lady friend? Where are they?' And they would say, 'Oh, they're doing the typing back in the office.'"

Yoko added, "Or 'taking care of the baby.'"

John once said, "I'm always interested to know how people who claim to be radical treat women. . . . It's ridiculous. How can you talk about power to the people unless you realize the people is both sexes?"

———

YOKO AND JOHN WERE ARGUABLY the world's most famous peaceniks. Though they were having doubts about Rubin, Hoffman, and the other leaders of the anti-war movement, they still worked with them and agreed to headline a national concert tour "to bring rock 'n' roll together with radical politics in a dozen cities," as Wiener wrote in his book *Gimme Some Truth*. The radical leaders wanted to end the tour in San Diego so they could disrupt the Republican National Convention at which Nixon would be renominated.

Word of these plans, which included a campaign to register young voters, escalated the Nixon administration's efforts to deport John.

The Republican National Convention was scheduled for August 1972. Some of the radical leaders talked about replicating in San Diego the riots that had taken place during the 1968 Democratic National Convention in Chicago. There, thousands of police officers and the National Guard had faced off against protesters, who were clubbed and tear-gassed.

"When they described their plans, we just kept looking at each other," John told me. "[Allen] Ginsberg was with us. He kept saying, 'What are we trying to do, create another Chicago?' That's what they wanted. We said, 'We ain't buying this. We're not going to draw children into a situation to create violence—so you can overthrow *what*?—and replace it with *what*?'"

The concert tour was canceled. Along with not wanting to be responsible for violence in San Diego, Yoko and John had another reason not to do it: Leon Wildes, their immigration lawyer, told them that concerts would increase the government's efforts to deport John. (The 1972 Republican convention was moved from San Diego to Miami, where Nixon was renominated as the party's candidate.)

IN MAY, 1972, YOKO AND John went on *The Dick Cavett Show* to promote a new album, *Some Time in New York City*. On the show, John announced that he had reason to believe that the FBI was wiretapping their phone in order to gather evidence for his deportation.

Next, they broached the subject they most wanted to talk about: Kyoko. John summed up the saga with Kyoko, adding new details. He told about the hearing in the US Virgin Islands. "We won the court case. . . . We got custody." Then he explained what had happened in Houston. "Finally as we start winning the case in Texas, Mr. Cox runs away with Kyoko again."

Yoko said, "As usual," and John continued, "They give us custody. Again. And this is temporary custody only if we bring the child up in America. And we don't mind. We agree. We'd like to be here and bring her up. We have two papers [stating we have] custody but haven't a clue where she is."

John made a plea directly to Tony. "We're saying it now if you're watching. There's nothing John and Yoko could do to Kyoko. We couldn't hide her anywhere like you because we're too famous. There's nowhere we could go. And Yoko always said in court and out of court, she thinks the child should have both parents, be able to see both parents, and we don't care what kind of arrangement he wants to make just so the child has the benefit of both parents."

Yoko showed a picture of Kyoko, and Cavett said, "[It] would be on your mind all the time." She responded, "John has to switch the TV to another channel whenever I see a child, because I just can't stand seeing a child."

MUCH LATER YOKO DID AN in-depth interview for *Cosmopolitan* magazine with the artist and writer Caroline Coon. The piece never ran, because, Coon would explain, "The editor of *Cosmopolitan* wanted me to be more critical of Yoko, especially regarding the 'fact' that Yoko 'had deserted her daughter.' I refused to add this into the interview, not least because I had never been asked to make such a comment about any of the divorced men I interviewed."

Yoko hadn't deserted her daughter—Tony had disappeared with Kyoko, and Yoko was desperate to find her—but the response by the magazine's editors was another example of the sexism Yoko continued to face.

THE CUSTODY ORDER THAT YOKO and John hoped would bring Kyoko to them was in jeopardy as the US government continued its efforts to deport John. The extent of the government's efforts to "neutralize" him came to light years later through a decades-long investigation by Wiener. Among much more evidence, Wiener uncovered a secret memo that the Senate Internal Security Subcommittee staff wrote in February 1972 to accompany a memo from US Senator Strom Thurmond. Entitled "John Lennon," it noted that "Radical New Left" leader Rennie Davis "and his cohorts . . . intend to use John Lennon as a drawing card to promote the success of the rock festivals and rallies. The source feels that this will pour tremendous amounts of money into the coffers of the New Left and can only inevitably lead to a clash between a controlled mob organized by this group and law enforcement in San Diego." The report recommended that Lennon's visa be terminated.

According to Wiener's investigation, Thurmond sent the memo to John Mitchell, Nixon's attorney general, on February 4, 1972. He wrote that "many headaches might be avoided if appropiate action be taken in time."

The next month, someone knocked on Yoko and John's door. A deportation notice was slipped under it.

It was the first of a series of such notices that Yoko and John fought for years.

CHAPTER 16

YOKO SAID THEY'D GOTTEN THE wrong information about methadone. It's a drug that people use to stay off heroin and other opiates because it prevents withdrawal and quells cravings, but Yoko and John had been under the impression that it would give them the same high as heroin without being addictive. Yoko said, "So most people take methadone because they want to withdraw from smack and we weren't taking smack, we weren't taking anything, so it was the silliest thing to do. So we got hooked on methadone."

They used the drug for five months, intermittently trying—but failing—to stop. They remained determined to quit and decided to do it in California. They'd never seen the part of America between the coasts and chose to embark on a cross-country drive. In spring of 1972, they headed to Los Angeles in a nondescript station wagon. An assistant, Peter Bendrey, served as their driver. John had Bendrey install a record player and a stock of 1950s rock-and-roll 45s. The records skipped whenever the car hit a bump.

They stayed at motels and hotels and ate at diners. They managed to remain under the press's radar, and when they were recognized by the public, they politely said hello and gave autographs. When they reached the West Coast, they went to Ojai, a haven for artists, musicians, and spiritual seekers an hour and a half north of Los Angeles, and rented an unassuming home with a swimming pool.

Soon after they arrived in Ojai, Yoko called Elliot Mintz at his Laurel Canyon home. Mintz, a late-night FM radio DJ, regularly received promotional records from record companies, and a year earlier, he'd been sent a copy of Yoko's *Fly* album. He loved it and called the record company to ask if he could interview Yoko on his radio show. Since everyone wanted to talk to John but almost no one was interested in Yoko, she and John were thrilled.

Elliot interviewed Yoko by phone. After the interview aired in LA, he sent her a recording of the conversation. She was pleased and called to thank him, and they talked until five in the morning. Elliot learned that Yoko was an insomniac like him, and after that, they spent many nights in conversation. One day, she asked if he'd like to interview John. That interview took place on October 9, 1971, the day John turned thirty-one. It led to more phone calls with them both. They became "phone pals." "We would have occasions where we would talk five, six, seven hours a day," he said.

Yoko called Elliot from Ojai, explained where she and John were, and asked Elliot to meet them there. As a security precaution, they didn't give him the address of the house. Elliot followed assistant Peter Bendrey's directions to an abandoned field outside the small town, where Yoko and John were waiting in their station wagon. Yoko emerged from the back seat, then John got out. They greeted each other with hugs.

Elliot followed their car back to the house; there, Yoko changed into a chartreuse one-piece bathing suit and John changed into shorts, and they all talked around the pool. Elliot recalled Yoko lying on her back on the diving board. She had on her sunglasses, and she was looking at the sky.

Eventually, Yoko came over to Elliot and instructed him to follow her. She led him into a bathroom and closed the door. They sat on the edge of the bathtub, and she turned the water on. She whispered, "We think this house is bugged, so we have to be very careful what we say. You understand, don't you?"

Later that day, John told Elliot he had something for him. He handed Elliot a record with no label on it. It had just arrived from New York, and John said,

"We've decided that you're going to be able to play the record before anyone else. We want you to take this back to LA and play it on the radio." The record was *Some Time in New York City*, which hadn't yet been released.

In LA that night, Elliot told his radio audience, "For the next hour, let's just all kick back and listen to something by John and Yoko. You've never heard it before. It's brand-new, and I'm fortunate enough to share it with you exclusively." And he played the record without commercial interruption or comment.

Later, Elliot said that as soon as he heard the first song, "Woman Is the N----- of the World," he knew he'd have to get out his résumé. Indeed, he was fired for playing the song because it contained the n-word in its title and chorus.

The next day, Yoko and John called Elliot to ask how it had gone. He reported that the good news was that he played the entire album. The bad news was that he had been fired. Yoko and John laughed. John said, "Pack a bag and come with us."

Elliot joined Yoko and John on their road trip. From Ojai, the three of them drove north to San Francisco, where they checked into the Miyako Hotel. They seldom ventured out of their room. "It was not a great time for them physically," Elliot said. They were desperate to get off methadone. Craig Pyes, editor of *SunDance* magazine, recommended a Chinese herbalist and acupuncturist named Yuan Bain Hong to help them quit. For a week, Yoko and John stayed with Hong's family in their San Mateo duplex, sleeping on the couch. Hong's treatments worked; the couple kicked their habit. John wrote, "It was [Hong] who was responsible for helping us survive methadone withdrawal, which had almost killed Yoko."

A few days after they arrived in San Francisco, on June 12, 1972, *Some Time in New York City* was released. "Woman Is the N----- of the World" was immediately banned from radio play. There were other political songs, including ones about John Sinclair and the Attica Prison riots, and a sixteen-minute version of Yoko's "Don't Worry Kyoko." The cover had a collage of lyrics and pictures laid out like a newspaper. One picture was an illustration of a line in

Yoko's song "We're All Water": "There may be not much difference between Chairman Mao and Richard Nixon / If we strip them naked." In the picture on the cover, Nixon and Mao dance together—nude. The record was mostly trashed, and it was a commercial flop. *Rolling Stone* slammed it, calling it "incipient artistic suicide." In the *NME*, critic Tony Tyler wrote an open letter to John titled "Lennon, You're a Pathetic, Ageing Revolutionary."

John later recalled, "[Yoko] and I started getting down about that record, saying it was a mistake, even though we tried to say something about women, and we tried to say something about love and peace or whatever . . . the war. We got into so much trouble."

YOKO AND JOHN SENT BENDREY back east with the car, and they flew to New York. They were off methadone but felt the aftereffects of withdrawal—melancholia, depletion. They were also depressed because of the negative response to *Some Time in New York City* and to a live performance at Madison Square Garden at which they played songs from the album with the group that had backed them on the record, Elephant's Memory. Though they were on a health-food diet of rice and vegetables, John was drinking heavily.

THREE MONTHS AFTER THE REPUBLICAN National Convention, Nixon was reelected president in a landslide, trouncing the Democratic candidate, George McGovern. Like many McGovern supporters, Yoko, John, and their radical cohorts had naively believed McGovern would win, but he lost in every state except Massachusetts and the District of Columbia. It was a major blow. McGovern had promised to end the war in Vietnam, and Nixon would continue it. Also, with Nixon's reelection, it was more likely that John would be deported.

Election night would turn out to be one of the worst nights Yoko ever experienced. Photographer Bob Gruen, a friend, was with Yoko and John at a party at Jerry Rubin's home in the Village, where they expected they'd be celebrating McGovern's victory. As the night wore on, and it became clear that McGovern was being clobbered, John, who was high, "was spewing curses and screaming like a Liverpool sailor," Gruen recalled.

He remembered, "There were few people left at the party and a girl started caressing John. In front of everyone, they started to make love, moved to the next room with a paper-thin wall. And we could all hear what was going on. And we were sitting with Yoko in the next room, and it got really awkward."

Gruen put on a record to drown out the sound, but the album he grabbed was an unfortunate choice. It was Bob Dylan's *Blonde on Blonde*, and the song that played was "Sad Eyed Lady of the Lowlands," which Gruen categorized as "the longest, slowest dirge Dylan ever wrote."

Yoko recalled, "I was just frozen, stuck there, sitting. And all that time [another] woman was saying, 'You don't understand how we feel about John, do you? He's the most lovely, the most beautiful person, and we all love him' to me. . . . And I was saying, 'Yes. Thank you.' I didn't know what to say."

All the coats were in the room John was in with the woman, so no one could leave the party.

YOKO AND JOHN HAD BEEN working on a new album of Yoko's, but no one showed up in the studio the next day. The day after that, everyone did return, but John was hungover and Yoko was silent. In spite of that, they worked through the night, and in the morning, they all went out to breakfast.

On December 23, 1972, the *Imagine* film was released. For them personally, it was poorly timed, as it was a reminder of better days—how much fun they'd had, how in love they'd been.

YOKO'S NEXT RELEASE, *Approximately Infinite Universe,* a stunning double album, was, in part, an overt expression of sadness and seething. In the song "What a Bastard the World Is" she raged: "You pig, you bastard, you scum of the earth." Then she weakened: "Please, don't go, I didn't mean it, I'm just in pain."

In interviews, Yoko insisted that the record wasn't about John ("It's a story of all of us women," she said once). She might have been telling the truth, but after his flagrant public infidelity, John was almost certainly at least an unconscious target for her.

"It was almost a mistake to make the album," Yoko observed. Yet she also said the record released some of the tension that had been building inside her.

Yoko and John worked. Sometimes they socialized. They saw a few friends. The McCartneys stopped by when they were in New York. They saw Fluxus artists, including Maciunas and La Monte Young, and other artists. But they mostly hid. John watched a lot of TV. He had replaced methadone with alcohol, and his drinking increased. Sometimes Yoko was fine, but other times she was melancholy and distant. And meanwhile the government continued its harassment. According to Wiener, after Nixon was reelected in November, the FBI lost interest in John and said it was closing its file. However, the INS continued its efforts to deport him for another year and a half.

They met with Leon Wildes, the immigration lawyer, often and spoke to him most days. In March 1973, John's application to stay in the country was denied because of his drug conviction.

The next week, they filed an appeal with the INS. Yoko, John, and Wildes held a press conference about the case during which Yoko and John announced they were forming "a conceptual country," Nutopia. It had "no land, no boundaries, no passports, only people . . . no laws other than cosmic." The *New York Times* reported, "With a characteristic instinct for showmanship, they each whipped out a white tissue and said, 'This is the flag of Nutopia—we surrender, to peace and to love.'

"Then Mr. Lennon blew his nose on it."

THEY FELT LIKE THE BANK Street apartment was closing in on them, and they thought a move would help. They started looking outside the city and almost bought a house in Connecticut. Then they were shown an apartment owned by the actor Robert Ryan in the storied Dakota apartment building on the Upper West Side of Manhattan. They made an offer on the high-ceilinged, ten-room seventh-floor apartment that wrapped around Central Park West and West Seventy-Second Street with spectacular views of the park. When Yoko and John were approved by the Dakota's board, they saw it as a fresh start.

In the spring of 1973, Yoko and John moved into the Dakota. They were keeping on, but there was a pall over them—their problems had moved into the building with them. John was becoming difficult to live with. Sometimes Yoko felt smothered by him; he was needier than ever. But sometimes he blew up at her.

"John was getting drunk a lot and he was depressed," Gruen said. "She was working and wanted to make music and he just was, you know, kind of wallowing. By the summer, Yoko was tired of John being an asshole and said, 'Well, if you're not gonna work, you're just gonna drink, do that somewhere else.'"

Yoko told me, "I really needed some space because I was used to being an artist and free. . . . So I thought it would be a good idea that he would go to LA and just leave me alone for a while."

YOKO NEVER DID ANYTHING CONVENTIONALLY, and her separation from John was no exception. Much has been made of her decision to kick him out and even more of her decision to "give" her husband a lover. Yoko wanted a break but she believed John needed to be taken care of. She chose May Pang, an assistant, as the ideal candidate. Yoko said she never felt jealous when John and May got together. "The affair was something that was not hurtful to me," she said. "I needed a rest. I needed space."

Maybe it wasn't hurtful to her, but as the story circulated and became part of the ballad of Yoko and John, it added to the impression that she was cold and manipulative.

Yoko and John had met Pang when she worked in the office of Allen Klein as an assistant. In December 1970, Pang had been assigned to help Yoko and John with their movie *Up Your Legs Forever* (it was similar to *Bottoms*, but it focused on another body part). Later, Yoko hired her as a personal assistant. Pang did whatever was needed, helping Yoko and John in the apartment, at the studio, with art projects, shopping, and other errands. Pang said it was a dream job. "A typical day would consist of the mundane (like brewing the morning coffee and opening mail) to calling Jackie Kennedy Onassis or Andy Warhol."

The oft-repeated story has Yoko startling Pang with an unexpected new assignment. "Yoko came to me at 9:30 in the morning and said, 'May, I've got to talk to you. John and I are not getting along,' which I knew because the tension was thick," Pang said. "She said, 'He's going to start going out with other people. I know you don't have a boyfriend, and you would be good for him.' I said I didn't think so, but she said, 'You don't want him to go out with somebody who is going to be nasty to him, do you?' I said, 'Of course not,' and she said, 'You will be perfect,' and walked out."

Yoko said, "May Pang was a very intelligent, attractive woman and extremely efficient. I thought they'd be okay."

It's been reported that the affair with John started when Yoko went to Chicago for a week for a feminist conference. Whenever it happened, she was pleased they'd gotten together.

BESIDES JOHN'S SULLEN MOOD, his drinking and the betrayal at Jerry Rubin's, Yoko was struggling with what it meant to be John's wife. She said,

"Can you imagine every day of getting this vibration from people of hate? You want to get out of that."

In addition, as Gruen recalled, "Wherever we went, everyone wants to talk to John. She was elbowed aside, literally." Initially her friends in the art world seemed too cool to be impressed by John's celebrity, but they weren't immune; they were seduced too. Everyone wanted John.

In an interview with me, John recalled, "One Beatle assistant who shall be nameless, in the upper echelon of Beatle assistants, in the early days when we were doing a lot of stuff together . . . he leaned over and said [to Yoko]: 'You know, you don't have to work, you've got enough money, now that you're Mrs. Lennon . . . ' That was in '68 or something. . . . But by the time we got to '73, you know, a good few years of that kind of attitude emasculates you."

He asked Yoko, "Is that the word?"

"Exactly!" she said. "I was emasculated."

"And on top of that, me being me is enough without the pandemonium."

Once she told Alexandra Munroe, "Before meeting John, I was doing two concerts and lectures a month. I was in demand. I was able to express myself all the time. Suddenly, by becoming the wife of a Beatle, what was required of me was to shut up."

She was the woman he'd looked for his whole life, someone to save him—a mother. He needed her to be his salvation but she didn't want to be any man's salvation and didn't want to need any man for *her* salvation. She needed to save herself.

Yoko said, "When I met John, women to him were basically people around who were serving him. He had to open himself up and face me—and I had to see what he was going through. But . . . I thought I had to 'move on' again because I was suffering being with John. I thought I wanted to be free from being Mrs. Lennon."

CHAPTER 17

"WHEN TWO PEOPLE ARE SEPARATED, they automatically assume the guy left the girl and the poor girl is suffering and in tears," Yoko said.

Yoko and John would spend eighteen months apart, a time that John famously referred to as the "lost weekend." John was indeed lost, as he often said, but Yoko wasn't.

John and May left for Los Angeles in the fall of 1973. They flew to LAX, where Elliot Mintz picked them up. When Elliot asked John what was up, he told him Yoko had kicked him out.

John had friends in LA. Besides Elliot, Ringo was frequently in town, and the producer Phil Spector lived there. Other friends and acquaintances in LA included the musicians Harry Nilsson, Micky Dolenz of the Monkees, and Keith Moon, the drummer for the Who. With them and others, John and May went out to clubs and parties. "Well, first I thought, Whoopee! Bachelor life! Whoopee, whoopee."

To all appearances, John was living it up. During that period, he worked on several albums with Ringo, Moon, Nilsson, Spector, and others—and he partied and drank heavily.

But John's excitement waned quickly. "I woke up one day and thought,

What is this? I want to go home. But she wouldn't let me come home," John said.

"I was haunted, all right, because I realized that I needed her more than she needed me, and I always thought the boot was on the other foot, you know?" John later said. "And that's as honest as I can get. . . . It was God-awful."

He told me, "I was trying to hide what I felt in a bottle, and it wasn't doing me any good. Physically and mentally it was killing me."

John's lost weekend is well documented, but Yoko's experience over that period has been mostly ignored. Her interlude was far different from John's. With him gone, Yoko initially reeled. It was a shock to her system. "My body was shaking," she said. "It was almost like a withdrawal. It's a withdrawal from intimacy."

But after a few weeks, something shifted. She relaxed. She lived relatively quietly. As always, she slept only four or five hours a night (during the day, she took catnaps). She normally started her days at four or five a.m., took an ice bath, then had tea. After scanning the newspapers, she went to her office, where she attended to business. She met with accountants and lawyers and dealt with practical matters. She dealt with spiritual matters too, consulting in person and on the phone with psychics. She took breaks, resting on the couch and meditating. She saw friends—musicians and artists, mostly. She went to the movies and to galleries and played mah-jongg with a group of friends who came to the Dakota. She read voraciously—history, philosophy, and books about spirituality and psychic phenomena; in the evenings, she read mystery novels to wind down. She continually made art and wrote songs and soon returned to the studio with Plastic Ono Band musicians but not John. She planned another album.

In LA, John worked in the studio with Phil Spector on a compilation of cover versions of classic rock-and-roll songs. The sessions for what became the *Rock 'n' Roll* album were fueled by alcohol. There were parties attended by celebrities every night. Of the music being made in the recording studio, drummer Jim Keltner told writer Philip Norman, "There were some flashes of brilliance—with Phil and John working together, there had to be. But mostly the music crashed and burned."

Norman wrote about a particularly bad evening: "Keltner and guitarist Jesse Ed Davis were called on to restrain John one night when the cocktail of vodka and 100-proof rock 'n' roll unlocked all his pent-up anguish over Yoko, and he went literally berserk. 'We had to hold him down in the back of the car to stop him kicking the windows in . . .' Keltner recalled. 'He was lashing out at Jesse, and pulling my hair and screaming Yoko's name.'"

Yoko and John talked on the telephone most days. He asked to come home. Every time, she said the same thing: "You're not ready." On trips back to New York, John visited Yoko at the Dakota. He told her what he was up to and she updated him on her life. He inevitably begged to come home, but she said no.

YOKO WORKED ON A NEW record with virtuoso guitarist David Spinozza, who served as her bandleader, and a new configuration of the Plastic Ono Band. In October 1973, she performed twelve sold-out concerts over six nights at Kenny's Castaways, a bar on the Upper East Side.

The Kenny's Castaways concerts were pure Yoko. She played songs from the album she was working on and staged events.

She received scathing reviews, including one in the *New York Times*. Critic John Rockwell wrote, "Let us start with the premise that Yoko Ono . . . is a simply terrible pop music performer. She can't sing, her tunes are tuneless, and her lyrics are clumsy. . . .

"Surely she must realize that by any normal criterion she is terrible; in fact, she deliberately emphasizes the abrasive aspects of her singing. So what is she up to? Perhaps she is simply working out her neuroses in public. But perhaps she is fascinated with the tension between herself and her audiences. After years as a leading avant-gardist, with the bland acceptance common at avant-garde events, perhaps she relishes any kind of electricity in the air, positive or negative."

Maybe she *did* relish any kind of electricity. Though she wanted to be accepted and appreciated, she also once told Bob Gruen that she didn't succeed in a performance unless half the audience walked out.

Yoko moved on. A month later, in November 1973, she released the new album called *Feeling the Space*. She *was* feeling the space and the album was exuberant. The new album had feminist anthems such as "Woman Power" and "Angry Young Woman."

"Men, Men, Men" reversed roles, parodying the way men look at and treat women. The credits on the LP listed the male musicians' measurements as if they were Playboy bunnies.

Feeling the Space has been called Yoko's "feminist manifesto." "The album's theme is female liberation," wrote Madeline Bocaro, author of *In Her Mind: The Infinite Universe of Yoko Ono*. "Side One tells stories of individual women oppressed by society. On Side Two women unite, wake up, rise up and kick ass!" Yoko dedicated the album "to the sisters who died in pain and sorrow and those who are now in prisons and in mental hospitals for being unable to survive in the male society."

EVEN AS YOKO WAS THRIVING alone, she heard from John, who, though living with May, continued to beg to come home. She also heard from mutual friends, including Paul McCartney, who pleaded with Yoko on his behalf. But in addition to feeling that John wasn't ready to come home, Yoko hadn't yet answered her own questions about the relationship.

One of the things that bothered her during that time was the fact that reporters were writing about her as the poor deserted wife. "And wherever I'd go they'd all look at me like, 'Oh, I'm so sorry for you,'" she told me.

John agreed that was how people saw it. He said everyone assumed she was the one who was bereft, but in fact she was "carrying on normally" while he was going to pieces; he explained, "I'm the one that freaked out. When we were separated it was me making an asshole of myself in the clubs and in the newspapers. It wasn't her. Her life was ordered."

John—with May—came to New York in early 1974. They visited Yoko at the Dakota on her birthday. During that time Yoko was working in the studio on a new project, *A Story*, an intensely personal record. The songs indicated her working through her relationship with John—and with herself. Yoko would end up postponing the album's release for almost two decades.

On the album, the song "Yes, I'm a Witch" was another exuberant and defiant statement.

Yes, I'm a witch
I'm a bitch
I don't care what you say
My voice is real
My voice is truth
I don't fit in your ways
I'm not gonna die for you
You might as well face the truth
I'm gonna stick around for quite awhile.

JOHN MADE MUSIC TOO, BUT he was miserable. He worked on *Rock 'n' Roll* as well as a new album to be called *Walls and Bridges*. On that record, John's song "Nobody Loves You (When You're Down and Out)" expressed how he was feeling in LA. Another song on the record was "Whatever Gets You Thru the Night." Elton John happened to visit the studio when John was recording it. Elton played piano and sang on the record. John said he "sort of halfheartedly promised" Elton that if "Whatever Gets You Thru the Night" became number one, he'd perform onstage with him at an upcoming concert at Madison Square Garden. John didn't think there was a chance that would happen.

———

JOHN CONTINUED TO WORK—AND party—as Yoko set out on a concert tour of Japan with the Plastic Ono Super Band. Bob Gruen was with her when the plane landed at Tokyo's Haneda Airport in August 1974. The reception she received was different from the previous time. "It was like Beatlemania," Gruen recalled. "Like she was the Japanese Elvis."

He documented the scene in a series of photos that showed throngs of journalists, photographers, and fans. She granted interviews and held a press conference.

Yoko performed six sold-out Plastic Ono Super Band concerts. She gave away a piece she created, a new "Self-Portrait," which was a folded mirror. When you opened it, you saw yourself. An alarm clock went off in the middle of the show. She tossed underwear into the audience.

Unlike her earlier concerts in Japan, this time the audience loved her; she was exhilarated, and not only because of the reception. She felt freer. She'd been with a man since she'd married Toshi when she was twenty-three. Now she was on her own. This was another turning point in her life: She discovered an inner strength she had not fully realized she had before.

Yoko thrived on the raw, unfiltered expression that she poured into her performances. The applause in Japan was thunderous, resonating with her sense of personal victory. Yoko stood on the stage not as John's muse or partner but—like in the old days before she knew him—as an artist in her own right.

CHAPTER 18

AFTER YOKO FINISHED HER JAPANESE tour, a numerologist advised her to travel back to New York by way of Europe, to complete her circumnavigation of the Earth. The normal route would have her fly east over the States, but she readily agreed to continue west.

Yoko had always been drawn to the occult, and she regularly consulted astrologers, numerologists, tarot card readers, palm readers, witches, and other mystics and seers. Her friend Tadanori Yokoo said she was always interested in "very unscientific things." He said, "For her it was something really important. Something invisible, something incredible. To believe in something that you can't see is a core principle of her art."

Yoko believed in magic. Things were "meant to be." She read about spirituality, reincarnation, "separate realities," and how to use one's psychic powers. She could be alarmed by bad signs and bolstered by good ones. She believed in positive affirmations. When something went well, she said "Thank you" three times, aloud, "to the universe."

When I asked why she'd consulted the stars and numerology, she said, "Because it's a larger force than us, in a way. And I was dealing with that, not man-made forces." Also, she relied on those systems as a way to "free my brain, think about problems from different angles."

She meditated and practiced visualizing. She fervently believed she could create a different reality by visualizing it—*imagining* it. She believed that the words she used—in everything from song titles to conversation—would influence the future. She wanted to fill her brain with positive thoughts, not negative ones.

One of the numerologists and other psychics Yoko relied on (and paid handsomely) advised her about "directional travel," instructing her to journey in one or another direction around the globe to either amass power or prevent calamities. Sara Seagull, an assistant who accompanied her on the trip to Japan, flew west with her to London, where she spent a week. (The band flew back to the United States via the conventional eastward route.) Yoko visited Paul and Linda McCartney and George Harrison and took Sara to see Stonehenge. They went to Tittenhurst Park, then owned by Ringo. She completed the circumnavigation by flying back to New York.

She also sent John on directional trips to protect him. Once he traveled from New York to South Africa and back because a psychic said it would benefit him. On another occasion, returning from a trip to Japan, John flew to New York by way of Hong Kong, Dubai, and Frankfurt.

In his song "God," John stated clearly that he *didn't* believe in the tarot, the I Ching, or magic—so why then would he spend days flying all over the world because his wife's psychic said he should? Elliot Mintz said it came back to one of the first things John told him when they'd met: "There will be times you'll think she's bloody mad. Just do what she tells you to do. She's almost always right. She sees things other people can't see."

Yoko's belief in the supernatural might have helped reassure and guide her, but it also opened her up to manipulation and exploitation.

A MONTH AFTER YOKO'S JAPANESE tour, she was back home, working in New York. John's *Walls and Bridges* album was released, and the single "Whatever Gets You Thru the Night" reached number one in the United States.

John had said he'd perform with Elton John live if the song hit number one. "I promised him," John told me, "so now I was stuck."

The concert was set for Madison Square Garden on Thanksgiving–November 28, 1974. Yoko contemplated attending. She was hesitant but decided to go to see how John was doing. "Everyone was telling me how worried they were about him, so I thought maybe I should go."

She didn't tell John her plans and requested a seat where John wouldn't see her from the stage. Before the concert, she sent John and Elton gardenias but didn't say she'd be there.

"I didn't know she was there because if I'd known she was there I'd have been too nervous to go on," John said. "I would have been terrified."

In the middle of his set, Elton brought out John. "In my whole career, I've honestly never heard a crowd make a noise like the one they made when I introduced him," Elton wrote. They played "Whatever Gets You Thru the Night," "Lucy in the Sky with Diamonds," and "I Saw Her Standing There."

As Yoko explained, "The whole house shook. But what I saw of him was a totally different thing. I saw this lonely person and that really touched me, and I started crying. . . . It was like my soul suddenly saw it . . . saw his soul, which was not what the audience saw, obviously, because they were just applauding. And that's why I went backstage—to say hello."

This decision was a concession on Yoko's part. When she went backstage, she said, "We looked at each other for the longest time. We couldn't take our eyes off each other."

THE NEXT THING THAT HAPPENED: "We dated," Yoko said. "We laughed about it."

They met at an art opening. They gossiped and turned over and over what had happened to them while they'd been separated. John was still living with May in an apartment he'd rented. After the date, he returned to May, and Yoko returned to the Dakota.

They went on more dates. Yoko was cautious. She was wary of being sucked back in—afraid of losing herself.

They sat together and didn't talk much. Sometimes they cried. When the strain became too great, she told him, "You'd better go now."

But finally Yoko was ready to try again.

They were both nervous. John said, "We realized that there were a lot of, as we call it, holes in our aura—space that we had to be gently healing between us."

She said, "We had to clean our aura."

He explained, "We had to clean the . . . separation period from us, you know. We had to sort of wash it off, somehow, and that was a delicate operation. Almost as delicate as first meeting, and that sort of getting-to-know-each-other business and all that."

Yoko said, "So then when we came back together again, I think that he really tried hard in a way to make it work. . . . I started to have just a great respect for him."

John left May. "John [called and] said, 'Yoko's allowed me to come home,'" she said. May was devastated when John left her.

When John moved back into the Dakota, no one, other than the small staff, knew until John phoned Elliot, who'd begun serving as a spokesperson, and said he could make an announcement. "Let the media know that the separation did not work."

YOKO WAS STILL TREPIDATIOUS, BUT the separation had changed her. She had more confidence than before. She was comfortable in herself. She felt that although John had work to do on himself, he was pretty evolved for a man, especially considering his background. He was deeply regretful about the night at Jerry Rubin's. After the hellish lost weekend, he'd concluded that the self-indulgent rock-star lifestyle was not for him. "I was the real pig,"

John told me later, "and it is a relief not to be a pig. The pressures of being a pig were enormous. They were killing me."

They talked about conditions for reconciling and made the decision to "reorder our priorities." They defined new roles that would allow them to work on what they needed to work on.

Yoko would take care of the business, which she'd begun to focus on when they were separated. "He was intelligent enough to know that this was the only way that we could save our marriage," she said. "Not because we didn't love each other, but because it was too much for me. Nothing would have changed if I had come back as Mrs. Lennon again. It was good for me to do the business and regain my pride about what I can do."

John knew he had to be sober. "When I was still drunk, I would just ramble on or scream abuse at her or beg to come back, you know—between Dr. Jekyll and Mr. Hyde," he said. "I don't know what I was saying or doing half the time when I was still drinking."

Also, as John said, he'd been a "performing flea" since he was a teenager. He decided he needed to stop living life as the Beatle or ex-Beatle. "I was the walrus, but now I'm John," he sang in "God." But he had no experience being just John; could he function as a person not in the center of the maelstrom of press, musicians, events, producing records—chaos? He decided there would be no recording studios, no media.

Their lives were simplified. John was humbled. Yoko seemed different too. Bob Gruen said, "She was less restless. . . . They were in love—like at first but it felt more solid, like two people who'd gone through the gauntlet."

On March 1, 1975, Yoko and John went to the Grammy Awards, where John was a presenter. He explained that the Grammys provided an opportunity to show the world that he was sober and he and Yoko were together. He thanked Yoko from the stage: "Thank you, Mother, thank you."

At the after-party, Gruen photographed them. Yoko, all in white with a feather boa, and John, wearing a white fringed scarf and a black beret with his long coat, looked euphoric. Three weeks later, on March 20, they celebrated their sixth wedding anniversary. They had made it—barely. At the Dakota, amid a sea of white carnations and white candles burning, dressed in white, they renewed their vows.

THEY WANTED A CHILD. OF course, they each had a child from a previous marriage, and both had been—by their own admission—less than stellar parents. But having renewed their commitment to each other, they were reassessing what mattered most, and they were consciously building their future together.

They'd been gravely disappointed by Yoko's miscarriages and had begun to accept they might never have a child. But back in 1972, Hong, the acupuncturist and herbalist in San Francisco who'd helped them get off methadone, had instructed them on how Yoko could get pregnant. Cryptically, he'd told them to take time apart, which had been unthinkable then. But now they had. Hong had also said to stop drinking and doing drugs. They had done that too.

Yoko soon got pregnant. In the past, they'd announced their pregnancies immediately, but Yoko asked John to wait this time. "We had many miscarriages that way because the minute we announced I was pregnant, there were a lot of negative vibes sent to us from crazy people in the world," Yoko said. "We'd get a doll in the mail with a pin stuck in it or something, wishing I didn't have the child. We had to separate ourselves and protect ourselves from that to nourish our child."

The doctor told Yoko to rest and stay in bed. John doted on her—brought her tea, accompanied her to doctor appointments, and took a Lamaze course with her. After Yoko's first trimester, their doctor said it was safe to make the announcement.

The baby would be born to parents who were legally permitted to be in the United States. There had been more developments in the immigration case over the previous year and a half. At one point, the Board of Immigration Appeals ordered John to leave the country. He had sixty days to comply. A series of appeals and countersuits were filed. It became a familiar routine. Eventually the case moved up to the US court of appeals. On October 7, 1975, that court overturned the order to deport him. The decision noted, "Lennon's four-year battle to remain in our country is testimony to his faith in this American dream." (Almost a year later, at a press conference after John's application to be a permanent resident was approved, John thanked Yoko. "As usual, there's a great woman behind every idiot.")

ON OCTOBER 9, 1975, JOHN'S thirty-fifth birthday and two days after the court overturned the deportation order, Sean Taro Ono Lennon was born.

People have speculated that they scheduled a cesarean section so the baby would be born on John's birthday, but that's not what happened. In the early morning of October 9, Yoko began having contractions, and they went to the hospital. Because of complications, Yoko received a blood transfusion, but she had a bad reaction to it. "I was there when it happened and she starts to go rigid, and then shake from the pain and the trauma," John said. "I run up to this nurse and say, 'Go get the doctor!' I'm holding on tight to Yoko while this guy gets to the hospital room. He walks in, hardly notices that Yoko is going through fucking *convulsions*, goes straight for me, smiles, shakes my hand, and says, 'I've always wanted to meet you, Mr. Lennon, I always enjoyed your music.'

"I start screaming: 'My wife's dying and you wanna talk about my music!' Christ!"

Although they'd planned on having natural childbirth, the baby ended up being delivered by cesarean section.

They were elated when they brought Sean home. Yoko and John's world mostly became the Dakota. It had been a year since the Elton John concert, and they were excited about a new way to be. It was just like starting over.

CHAPTER 19

"THE QUEEN IS IN THE counting house counting out the money; the King is in the kitchen making bread and honey." Those were among the lyrics of "Cleanup Time," a song John wrote about that period. "It's sort of a description of John and Yoko and their little palace. The Palace of Versailles—the Dakota," he said.

Their friend the comedian Dick Gregory promoted "juicitarianism" and Yoko and John had tried it in Denmark with Tony and Melinda. Now they went on a forty-day juice fast. "I've never been so clear," John told Bob Gruen. "My mind is flying."

After that, with the baby in a snuggly pack or stroller, they walked to Café La Fortuna, their hangout a block from the Dakota, for coffee or they walked in the park. Yoko and John occasionally went out to restaurants, leaving Sean with the nanny, but they saw only a few people. Gruen visited; so did Elliot Mintz when he was in New York. They were friends with the actor Peter Boyle and his wife, Loraine Alterman. They saw the McCartneys occasionally.

On April 24, 1976, Paul and Linda McCartney were over, and the four of them watched *Saturday Night Live* together. Producer Lorne Michaels joked on the air that he'd pay the Beatles to reunite on the show. They'd been offered millions, but he offered $3,200. John and Paul talked about heading to the *SNL* studio at Rockefeller Center. They almost went but were too tired.

Klaus Voormann stopped by a few times with his son. "At one point [John] said, 'I'm so happy, Klaus. This is the first time I don't have to do any records and any obligations, I'm completely free.' The next minute he picks up the guitar—because he enjoys it, not because he had a job." Voormann said Lennon as househusband was a complete contrast to the Lennon of the past, who was "always uptight and frustrated. . . . He was completely different than he was before. Even though he had success, you always had the feeling that John was not sure about the future, how his life would go. Now he was happy."

There was a nanny and domestic staff as backup, but John was hands-on. Being his son's primary caretaker thrilled him. He attended to Sean's meals, played with the baby, and put him to sleep at night. He sat by the crib and played guitar and sang to him.

And Yoko? Before Sean was born, she said to John the same thing she had said to Tony Cox: "I am carrying the baby nine months and that is enough. You take care of it afterwards." And John had agreed.

She explained to me, "If a father raises the child and a mother carries it, the responsibility is shared. That is a better way. I am not criticizing myself. This is what I am, and I can't be anything else." Her reasoning flew in the face of conventional gender roles at the time.

But as a mother, Yoko wasn't completely uninvolved. Focused as she was on business and investments, she downplayed her maternal instincts, but John defended her. He said, "She puts herself down as a mother, which is garbage!" He saw a natural connection between Yoko and Sean. He explained, "She can still allow him to climb all over her when she's doing something else, which I cannot do. I'm either doing him or I'm not doing him. Sean can wake her up without her being irritated, whereas it still irritates me if he wakes me up before I've woken up naturally."

A friend recounted going for a walk and then to lunch with Yoko, John, and Sean. He described seeing "Yoko always riffling with the baby's hair. Gently touching him. So happy."

MONTHS WENT BY. THERE WERE a few public appearances; one was on July 27, 1976, when John finally got his green card granting him permanent residency in the United States. Yoko wore a white dress, her hair pulled back, and John was in a black suit and tie when they stood in the Immigration and Naturalization Service hearing room. It was reported in the *Times*. The article began: "Yesterday, all of John Lennon's troubles seemed so far away and now it looks as though he's here to stay."

Yoko's office, downstairs at the Dakota, was a hive of activity. Yoko never wanted to lose herself in John's world again or be treated as a nonentity in their partnership. Ironically, the world she immersed herself in was one of lawyers and accountants and bankers—her father's world.

The Beatles had dissolved, but Apple continued to manage a sizable and complex web of business holdings. "Every lawyer had a lawyer," John said.

Yoko fired "the daddies" they'd relied on—or at least some of the lawyers and other advisers. "These lawyers were getting a quarter of a million dollars a year to sit around a table and eat salmon at the Plaza," John said. "They're all male, you know, just big and fat, vodka lunch, shouting males, like trained dogs, trained to attack all the time."

Yoko described the other Beatles' representatives as being "terribly antagonistic" toward her, but she said, "It's a fascinating world . . . It's like another chess game."

It was rumored that the other Beatles and their lawyers held a secret gathering at which they discussed how to deal with Yoko. Initially when she tried to speak, the others cut her off or ignored her. John said, "There was a bit of an attitude that this is John's wife, but surely she can't really be representing him. . . . They can't stand it. But they have to stand it because it is she who represents us."

She shuffled tarot cards during meetings. "They thought I was very strange, but they had to listen to me," she said.

Yoko consulted psychics about every decision she made. She had John consult with them too. Her mystical approach tested the patience of the other Beatles. Talking about one meeting, Linda McCartney said, "The numbers weren't right, the planets weren't right, and John wasn't coming. . . . Had we known there was some guy flipping cards on his bed to help him make his decision, we would have all gone over there. George blew his top, but it didn't change anything."

Yoko told Barbara Graustark, who interviewed her for *Rolling Stone*, about her modus operandi: "For instance, when I was going to Apple meetings with lawyers who represented the other Beatles, if I tried to play the same game they were playing, I would lose because I didn't have their experience. In confronting them, I had to be myself, which meant using my instinct. In one meeting that was very important, I knew I didn't have the power to stop the dangerous things that the lawyers would try to do. The only power I had was to manage to move the date of the meeting to when the moon was void astrologically—not in line with the earth. If you have a meeting when the moon is void, everything you decide will later be annulled. I said, 'Well, we have to meet on this particular date because it is the only one available to me.' And we met, and they decided on a lot of things I couldn't stop, and later the decisions were annulled."

While doing business, Yoko consulted her tarot card readers, numerologists, astrologers, and other psychics multiple times a day. Some of those who knew her well claimed she relied blindly on their business advice, while others maintained that she used them to disorient her adversaries. Both were true. She believed, but the advice from tarot and other belief systems also freed her mind from preset patterns and traditional thinking; it prompted her to consider problems from fresh angles. She believed the universe had its own force, and she was an extension of that force. She felt more comfortable making business moves knowing she was channeling a force bigger than herself.

BESIDES THE MUSIC BUSINESS, YOKO also conducted personal business, which included investments in everything from art to Egyptian artifacts to real estate. For weekends and summers, she bought a mansion with a swimming pool and rolling grass lawns near Billy Joel's home in Cold Spring Harbor on Long Island. She bought a massive estate as a vacation home on Palm Beach's "Billionaire's Row." There were properties in Virginia (a psychic found them; the purchases would fulfill prophecies). "Buying houses was a practical decision—John was starting to feel stuck in the Dakota and we get bothered in hotels," she said.

"People advised us to invest in stocks and oil, but we didn't believe in it," Yoko told *Newsweek*. "You have to invest in things you love. Like cows, which are sacred animals in India." In upstate New York, she bought dairy farms and a herd of Holstein cows. (Years later, Elton John asked Yoko about the Holsteins, and she said she'd gotten rid of them. When he asked why, she responded, "All that *mooing*.")

Yoko loved, and wanted, anything magical—"power objects"—and she collected Egyptian artifacts. "To make money, you have to spend money," she said. "But if you are going to make money, you have to make it with love. I love Egyptian art. I make sure to get all the Egyptian things, not for their value but for their magic power. Each piece has a certain magic power. Also with houses. I just buy ones we love, not the ones that people say are good investments."

MOST MORNINGS, AS YOKO AND John had coffee or tea, Yoko went through the day's mail, delivered to the kitchen on the seventh floor from Studio One by an assistant. Then she left John with Sean upstairs and went down to the office, where she was in meetings or on the phone throughout the morning, consulting her lawyers, accountants, and psychics. She smoked endless cigarettes, meditated, and read.

Yoko and John generally had lunch together on the seventh floor, where John spent much of the day with the baby. Sometimes Yoko joined John and Sean on walks. Other times he took Sean out by himself. They walked in

Central Park and throughout their Upper West Side neighborhood. Sometimes paparazzi and fans intruded, but most kept a respectful distance from a dad out with his baby son.

Afternoons were more of the same. Yoko took breaks for quick catnaps—she'd be recharged after fifteen minutes. Sean took his nap, and John drew, read, wrote, and noodled on guitar and piano.

After Yoko finished work for the day, they ate dinner together. John made stews, steamed vegetables, rice. Yoko cooked sometimes too, simple macrobiotic or Japanese fare. Sometimes they had meals delivered. Sushi was a staple. They tried to eat healthy but lapsed frequently. The kitchen was stocked with Hershey Bars.

After dinner, they played with Sean, and then John put him to bed. Late at night, Yoko and John retreated to their bedroom, where they read books and the newspapers, listened to the radio, and watched a large-screen TV. And they talked. About everything. John sketched the family. In one portrait of the three of them together in the kitchen, Sean is playing on the floor and Yoko is on the phone—she was often on the phone with Elliot or psychics, sometimes talking through the night.

WITH HIS GREEN CARD, JOHN was free to travel outside the United States without fearing that he wouldn't be able to get back in. In winter, he spent two months studying Japanese at the Berlitz language school, preparing for a trip to Japan so they could introduce Sean to Yoko's family. Evenings, he practiced vocabulary with Yoko.

Yoko had first brought John to Japan in 1971 when he suggested that he should meet her family. She had asked him, "Why would I want to see these boring people?" She said, "They're the kind of people I left to make my own life." Yoko had been nervous to introduce John to her parents. She resented Eisuke and Isoko but still wanted their approval.

Before going with Yoko to Japan, John had been there with the Beatles.

In 1966, they had performed five concerts at the Nippon Budokan in Tokyo, and the nation had experienced fervent Beatlemania. But Yoko's family was unimpressed by Lennon's pop fame, and when John met them in 1971, he did not make an effort to impress Yoko's family. Though he'd wanted to meet them, he didn't shave. He didn't dress up; instead, he wore a ragged army-surplus coat. "He was just looking like a bum. This kind of 'here I am' attitude," she said. "My family was not enamored."

There was a party—a reunion of sorts. Eisuke took Yoko aside and said, "The other one"—meaning Tony Cox—"was more handsome," and there had been no love lost between Tony and Eisuke. For his part, John "expected to meet these two little Japanese people," Yoko said, but Eisuke was taller than he was. Her parents were modern and sophisticated. Isoko was disquietingly self-possessed and curt.

In spite of Yoko's trepidation, she had enjoyed showing John her home country. She introduced him to her brother, Keisuke, and his wife, Masako. She brought John sightseeing to Kyoto and other cities. He fell in love with the country.

The 1977 trip was their first time bringing Sean to Japan. The couple's trips to Japan with their son were some of the happiest days of their lives. John took Sean to the zoo and parks. Yoko, John, and Sean visited Kei, Masako, and their children and went around by bicycle in Karuizawa in the mountains, where they stayed at the Mampei Hotel.

Most days they bicycled a half hour from the hotel to Rizanbo, a café set in the woods. There was a hammock in the backyard, and Yoko and John, with the baby, spent hours "lying in it, giggling, singing, and watching the sky," Yoko recalled.

Visitors to the café now can see photos of Yoko, John, and Sean on the walls taken that summer and the ones that followed. Outside the main building there's a tree with a nail in it. John marked the top of Sean's head with chalk but realized it wouldn't last. With the owners' permission, he hammered in a nail. It's still there.

On that first trip with Sean, John organized an Ono/Yasuda family reunion.

More than fifty people attended. In contrast to his first meeting with her parents, John put in some effort, dressing up in a suit and tie. He was gracious, shaking hands and thanking people for coming. The reunion was considered a success; this time Yoko's family seemed duly impressed with her husband and enchanted by their son.

CHAPTER 20

SINCE YOKO AND JOHN WERE living a quiet, private life, stories spread that they had become recluses. John said it wasn't true. "We just stopped talking to the press," he told me. "The rest of our life was just as busy and full of things happening as it ever was. You see? Our life is quite as interesting without the media as it is with the media."

Yoko and John did see less of some friends, and those people didn't take it well. Mick Jagger later wrote, "He was living close to where I was living in New York City, but I was probably considered one of the 'bad influences,' so I was never allowed to see him after that. On one or two occasions when I went to visit someone in the Dakota, I'd leave him a note saying: 'I live next door. I know you don't want to see anyone, but if you do, please call.' He never did."

One Christmas, Linda and Paul came to the Dakota, and they all went out to lunch together at Elaine's, the Upper East Side celebrity haunt. Nothing on the menu appealed to the group, so they ordered pizza to be delivered to the restaurant.

On another occasion, Paul stopped by again, but that time it pissed John off. John turned him away, saying, "Please call before you come over. It's not 1956, and turning up at the door isn't the same anymore. You know, just give me a ring [before you turn up]." John said that Paul was upset by that, but that he hadn't meant anything by it. "I just meant please give me time . . . I'm tired, I've just been with the baby all day and some guy turns up at the door."

John was "just a dad," he said, though not all fathers had to answer a question that Sean asked one day after playing with Max LeRoy, who lived in the adjacent apartment on the seventh floor. Max was the son of Warner LeRoy, owner of Tavern on the Green, a restaurant in Central Park. One evening, Sean was over at Max's and a nanny popped a video in the player: *Yellow Submarine.* Sean came home and asked John, "Daddy, were you a Beatle?"

They escaped New York sometimes. They went to the Cold Spring Harbor and Palm Beach mansions. In New York City, there were frequent Yoko and John sightings in Central Park and in restaurants. They went to the Palm Court at the Plaza Hotel for tea. It's often written that they loved New York because they were left alone to go about their business—John once said they were "just another couple." However, they weren't just another couple. When they attended an exhibition at the Guggenheim, art critic Jerry Saltz wrote about seeing them:

> We have all seen the power of fame. My most vivid experience of it occurred in the fall of 1978 when I saw John Lennon and Yoko Ono leaving the Guggenheim Museum. Dazzled by the sight, I couldn't stop looking and fell into step behind them. I ended up following in their wake for about twenty blocks, watching the waves of recognition spread down Madison Avenue, the marvelous shock, the astonishment, the joy. It was like an emotional landslide. People staggered or seemed to buckle as the couple passed. Space distorted, time fell into a trance. The light of forever appeared to glow around them. At that exact moment in the exact place they seemed the sum of all sums. I still feel the reverberations on that particular stretch of upper Madison Avenue.
>
> That was old-fashioned fame: God-like, classical, aristocratic, transcendental, almost religious: a strange, strange love.

When Yoko was busy, John took Sean to the playgrounds in the park and for swimming lessons at the YMCA, and when they were in Cold Spring Harbor or Florida, he took him to the pool and the ocean. He relished parenting. "He didn't come out of my belly, but, *by God,* I made his bones, because I've attended to every meal, and to how he sleeps, and to the fact that he swims like a fish. That's because I took him to the Y, I took him to the ocean. I'm so proud of those things. He is my biggest pride."

John wrote about what he felt for Sean in the lullaby he sang to him at night: "Beautiful Boy," a song that countless parents would sing to their children in the years to come.

JOHN HAD ALWAYS WANTED TO sail, and after Yoko essentially told him to put up or shut up about it, he hired an instructor on Long Island and took sailing lessons. Then in June 1980 he chartered a yacht and set sail for Bermuda, a location approved by Yoko's psychics. He arrived in Freeport, and Sean was flown to Bermuda with an assistant. The plan was that they'd holiday there. Yoko would join them when she could take breaks, but she stayed in New York most of the time to conduct business.

In Bermuda, John settled into a rented villa. He and Sean sailed, swam, and played on the beach. John took Sean for walks in a botanical garden where the plants were identified with small plaques, the English name under the Latin name. John noticed one—a freesia, commonly known as double fantasy, a name that would stick in his head.

In New York, besides working, Yoko saw friends. She went to restaurants. She shopped for furniture for the ongoing redecorations of their houses, often with her interior decorator Sam Havadtoy. With Sam, she attended plays and movies. She shopped for clothes. For Yoko, shopping meant buying multiple sizes and every color of whatever she liked. "She never wore most of it—she gave it away," according to Sam.

One night, John asked an assistant who'd been flown to Bermuda to take him to hear some music, and they went to a nightclub. "Upstairs, they were playing disco, and downstairs I suddenly heard 'Rock Lobster' by the B-52's for the first time," John told *Rolling Stone*'s Jonathan Cott. "Do you know it? It sounds just like Yoko's music, so I said to myself, 'It's time to get out the old ax and wake the wife up!'"

Yoko had never stopped writing songs—even if she wasn't going to record them, she couldn't help write them when she was inspired—but now John wrote songs at a "furious pace," recording them on a portable tape recorder.

John played the tapes for Yoko on the phone, and in the Dakota, she played songs she was writing for him.

John and Sean returned to New York at the end of July. Yoko wrote the song "Yes, I'm Your Angel" that night. "The first night when he came back from Bermuda, I took him to a restaurant and we had a nice dinner, and we felt so good because after about a month of separation and just feeling a bit tipsy—we'd had a little wine and everything—and coming home, but we had to come home a bit early because of Sean," she said. "'Oh, well, we should go home before twelve.' That sort of thing. And that sounded like Cinderella to me, you know? And it was a beautiful night, early summer, and the carriage was going in Central Park, and you hear all these sort of carriage sounds and everything. It almost made me feel like it was not this era. It could be any era. So it was a very romantic feeling, and coming back, and the gate was still open at the Dakota. We just strolled in, and I just went to the piano. And I just started writing the whole thing. So good, that's how it was."

FOR FIVE YEARS YOKO AND John had honored their commitment to focus on the family. But now they decided it was time to make an album together.

Jack Douglas had been an engineer on the *Imagine* album and the "Happy Xmas (War Is Over)" single and had gone on to produce Aerosmith, Patti Smith, and Cheap Trick. Yoko and John hired him to coproduce the album, and John asked Jack to recruit musicians. After John returned from Bermuda, he and Yoko spent most of July polishing the new songs. They began recording at the Hit Factory Studios, on West Forty-Eighth Street, on August 7.

John was direct and clear about the recording of his and Yoko's music. He instructed Douglas and the others working on the album, "Do not take Yoko's music any less seriously than you are taking my music, gentlemen," according to drummer Andy Newmark, who played on the record. "He not only said it, he conveyed it. . . . It was very loving and democratic the way he shared the bill with her, and never once pulled rank as John Lennon."

Yoko intentionally wrote pop songs this time, not because she wanted sales so much as because she wanted to use a common language that reached a broader audience. Making pop songs was also a way of reining herself in so she wouldn't alienate John's fans.

At first, Yoko and John disagreed about the structure of the album. Yoko thought John's songs should make up the A-side and hers should be on side B, but he wanted to alternate them throughout the record "like a dialogue."

Yoko worried that switching back and forth from his songs to hers would hurt John's chances of having a hit. As she said in 1981, "I thought, If John wasn't with me, he would still be making Number One records." She said, "John was artistic, quote unquote. He needed somebody with the ability to be more commercial than he if he was to make it in the world. But he had teamed up with somebody who was less [commercial]. We were a sinking boat. I felt guilty about that. From a purely record-industry point of view, I did damage to him. But if you had asked him, he probably would have said he wouldn't have wanted to miss it for anything."

David Geffen, whose eponymous label would release the album, confirmed that John pushed to alternate his and Yoko's songs on the album. "John said if they had her on one side and him on one side, they'd only end up listening to one side. I don't think at that point in his life he was concerned with whether that was the most commercial choice to make."

Yoko kept changing the order of the songs. She checked her decisions with tarot cards, which she shuffled incessantly. She even consulted the cards to determine how much time there should be between tracks.

On the record, John's "Beautiful Boy" was pure love from a father to his son. Yoko's response, "Beautiful Boys," was for Sean and John but it was also a (poignant) message to all men: "Don't be afraid to go to hell and back. Don't be afraid to be afraid." John wrote about how it was "(Just Like) Starting Over" after the separation. "Cleanup Time" also followed the period when they were apart and addressed their new roles. "Dear Yoko" was a straight-up love song. "Woman" was pure love too. Yoko's songs were multilayered. Like John, she processed it all—the separation, reunion, healing, and reevaluation of their roles in the family. There was the love song "Yes, I'm Your Angel," but in "I'm Moving On," written earlier, she chastised John: "You didn't have to tell a white lie / you know you scarred me for life," she sang. His response was in "I'm Losing You." "Well, well, well, I know I hurt you then / but hell, that was way back then / Well, do you still have to carry that cross?"

They decided that "Starting Over" would be the first single. The B-side would be Yoko's "Kiss Kiss Kiss." That song included the sound of a mock orgasm. She recorded it while lying on the floor in the darkened studio.

The final song on the album was one written and sung by Yoko, "Hard Times Are Over." A full choir was brought into the studio, and when the session was over, John said, "Here must be the world's first Japanese gospel song." After listening to the final mix, Yoko and John thanked the choir. She had tears in her eyes.

Yoko was elated and not only because the album was going so well. Things were different with John. Their love felt purer. There was the new album expressing their love. Acknowledging the struggle. Celebrating starting over. Yoko felt safe and secure and as content as she ever had. At last. She spoke about surrendering to love, and for her it really was a surrender—with John, her protective walls finally came down.

CHAPTER 21

I N ANTICIPATION OF THE RECORD'S release, Yoko hired a publicist, who, in mid-August, announced that Yoko and John were working on a new album.

This was big news in the music world. Initially it was thought there'd be a bidding war for the record; Yoko was offered huge advances, but she wasn't looking for money, according to David Geffen. Geffen had been instrumental in the careers of Joni Mitchell; Crosby, Stills, Nash, and Young; and others and was just founding a new label, Geffen Records.

"I knew it would be quite a coup to sign them, but I didn't think I had a chance," Geffen said. "I wrote Yoko a letter—because I knew that the only person who could make it happen was her. John had complete faith in her; he trusted her in all decisions about business. His motive in recording *Double Fantasy* was completely romantic in that he wanted the record to show the world Yoko's talents and for his wife to finally get the recognition he felt she deserved. He wanted the light to shine on her. 'We have to take care of Yoko,' he would say to me. 'That is our goal with this record.'"

In a series of conversations with Yoko, Geffen expressed his commitment to them both. He made clear that he wasn't interested in just signing John—he was a Yoko fan. Yoko did his numbers and consulted the tarot cards. "She called and said, 'We're going to make a deal with you.'"

There was no bidding war, Geffen told me. "What I offered her was a fifty-fifty split of profits. That was the deal. I didn't ask to hear a note. It's John Lennon. Do I know better than him?"

Yoko asked him to provide a one-page contract. That was unprecedented.

Geffen told her, "Yoko, it's not in your best interest to have a contract that's one page."

She said, "Well, you give me a one-page contract that's in my best interest."

Geffen said, "When I said to my lawyer that it had to be on one page, he said, 'It's gotta be at least two pages.' So I called and said, 'My lawyer says it has to be at least two pages.' Anyway, I sent the contract to her, she had her lawyer look at it, then she said, 'We'll never have to rely on this contract because we have a relationship.' At that point we didn't actually have a relationship. We were beginning a relationship. But that was her faith in relationships."

Preparing for the release of the album, they did several interviews, the most extensive for *Playboy*, which I conducted in September as they continued to work on the album. "The word is out," I began. "John and Yoko are back in the studio."

In the far-reaching interview, they spoke about the new album, their backgrounds, their lives together from their meeting to their marriage to the split and reconciliation, the Beatles and the band's breakup, music, art, politics, feminism, racism, spirituality, and the power of wishing.

The interview took place in recording studios, cafés, and other locations, but we mostly talked at their Dakota apartment and in Studio One, Yoko's office. It was an unconventional environment. The staff included Richard De Palma, the office manager, and a rotating cast of assistants, among them a young man named Fred Seaman, who'd been with John and Sean in Bermuda. Norman Seaman, Fred's uncle, was a longtime friend of the Lennons, and Helen Seaman, Fred's aunt, was Sean's babysitter. There were two young brothers, Rich and Greg Martello, who some months earlier had broken into the apartment building of their hero John Lennon as a prank and, since they seemed harmless enough, were hired by Yoko to work as gofers. There was Dane Worthington, caretaker of the Cold Spring Harbor estate, who was in town working in the studio. Like the upstairs staff—including the maid, Miyoko Onoda, whom Yoko brought over from Japan, and Sean's nanny, Helen—everyone in the office had one thing in common: Their numbers and astrological signs had been assessed by Yoko, and they'd been approved by the tarot.

For these interviews, we generally started talking in the kitchen and then walked to Café La Fortuna, where they ordered coffee and pastries. They were trying to stay on a macrobiotic diet but fell off the wagon a lot.

After coffee, we headed back to the Dakota to Studio One. John went upstairs to be with Sean while Yoko checked her messages and did other business—signing checks, responding to interview requests (from Barbara Walters, for one), and checking in with business and spiritual advisers. Between calls, and sometimes during them, she shuffled a deck of tarot cards and carefully placed them on the table to read. She would work for an hour or more and then buzz John and ask if he was ready to go to the studio. John left Sean in the care of his nanny and minutes later was downstairs.

Arm in arm leaving the Dakota, he and Yoko passed the reception desk, where they said good morning to a silver-haired woman who had worked in the building for fifty years. She was retiring soon, and in appreciation, Yoko had recently given her a mink coat. Yoko's long, thick black hair was tied back tightly; her sunglasses shielded her eyes from the daylight.

Outside, there were always a gathering of fans waiting for a glimpse of the couple. Yoko and John were gracious; they gave autographs and posed for photos. One day a boy thrust a record in John's face, a collector's item—a mint 45 of "All You Need Is Love" from 1967—and asked him to autograph the sleeve. As John signed, the boy asked the tediously familiar question: "Hey, John, when are the Beatles getting back together?" John smiled wryly and offered his well-worn response: "When are you going back to high school?" The quip came off snippier than he'd intended; to soften it, John made a joke and told the boy to enjoy the record.

We would pile into the limo's back seat and head to the recording studio. There, inside the glass booth with the photo of Sean tacked above it, they worked on the songs that would make up the new album. Sometimes while one worked, I interviewed the other in a small side room; sometimes I interviewed them together, and sometimes I just watched as they recorded and mixed the album. Dinner—usually sushi—was delivered. When they wrapped up for the night, we returned to the Dakota, where we continued talking in the kitchen until they were ready to call it a night.

The interview continued through late September. The last night I was with them in the studio, they worked on the album and didn't get out until late, but that wasn't unusual.

In fact, nothing that happened during that period was remarkable for the couple who were as content as they'd ever been. They were enjoying working again and especially working together. They were thinking about the future. Yoko talked about a Broadway musical and the possibility of touring. John also talked about touring. "Well, we probably will, you know. I wouldn't have believed it a month ago. But then I thought, What the hell, why not?"

After leaving the studio that last night, we returned to the Dakota. We sat at the kitchen table and talked about the record. I asked Yoko about the song that was expected to end the album, her "Hard Times Are Over."

"What inspired me," she explained, "was remembering when John and I went cross-country from New York to San Francisco in a car, and we had to stop. . . . While our driver was getting gas, John and I were standing on the corner of the street looking at each other. I didn't know the name of the city or anything. It didn't matter where we were when we looked into each other's eyes."

Yoko and John were quiet. After a moment, I said, "So that's *Double Fantasy*." They had said that was the album's title, after the freesia John had seen in Bermuda.

"Well," Yoko said.

John jumped in. "That might not be the title, so you better check."

"It will be," Yoko responded.

"It will be?" I asked. "Okay."

"Yeah. You heard it from above," John said.

Yoko laughed, and he continued, "I'm only saying that 'cause she's liable to change it. Something could change. Like now I'm in the new studio, or now I'm in the middle of the ocean. Who knows what's going to happen?"

TO CELEBRATE JOHN'S FORTIETH AND Sean's fifth birthdays on October 9, 1980, Yoko arranged for a plane to write a message in the sky above Manhattan. In puffs of white smoke, it read HAPPY BIRTHDAY JOHN AND SEAN LOVE YOKO. Her gifts to John included a tie she'd knitted and, from Tiffany, a $25,000 yellow-gold Patek Philippe 2499 wristwatch.

Later in October, John's "(Just Like) Starting Over" was released as a single backed by Yoko's "Kiss Kiss Kiss." Yoko and John were officially back. "Starting Over" jumped onto the *Billboard* charts and received wide radio play. The album was released in mid-November.

Yoko and John continued working at the Hit Factory on a song that would come out after *Double Fantasy* (yes, that was the album's name), a track of Yoko's that John loved, "Walking on Thin Ice."

ON A QUIET NOVEMBER MORNING, the winter light streamed into the Dakota kitchen. Yoko and John were having breakfast and flipping through the newspapers. An assistant entered the rear kitchen door. Fred Seaman, wearing an IMAGINE T-shirt, had a stack of mail and magazines in his arms. Without looking up from the *Times*, John held out his hand and asked for the music papers. Seaman handed John copies of *Billboard* and *Cashbox*, and Yoko moved closer so she could see as John flipped to the *Billboard* Top 200 chart.

Double Fantasy had been out for two weeks and Yoko and John were excited about the buzz it was generating. The album had entered the chart at number twenty-five with a bullet, indicating it was ascending. John broke into a wide grin and glanced up at Yoko. "Not bad, eh, Mother?" He grabbed a red Sharpie and circled the entry. With the marker's bold line, he drew an arrow from number twenty-five to number one and crossed out Barbra Streisand's album *Guilty.* "We're on our way, Mother," he said.

Yoko was pleased, but she was determined to make the album go to number one "for John," as she told Geffen. She asked him to send people to record stores to buy copies of the album so it would sell out. He explained that that was not the way things worked. He told me it was clear that she wanted it to succeed "for him, not for her."

The following week was filled with more work on "Walking on Thin Ice" and more interviews and photo sessions. On Sunday, December 7, they received a copy of their longest interview ever from my *Playboy* editor, Barry Golson, who messengered over the new issue. In that interview, John had anticipated turning forty years old. "Life begins at forty, so they promise," he told me. "Oh, I *believe* it, too. Because I feel *fine.* I'm, like, *excited.* It's like twenty-one. You know, hitting twenty-one. It's like: *Wow!* What's going to happen next?"

THE NEXT MORNING, DECEMBER 8, Yoko and John went for coffee at La Fortuna and John had his hair cut. They then did a photo session with Annie Leibovitz for *Rolling Stone.* Leibovitz took a photograph that became one of the most famous ever. It was John's idea. Yoko lay on the floor while he curled up next to her in the fetal position, clutching her. Yoko wore all black. John was nude. John explained that the image showed the truth of his and Yoko's relationship. He wanted to expose his vulnerability and dependence, reveal a portrait of a couple in which the man finally let his guard down after suffering from machismo that nearly killed him and almost destroyed his marriage, show that he was saved by and dependent on a woman: Yoko.

After the photo session, they did a radio interview. At five p.m. they headed out to the studio. John was stopped on his way to the limousine by a fan. He signed the man's copy of *Double Fantasy*.

At the studio, they worked on "Walking on Thin Ice" throughout the evening. Geffen stopped by and told them the album was about to go gold, indicating sales of five hundred thousand copies. After several hours, they listened to a playback of "Thin Ice."

They stopped working around ten thirty. Yoko suggested they go out for dinner, but John wanted to head to the Dakota to see Sean before he went to bed.

On their way out, John said good night to Jack Douglas, the coproducer. John was thrilled about the day's session. Geffen jumped in their car, and Yoko and John dropped him off at his apartment on their way home.

IT WAS A CLEAR, MILD night. Yoko and John didn't speak much as the car rolled uptown—it had been a long day and they were tired. At the Dakota's stone carriageway, they thanked the driver and were walking toward the portico when someone called John's name. The man was clutching an autographed copy of *Double Fantasy* that John had signed earlier that day. The man drew a revolver and fired.

PART THREE

YOKO ONLY

1980–2024

CHAPTER 22

THE ASSASSIN FIRED FIVE SHOTS, four of which struck John in the back and shoulder. He staggered into the reception area and fell. Yoko yelled, "John's been shot!" She cried out for help. *"Get an ambulance!"*

The concierge at the Dakota front desk called the police. Meanwhile, the shooter placed the gun on the ground, and the doorman kicked it away.

"Do you know what you've done?" the doorman asked him.

"I've just shot John Lennon."

The gunman waited, calmly reading a book: *Catcher in the Rye.*

John lay on the ground in a pool of blood.

POLICE CARS ARRIVED WITHIN MINUTES and the assassin was arrested. An officer decided there wasn't time to wait for an ambulance, so he and his partner gently lifted John and laid him down in the back seat of their squad car. They sped to Roosevelt Hospital on West Fifty-Ninth Street. Yoko was driven in a second police car.

At the hospital, Yoko was ushered into a private room down the hall from the trauma room to wait while doctors attempted to resuscitate John. She shakily called Geffen, and he rushed to the hospital and waited with her. "She just sat, frozen, and it was terrifying," he recalled.

Fifteen minutes or so later, a doctor came in.

She pleaded with him, "Please tell me he's okay."

The doctor took a breath. "I can't tell you that."

"It's not true," Yoko cried. "You're lying. It can't be. I don't believe you."

But she believed it when a nurse gave her John's wedding ring.

Yoko sobbed. She sobbed harder when she thought of Sean. Then it dawned on her: What if her son was awake and the TV was on? Through tears, she asked the doctor to delay announcing John's death so she could get home and tell Sean what happened before he saw it on TV.

ACCOMPANIED BY GEFFEN, YOKO LEFT the hospital. Back at the Dakota, they took a service elevator that led to the landing on the seventh floor outside the kitchen. Richard De Palma had been working late when the shooting happened and was waiting for news. The live-in maid and Sean's nanny were there too. When Yoko came in, she asked about Sean. Thankfully, he was asleep. Speaking numbly, she asked De Palma to call Julian, John's aunt Mimi, and the other Beatles and tell them what had happened. She also asked Geffen to place the calls. Yoko was hysterical. She wanted to be alone, and she retired to her bedroom.

JOHN HAD BEEN PRONOUNCED DEAD just after 11:00 p.m. At that time, televisions in millions of American homes were tuned to ABC's *Monday Night Football*. Announcer Howard Cosell's voice was familiar to sports fans, who'd grown up with him covering the careers of Muhammad Ali, Joe

Namath, and other sports stars, but he had never spoken as solemnly. "An unspeakable tragedy confirmed to us by ABC News in New York City—John Lennon, outside of his apartment building on the West Side of New York City—the most famous, perhaps, of all of the Beatles—shot twice in the back, rushed to Roosevelt Hospital, dead on arrival."

Other television and radio programs around the world were interrupted with the news. The media descended, and fans began to gather outside the Dakota. By 1 a.m., there were hundreds of people. By dawn, there were thousands, and the crowd continued to swell. People spread around the building, stopping traffic and spilling into Central Park. Someone had a radio or tape deck that played John's songs. Many cried as they sang along, and their voices wafted up to the seventh floor, where, in her and John's bedroom, Yoko couldn't escape the voices singing "She Loves You," "In My Life," and "Strawberry Fields Forever." They sang "Imagine" and "Give Peace a Chance," "Woman," and "Dear Yoko." Yoko was haunted by John's voice and words.

Even after all these years
I miss you when you're not here
I wish you were here, my dear Yoko . . .
Oh, oh, Yoko
I'm never, ever, ever, ever, ever gonna let you go.

DE PALMA KNOCKED LIGHTLY ON the door, and she told him to come in. He asked if she needed anything, and she issued instructions: She said that he and the others shouldn't go easy on her; she wanted to know and hear everything that happened. She had him switch on the television and, from bed, began to watch TV coverage of the murder. The news seemed surreal, unconnected to the events of the past few hours: There were clips of the Beatles performing and photos of her and John marrying in Gibraltar. There was film of them singing at the bed-in and walking together in Central Park just a month ago. Yoko didn't know if she could survive—or if she wanted to.

The Dakota office and kitchen were filling up. Along with Geffen, the family's lawyer had arrived. There were the domestic staff and a small handful of additional staffers who'd also made their way into the building. Someone said aloud what others were thinking: Would Yoko try to kill herself? De Palma was tasked with going into her room to search the bathroom for razors and other sharp objects. Yoko saw him and understood what he was doing. She told him not to worry, she wasn't going to kill herself—but she did fantasize about doing it to escape the horror. She'd been here before in her life—despairing, suicidal—and she had survived. But this nightmare was unlike anything she'd experienced. The horror replayed in her head. Meanwhile, fans outside sang along with John.

In the middle of the night I call your name.
Oh, Yoko.

THE MORNING AFTER THE SHOOTING, the front page of the *New York Times* featured a picture of Yoko, anguished, being held up by Geffen as they were led out of the hospital by a police officer. The staff in Studio One and those upstairs in the kitchen fielded calls. Elliot Mintz had taken a red-eye from Los Angeles. He reached the Dakota at about 7:30 a.m. "It was a crime scene," he said. "The yellow tape was up; the blood was on the sidewalk. It was everywhere." He was escorted through the crowd, past the outer offices rapidly filling with wreaths and flowers and packages, and took the elevator to the living quarters. Pausing outside the huge mahogany door to the apartment, he drew a breath, then knocked. Miyoko let him in.

"Yoko-san is in her bedroom," she said. Elliot went to the bedroom and knocked.

"It's Elliot," he said through the door. "I'll be right outside until you are ready to see me."

Yoko unlocked the door. "I had never been in the room with just Yoko before," Elliot later wrote. "John and Yoko had always been there together. This was their bedroom, their nest. But John . . . was not there. Yoko looked devastated, hollow, lost."

One of the first things Elliot did in Yoko's bedroom was close the curtains. He was partly worried that the occupants of the apartment opposite would let a photographer take photos, but he also worried about another assailant. With the curtains drawn, the room was darker, lit mostly by the big-screen TV, which remained on with the volume off. Yoko lay in bed and Elliot sat in the wicker chair at her bedside. There were endless news reports—twenty-four-hour, wall-to-wall coverage of the killing and remembrances of John. And then there was endless coverage of the killer, identified as a former security guard from Hawaii, Mark David Chapman, purportedly a fan of John's.

WHEN HE LEFT YOKO'S SIDE, Elliot went downstairs to Studio One and took over organizing the assistants to screen calls. He laid down some basic guidelines about who should be buzzing Yoko's bedroom and what they should say to the media.

A disturbing call came in. A receptionist at the Dakota's front desk reported that someone had called and said he was coming to New York from Los Angeles to "finish the job Chapman started."

Elliot phoned the Los Angeles police. He was right to take the threat seriously: A man had been arrested at the Los Angeles airport when he punched a police officer and vowed to "get" Yoko Ono. He had a history of psychiatric disorders.

YOKO KNEW SHE HAD TO tell Sean. The thought paralyzed her, and she put it off for the moment—there were other pressing matters that required her attention.

"When John died, I was so shocked that I couldn't move," she said. "There is nothing of you left. I could barely stand. But by the time I came back from the hospital, there was someone asking, 'What do you want to do with his body?'"

She asked that he be cremated at a mortuary in suburban Hartsdale, New York.

THE SHOOTING HAD PUT A fear in Yoko that nothing could dispel. Yoko and John had hired a former FBI agent to provide security for Sean, but they hadn't had their own bodyguards. Almost immediately, armed off-duty and retired police officers were patrolling the apartment twenty-four hours a day. It was surreal to have gun-toting guards around a household devoted to peace.

Neither De Palma nor Geffen had been able to reach Ringo, who was with his wife, Barbara Bach, in the Bahamas. When they heard what had happened from Ringo's stepchildren in Los Angeles, they immediately got on a plane to New York. They called from a pay phone at the airport and reached Elliot, who told them to come to a back entrance of the Dakota. Elliot sneaked them up in a freight elevator.

Ringo, trying to comfort Yoko, said, "I know how you're feeling."

"No, you don't," she said, "but I'm very glad you are here."

De Palma hadn't been able to reach Julian either. Yoko got on the phone to tell him, but his stepfather, who answered the phone, declined to wake Julian because Cynthia was away. Julian, then seventeen years old, woke up early on the morning of December 9. "I just came downstairs, and all the curtains were closed. And I knew something was wrong, I absolutely knew something was wrong. I peeked out from the curtains and just saw all the press and I just felt it already. I just knew it in my heart, and my stepfather wouldn't tell me."

Julian had a difficult relationship with his father, but it had been improving. The two of them talked on the phone frequently. The last time they had spoken, John played Julian songs from *Double Fantasy*. Now Julian flew to New York. He remembered, "Every person on that plane had the newspaper [with] Dad's, you know, picture and 'John Lennon, slain' and 'murdered,' and that was a toughie."

Yoko sent an assistant to pick him up at the airport and escort him back to the Dakota, where he was mobbed by fans and reporters. He went upstairs and met with Yoko.

Later, Yoko asked Elliot to look after Julian—"Take him around New York . . . make sure he isn't photographed," she said.

"She was asking partially as a kindness to Julian but also as a mercy to herself," according to Elliot. "Yoko was in no condition to deal with John's grieving teenage son."

In Tokyo, Keisuke, Yoko's younger brother, got the news about John from an acquaintance who worked at a newspaper. He told Isoko. Together they flew to New York the next day and went directly to the Dakota. They called the apartment but couldn't get through to Yoko. They never saw her. She later explained that she couldn't bear to see them yet.

During that time, some trusted visitors came to the apartment. Yoko's friend Sam Havadtoy sat with Yoko while she alternated between tears and stunned silence. "We were all afraid she was going to die," he said. "She was so frozen. It was the most frightening thing to see."

YOKO HAD POSTPONED TELLING SEAN. "I was like a person who was drowning—I didn't have the energy to reach out to him," she told Barbara Graustark. "And he reminded me so much of John. Because John was so close to Sean, I thought, 'Without John, we're not a family anymore.'" What would she say? But she had to break the news to him and instructed his nanny to bring him to her bedroom.

Sean recalled, "I remember someone telling me to go see my mom in the bedroom. There were already thousands of people in the park singing songs and it was chaotic and I felt that something was going on because everyone was just acting weird.

"My mother was alone in the bed, and I went in there and I remember seeing newspapers next to her and they all had this headline and seeing my dad's name. And she was sitting there, and she was silent, just looking at me, and said, 'I have to tell you something. Your dad's dead. He's been killed.' I think she might have said 'he's been murdered' or 'shot.' I remember that hitting me like a fucking ton of bricks.

"My first thought was *Oh my God. You promised that you weren't going to die.*"

John had made that promise when Sean's cat, Alice, died and Sean first recognized the existence of death. The three of them were in his parents' bedroom, and Sean asked, "Are *you* going to die?"

John said, "Don't worry. We're not going to die."

"Do you promise?" Sean asked.

John repeated, "Don't worry, we're not going to die."

Sean didn't know why John said it. "I think he thought I was such a baby, it didn't matter what he said. He died right after that."

To his mother, trying to sound grown up, Sean said, "Well, if he's dead, he's dead." He explained, "I wanted to be tough. And she said, 'Well, I'm glad you feel that way.' . . . She looked so vulnerable. Then I thought [I should] say something nice and said, 'Don't worry, Mom. You're still young. You'll find somebody.' I remember feeling like a waterfall or tornado of tears were about to explode from me. I felt like I was going to be overwhelmed and started tiptoeing out of the room because I didn't want her to see me crying. Then I remember running down the hall and slamming the door and I just exploded into an insane traumatic episode of weeping and uncontrollable sadness. I was so scared and so freaked out. I was just alone in my room."

The incessant singing downstairs haunted Sean as it did his mother. They couldn't escape John's words, including the song "Beautiful Boy," John's lullaby to Sean:

Before you go to sleep
Say a little prayer
Every day, in every way
It's getting better and better.
Beautiful, beautiful, beautiful
Beautiful boy.
Darling, darling, darling
Darling Sean.
Good night, Sean.
See you in the morning
Bright and early . . .

Later Yoko and Julian sat with Sean, who was trying to make sense of what had happened. He wanted to know why someone would shoot his father. Yoko explained that he was probably a confused person. As she wrote in a statement to the Associated Press, "Sean said we should find out if he was confused or if he really had meant to kill John."

She said that that was up to the court to decide. "I recall Yoko mentioning that the man who killed dad would have to go to court," Julian said, "and Sean was still not really grasping things, as he said, 'You mean like a tennis court?'"

OUTSIDE THE DAKOTA, MOURNERS CONTINUED to play John's songs and sing along with them. Yoko appreciated that fans needed to grieve, but hearing his voice was torturous.

She decided against a public funeral. "She wanted to avoid the circuslike atmosphere that had surrounded Elvis's funeral," Elliot explained to music critic Robert Hilburn. But she felt she owed an explanation to the masses she heard mourning John on the street below. She released a statement on December 10.

There is no funeral for John
Later in the week we will set the time
For silent vigil to pray for his soul.
We invite you to participate from wherever
You are at the time.
John loved and prayed for the human race.
Please pray the same for him.
Love, Yoko and Sean

Yoko's grief was punctuated by a stream of other crises. When she was told about the suicide of a distraught fan—the first of three—she cried uncontrollably.

"They asked me, 'What are you going to do about it?'" she recalled. "One side of me was saying, 'How do you expect me to deal with something like that?' But the other side of me just starts to deal with it."

She called a reporter at the *New York Daily News* and requested that they publish a statement asking for the suicides to stop. The paper printed her plea.

The phone rang constantly, and telegrams poured in. While most people who called or wrote were emotionally devastated, some were looking to cash in on the tragedy. De Palma was opening telegrams, most of them messages of condolence, but stopped after reading a particular one. He walked over to Elliot and handed it to him. The sender was a woman who claimed to know someone who was present at John's cremation and who'd said that the cremation had been both filmed and photographed. "You may want to contact me for more information," the message concluded. No public evidence that these films existed ever surfaced.

However, another macabre call came in. According to Elliot, the caller said an attendant at the morgue had sold to a photo syndicate some shots of John's body "with the sheet off." That set off a flurry of frantic phone calls to stop the photos' publication, but it was too late. One of the morgue photographs appeared on the front page of the *New York Post*; later, and in color, a photo appeared on the front page of the *National Enquirer*. It was later reported that the attendant was paid ten thousand dollars for the photographs. As Elliot observed, he became "the first one to make a buck off John's death."

In the meantime, on the first floor, the outer fringe was being heard from. A man called the Dakota from England to say, in a trembling voice, that he had absolute proof that John's murder was a conspiracy. Another man claimed he had just arrived from a distant planet with a message to Yoko from John. Mediums called with messages from John they insisted were matters of life and death. A boy phoned to say that John's spirit had taken over his body.

The speculation and rumors wouldn't stay on the fringe for long. Decades of efforts to reconstruct the shooting millisecond by millisecond followed. Details varied from account to account. Bill O'Reilly and James Patterson were among the writers who investigated and chronicled the murder. There were countless newspaper and magazine articles, documentaries, docudramas, and special reports on television. As they did after the assassination of John F. Kennedy, conspiracy theories abounded, allegations that the gunman hadn't acted alone, was an FBI operative, was a CIA operative, or was a hired assassin. But in fact, Chapman acted alone. He was deluded—he said voices told him to kill John. It was later revealed that Chapman was envious of John's fame and wealth and sought fame for himself. Instead, he achieved infamy.

WITHIN A WEEK, THE OFFICE of New York City mayor Ed Koch organized a vigil for John. Fans were asked to gather in Central Park at 2 p.m. on Sunday, December 14. Yoko asked that at the start of the vigil, radio stations around the world be silent for ten minutes. More than one hundred thousand people gathered around the band shell in Central Park upon which was a portrait of John. There was a sea of people crying in the cold. Some held signs—GIVE PEACE A CHANCE, IMAGINE, WE LOVE YOU, JOHN. At exactly 2 p.m., everyone fell silent. There were similar vigils in London, Liverpool, and other cities. After ten minutes, the meditation ended with

"Imagine" playing. More of John's songs played: "In My Life"; "All You Need Is Love"; "Give Peace a Chance."

Years later, Yoko remembered, "When he died, the sky became gray. It snowed on his vigil, as if the sky was crying with us. But that ten minutes of silence throughout the world we held together created the strongest ring on this planet and made us all family."

CHAPTER 23

T HE FIRST TIME I VISITED Yoko after John died, she was in bed. The curtains were drawn, the bedroom dark, and I sat next to the bed, and I felt the weight and could barely speak. I cried with her. She broke down in terrifying paroxysms. I'd never seen anyone as sad and scared.

She said she appreciated the outpouring of love from around the world, but clearly it was a hollow echo in the void of her grief.

After falling for each other, after splitting up and then surviving the lost weekend, Yoko and John had gotten back together—reunited, stronger, committed—and Yoko had spent the five years that followed awash in feelings she'd always craved: security, stability, safety in love. After a lifetime of chaos and depression, she experienced a kind of peace she'd never known. The fear had abated. "I never met anybody else who could understand me," she once said. "We understand each other so well, and I'm not lonely anymore—which is a shocking experience, really."

She and John had vowed to be together forever. "The two of us are really one," John sang in "Dear Yoko." "Did you slay the dragons?" John asked when she came upstairs to the kitchen from Studio One. They exchanged gentle looks. I'd never seen love like that.

I'd never seen love like that, but now, in the darkened bedroom, I'd never seen grief like that. John, her other half, was dead. She told me she felt as if the bullets had struck her. The horror replayed in her head. Gunshots. John falling. His blood. Her partner, friend, lover, collaborator. "I should be with him," she whispered. It took all her energy to speak his name: "Oh, John," she said, and she wept more. She gasped for breath. Then she whispered, "Sean." Thinking about Sean—what he lost—she sobbed harder.

IN THE FIRST WEEKS AFTER the murder, Yoko holed up in the Dakota; she left only once, when David Geffen and Calvin Klein snuck her out the back way and took her to a restaurant. They did it to give her a break from the nonstop singing—"the dirge," Geffen said. "And to get her to eat something." At the restaurant, she was almost catatonic.

Christmas came. Yoko and John had loved Christmas, and the holiday had taken on new meaning since Sean's birth. Yoko insisted, in spite of her depression, that a tree be put up and strung with lights and tinsel for Sean. Before he died, John had arranged to buy a puppy for Sean for Christmas, an Akita. One morning before Christmas, Yoko told Sean there was something for him in Studio One and he should go downstairs. The puppy was there with a ribbon and note saying *Merry Christmas from Daddy*. Sean thought it meant the dog's name was Merry Christmas, and the name stuck.

Yoko composed a Christmas message to the staff, apologizing for the burden of "the sudden trauma," but the composure she mustered when she faced people dissolved when she was alone.

NO ONE RECALLS EXACTLY WHEN it was that Yoko sent Sean to the estate in Palm Beach with his nanny. It was Sean's idea; he asked if he could go. She said, "I asked him why he wanted to go, and he said, 'The weather is good in Florida,' but I realized it was too much [for him] here."

"I had good memories of Florida with my father," Sean said. There were two swimming pools. A trampoline. And the ocean. Yoko let him go, knowing he would escape New York's winter and the funereal mood around the Dakota. But later she was frank enough to admit she found it too painful to be around Sean. She saw John in Sean's face. Sean had meant more to John than anything or anyone else ever had. John was Sean's rock, and now he was gone.

As he left for Florida with his nanny, Sean walked through the Dakota courtyard to the waiting limousine. "I remember the janitor was cleaning the floor with soapy water, scrubbing it," Sean said. "I remember hearing my babysitter say, 'Don't let him see that,' because that was the blood that was being cleaned off the ground. It was leading up to the staircase. I remember thinking, *Why would you say that?* It was just so obvious that I could hear her. Of course I saw it. I remember feeling so alone and so scared. I remember my dad's brownish-colored blood staining the cement and the janitor trying to clean it up and I still think of it every time I walk into the Dakota. I walk by that spot and I see it every time."

In Palm Beach, Sean was taken to his bedroom in the spacious home. "My dad had just died, and I was alone with my nanny and two bodyguards in this big house in Florida. I remember how scary that house was at night. I remember thinking every night that my bed was shaking, and I couldn't go to sleep. I called the nanny. 'My bed's shaking again.' 'No, it's not.'" It must have been Sean himself that was shaking.

The scary, lonesome nights in Florida were too much for Sean. He asked to come back to New York.

THE *ROLLING STONE* ISSUE WITH the Annie Leibovitz photograph on the cover hit the stands in mid-January. The image of John in the fetal position, nude, wrapped around Yoko, was startling. It was disturbing for people to see John so vulnerable so soon after his murder. Some supermarket chains refused to carry the issue. Leibovitz explained in the magazine, "I promised John that this would be the cover. I shot some test Polaroids first . . . John said, 'You've captured our relationship exactly.'" In spite of the ban, the issue sold out.

While members of the public either gazed upon or averted their eyes from the last images taken of John, now, only weeks after his murder, Yoko started to deal with the pain the way she always had: through work.

She returned to the studio to complete the song she and John had been working on the night he died. The lyrics to "Walking on Thin Ice" took on new meaning now: "I'm paying the price / For throwing the dice in the air." She sang,

> I may cry someday
> But the tears will dry whichever way
> And when our hearts return to ashes
> It'll be just a story.

When she wasn't in the studio, Yoko mostly stayed in her bedroom. From time to time, she emerged and went to the kitchen, and she made forays downstairs to Studio One. At first she could hardly bring herself to see Sean, but she knew she had to, and she began to spend more time with him. She tried not to fall apart in front of him, but she did sometimes. And Sean did the same. In front of her, he was mostly stoic, but he wept when he was alone. She told herself repeatedly that she had to survive for Sean.

Yoko was living day by day. She could see that John's fans were mourning too—many were devastated—and she wanted to thank them directly for sharing her grief. She obsessed over the wording of an open letter titled "In Gratitude" that she published on January 18, 1981, in the *New York Times* and the *Washington Post*, thanking those who grieved for John and sent "letters, telegrams and thoughts." She asked for time to herself, and she also wrote, "I thank you for your feeling of anger for John's death. I share your anger. I am angry at myself for not having been able to protect John. I am angry at myself and at all of us for allowing our society to fall apart to this extent. The only 'revenge' that would mean anything to us, is to turn the society around in time, to one that is based on love and trust as John felt it could be. The only solace is to show that it could be done, that we could create a world of peace on earth for each other and for our children."

She concluded, "Remember, there's nothing you can do that can't be done. Imagine, Love, Yoko."

YOKO KNEW SHE'D BE CRITICIZED for putting out a record so soon after John died, but she didn't care. She felt confident that John would want her to continue their work, and it was helping her survive. She explained, "If I had had to sit in the Dakota without doing anything—because I am a workaholic by nature—I would have jumped out the window. Music was the most natural thing I could think of. It was part of our life. For me to wear a black veil or go to the mountains or take John's body and bury it in a grave-yard—that would have been foreign. But going back to the studio where we had been making music up until his death was like going back to the family. And music was our family language."

At the end of January, she released "Walking on Thin Ice," a twelve-inch single. The song was Yoko's first chart success; later it would become a smash disco track. The *NME* would rate it number ten on its list of the best tracks of 1981.

She soon began working on an album, to be called *Season of Glass*. "Music was my salvation," she wrote. "When I started to sing, I noticed that my throat was all choked up and my voice was cracking. I seriously thought maybe I should quit making the album because, as some people had advised me, 'It was not the time.' But the question was, 'When would be the time?' I thought of all the people in the world whose voices were choking and cracking for many reasons. I could sing for them. I could call it a choke or a crackle. Well, wasn't that what the critics had been saying about me for all these years anyway? That gave me a laugh, and it became easier."

One song she included on *Season of Glass*, "Nobody Sees Me Like You

Do," had been written in 1980. She said, "It was a song John liked . . . and it was especially hard doing this song when he was not around anymore."

Another song, "I Don't Know Why," had been written two nights after John was killed. The quiet rage she expresses in the song is bone-chilling.

I don't know why, was getting so good with us,
I don't know why, was getting so good with us,
I don't know why, was getting so good,
Was getting so good with us . . .
You left me, you left me, you left me without words,
You left me, you left me, you left me without words,
You left me, you left me, you left me without words.

Finally she lets go with chilling ferocity:

You bastards!
Hate us! hate me! we had everything, you . . .

She said the song "No, No, No" was how she felt after the tragedy. "John was dead. I was alive. But John's side of the bed was still warm when I came back from the hospital. My side was cold. I was shivering. It was as if John were still alive. I wanted somebody to hold me. In my mind, I was saying please, hold me. I wanted to stop shivering. . . . My mind was like a shattered glass, the sharp points split in tangents. I made myself impossible for anybody to hold me."

Yoko conceived of the album's cover, called Bob Gruen, and told him that she was taking a picture of a glass of water on a windowsill and wanted help lighting it. She didn't tell him that next to the glass of water she had put John's glasses—the ones he was wearing when he was killed. Spattered with his dried blood.

"It was just too horrifying and sad to see the reality of John's blood," Gruen said. "We both were crying."

Gruen set up the lighting, and Yoko snapped the photograph. Later she used it in anti-gun campaigns.

As had happened with "Thin Ice," when the album was released, some criticized her: How could she put out a record so soon after John's death?

But Yoko said, "After *Season of Glass* was finished, I felt a relief. I finished the mastering, sent the disc to the record company and, for the first time in a long while, I took a walk in Central Park. I felt relaxed, and I thought, well, maybe I could go to a coffee shop. And then I thought, *I could possibly even go to the theater*. And slowly I worked my way back into the world."

Many of the responses to *Season of Glass* were not about the music, but about the cover. David Geffen told Yoko that some record stores refused to carry the record unless she changed it. She later explained, "They said it was in bad taste. I felt like a person soaked in blood coming into a living room full of people and reporting that my husband was dead, his body was taken away, and the pair of glasses were the only thing I had managed to salvage—and people looking at me saying it was in bad taste to show the glasses to them. 'I'm not changing. This is what John is now,' I said."

Aside from the criticisms of the decision to make the record and of her choice of a cover, like "Thin Ice," *Season of Glass* earned almost all positive reviews. In the *Record Mirror*, Mark Cooper wrote, "Yoko has made a record of fragility, grief, and ultimately, of great human strength. Pain too terrible to confront is confronted, experienced, and expressed . . . feeling can't be denied, but it can be messy and incoherent. Yoko's faithful to feeling here while controlling it. The sadness that pervades every song here is the season of glass."

"I remember *Season of Glass*, the music moving me so much," Sean Lennon would say. "It's an amazing accomplishment that she went into the studio after my dad died. She takes the most painful, most intense experiences and turns them into beautiful art. And I think that's what my dad loved so much about her." He told me, "People criticized her for making that record. They thought she should be in mourning. But that was her mourning."

"SOON AFTER JOHN WAS KILLED, I started going for a walk in Central Park every morning," Yoko said. "One morning I thought, 'This is not right. I should take a walk with Sean.' So I said to him, 'You want to come with me?' He was overjoyed. . . . But when we started out, he lay on the floor and closed his eyes and wouldn't move, he was so choked up. I said, 'It's not like going for a walk with Daddy, is it?' He shook his head."

A security guard wanted Yoko and Sean to wear bulletproof vests. She tried one on but it was uncomfortable. The other, specially made for a child, made her shudder. She said no to the vests but was closely followed by guards wherever she went.

For Sean, every landmark in the park evoked a bittersweet memory of his frequent walks with John, and he recounted the memories to Yoko. "Each time he said these things, my heart was breaking," she recalled. "I thought, 'No more walks in Central Park with Sean.' I couldn't stand it."

Yoko ventured out more—took more walks and visited restaurants and art exhibitions with friends. She kept her dark sunglasses on, and when people stopped her to express their condolences, she was gracious. Once she went to Tavern on the Green with her neighbors who owned the restaurant, and a young girl latched onto her and sobbed. The security guards were alarmed, but Yoko said it was okay. For these social engagements, she dressed up, steeled herself, and went through the motions. She was trying. On March 20, 1981, almost three and a half months after the murder, she went to Quo Vadis, a chic Upper East Side restaurant, where she ran into Andy Warhol, who documented the meeting in his diary.

"We were so stunned," he wrote. "She looked so elegant, like the Duchess of Windsor with her hair back and dark wraparound sunglasses, and beautiful makeup and Fendi furs and jewelry—an emerald ring with a big ruby in it and Elsa Peretti diamond earrings. . . . It was really strange, a whole new Yoko."

She was willing herself to be okay. She'd begun with *Season of Glass*. Much had been made of the photo on the front, with John's glasses, but few people noticed the photo on the back. It was a photograph of the same place in the

Dakota—the same table, the same window overlooking Central Park. However, the composition was different. Yoko had replaced John's bloody glasses with a plant—a geranium. The glass of water that was half empty on the front of the album was now full. She was trying to change her reality. It was a wish. If she could visualize things getting better, maybe they would.

CHAPTER 24

B Y MIDSUMMER OF 1981, YOKO was making definitive attempts to reclaim a normal life. She and Sean were constantly accompanied by bodyguards, but she socialized more, attended to business, and worked on music. In another sign of looking toward the future, she resumed redecorating the apartment, which she'd started before John died.

Yoko and John had met Sam Havadtoy, their decorator, when they were shopping for antiques. Sam had been born to Hungarian parents in London in 1952 and then returned with his family to Budapest, where he was raised. When his parents divorced, he was placed in an orphanage for several years. After that, Sam lived with his mother and brothers in a one-room basement apartment without electricity, water, or heat. Later he lived with his mother when she squatted in an apartment building. Eventually the family bought an apartment from the state.

From fourteen to seventeen years old, Sam went to trade school to become a waiter. Everything changed for him when he saw the movie *A Hard Day's Night*. "That's when I realized: I belong *there*." *There* was England. At eighteen, he escaped Hungary through Yugoslavia; he went to Italy and then, finally, to London, where he found work as a cook and butler for a French general and attended school to learn English.

Sam became a waiter in Covent Garden, where he met Stuart Greet, an antiques dealer and interior designer based in New York. Sam developed a romantic relationship with Greet, and, in 1972, followed him to Manhattan. Greet educated him about art and antiques and taught him interior decorating. Sam was a quick study with impeccable taste. He was also industrious and ambitious. By 1977, "I was rolling in decorating jobs."

One afternoon, Yoko and John were shopping and admired a pair of Egyptian revival chairs in the window of the Greet gallery. They stepped in.

"And how strange is life that I escaped because of *A Hard Day's Night* and . . . John and Yoko walk into the shop?" Sam said. "And I always tell the story that they liked the two Egyptian chairs. . . . Well, I was included in the price of those two chairs."

That day in the antiques shop, John saw an ivory chess set from India and he pulled Sam aside, out of Yoko's earshot. John asked Sam if he could make both sides white as a present for Yoko—re-creating her all-white "Play It by Trust" piece. "I couldn't believe he was asking me to bleach this old chess set, but I said, 'Of course we can. Why not?'" John slipped him a piece of paper on which he'd scribbled a dedication he wanted engraved on a plaque to be affixed to the chessboard.

Sam bleached the chess pieces and board, added the plaque, and delivered the set to John. "He went berserk," Sam recalled. "He told me that I'm an idiot. I didn't do it right." Sam didn't understand. Finally John explained that the words on the plaque were wrong. Sam said, "But you asked me to have it engraved 'From the kids to the queen' in your note!'"

Sam had misread John's scribble. John had written "From the king to the queen."

Sam apologized. John apparently forgave him because Yoko hired him to redecorate her Dakota office. That led to jobs redecorating the upstairs apartment and, eventually, their other apartment in the Dakota, the mansion in Cold Spring Harbor, the farm she'd acquired in upstate New York, the Virginia properties, and the Palm Beach estate. John asked Sam to help buy birthday and Christmas presents for Yoko, and Yoko asked him to help buy presents for John. "They kept trying to outdo each other," Sam said.

John bought jewelry for Yoko. Yoko once bought John an antique Wurlitzer jukebox. Another time she bought him a church. An entire church—or at least its contents. The church, in Louisville, Kentucky, was going to be demolished, so its contents were being auctioned off. Yoko saw that in a magazine, and a psychic advised her to buy everything. She dispatched Sam.

Sam was tall, slim, bespectacled, and handsome. He dressed in casual suits. He was charming and funny. Yoko considered him a good friend. After John died, he rushed to the Dakota to offer his support. Later in 1981, when he resumed the redecorating work he'd been doing for her, their relationship turned intimate.

"It just happened," Sam said of their romance. "Even when John was alive, we went to the theater, to lunch, we hung out. . . . We were really friends, good friends. Then it became a little bit more than that." Sam moved into the Dakota. Yoko was alone and scared, and Sam helped. As Jann Wenner, who became one of Yoko and Sam's closest friends during that period, observed, "Sam really took over taking care of her, and she was grateful. It kind of brought her back to life."

At the time, Jann was married to Jane Wenner. "Jane and I started having a kind of a normal couples relationship with them. . . . We took vacations together. A lot of the little girl in Yoko—giggling, funny, joyful—came out." Sam and Yoko visited them in East Hampton, staying at a local inn. "She'd be there knitting her sweater; they'd go for walks on the beach. She got back on her feet."

Wenner observed that one of the most important aspects of her relationship with Sam was that he protected her from the outside world. She had been afraid of people taking advantage of her even before John's death. "And then the king is gone and everyone is scrambling for position. It's that classic situation. And she had reason to be paranoid and afraid."

YOKO ONCE TOLD ME, "WHEN John died, I thought it was the worst thing that would ever happen. But that was only the beginning."

In March 1981, Yoko asked one of the off-duty police officers who served as bodyguards to manage security for her. In his off-hours, Dan Mahoney, then a sergeant with the New York Police Department Street Crimes division, protected celebrities (Elizabeth Taylor, Richard Burton, and Jerry Lewis, among others) and business executives through a detective agency. Responding to Yoko's request that security be increased—"because of continuous and credible threats," Mahoney said—he brought in a new team of bodyguards, all of them New York City cops.

One day a letter was delivered to the Dakota accompanied by a copy of *Double Fantasy* that was riddled with bullet holes. The sender wrote that he had come to New York to kill Yoko. Mahoney couldn't guarantee her safety at the Dakota, and he moved her, Sean, and Sam into a Midtown hotel for several days before she insisted on returning home. More threats came in the mail. Sam opened a letter and found a razor blade along with a threat to kill Yoko. Someone wrote, "To fulfill the prophecy, I am going to kill you. You were not supposed to have survived."

YOKO WAS PREOCCUPIED BY THESE physical threats and didn't yet know about a string of thefts and a plot to exploit John's death—and her—that had begun the day after John was killed.

That first betrayal came from the inner circle. Fred Seaman, Norman and Helen Seaman's nephew, had worked as an assistant to the couple at the Dakota and to John in Bermuda the summer of 1980. He was there when John wrote the songs that appeared on *Double Fantasy*. "He was the most trusted person," Sean said.

Almost immediately after John's death, Seaman began stealing documents, tapes, letters, and other precious memorabilia, lugging it out of the Dakota in shopping bags. Included in the thefts were John's diaries. Soon after the murder, Seaman drew up a contract for himself and a college friend, a writer named Bob Rosen, making them partners on a book about John and merchandise like John and Yoko dolls. Seaman named his scheme Project Walrus.

Before she found out about the thefts and the book Seaman and Rosen were working on, Yoko was upset to learn about another tell-all book in the works. The author was John Green, one of Yoko's former tarot card readers. Green, aka Charlie Swan, had been on salary for a while and had lived in a loft Yoko and John owned. He advised Yoko on real estate purchases and other business. He also read cards for Lauren Bacall and Andy Warhol. When Yoko and John were separated, she consulted him most days. Now he was writing a book.

In Sam's opinion, it wasn't surprising that Green—and, over time, other psychics—exploited her. "That's what they did."

Yoko's belief in the paranormal made her ripe for exploitation. She had regularly consulted psychics when John was alive, but after the murder, in a continual state of distress, she turned to dozens of people who claimed to be in touch with and connected to "larger forces." Her reliance on psychics came from a desperate attempt to find answers about what had happened and to protect herself from the very real threats.

She paid mediums to hold séances during which she attempted to communicate with John—and she believed some were successful.

Everyone close to Yoko witnessed her obsession with tarot cards. Whether she was in her office or in a recording studio or in the kitchen talking with friends, in person or on the phone, she constantly shuffled a deck of cards.

After John was killed, others asked her—and she asked herself: Why had none of the psychics anticipated John's death and protected him? Yoko obsessed over this, concluding, she told me, "There were premonitions and warnings." One tarot card reader warned Yoko, "[John] sleeps in blood," a vision that chilled her. She followed his and other psychics' advice to protect him. "It wasn't enough," Yoko said. "The forces against us were too powerful." In 2010, she said, "There is within me this feeling of guilt because I couldn't stop [John's murder]."

Sam loathed her obsession with the supernatural and, especially, her reliance on psychics. "I would always tell her, 'So why don't they play the lottery if they can predict the future? Why do they live in this shitty house? Why don't they have a car? I mean, if they see everything . . .' It's just so pathetic. But I come from a more practical world." He recalled a psychic giving a group reading in Palm Beach. "Everybody was always a princess, a queen, a pharaoh in their past life, you know. I never met somebody who was a normal person in a past life."

Sam saw some of the psychics manipulating her by issuing scary warnings of the tragedies that would befall Yoko and Sean and insisting that they—and only they—could prevent the calamities. And though he continually tried to convince her that the psychics were frauds, he also understood why she believed. "She was so insecure, she felt so alone, that she wanted some help for herself," he said. Yoko was desperate to feel safe.

One psychic who had Yoko's ear "was upsetting her—inflaming her paranoia," according to Sam. "I got to the point that I couldn't stomach it anymore, so I had [the psychic's] phone bugged."

The psychic whose phone he bugged would talk to Yoko, hang up, and call Yoko's other psychics. They used the information they exchanged to make their readings and advice consistent and therefore more believable. "They'd get their stories straight," Sam said. "They were disgusting. I wanted to get rid of them."

Sam played Yoko a week's worth of the psychic's calls with her cohorts. Yoko heard the psychics talking after they consulted with her, sharing stories. Sam thought he'd succeeded—"I thought it was a job well done"—but later he realized she'd continued to consult the psychics behind his back.

LETTERS CONTINUED TO POUR INTO the Dakota. Most expressed sympathy and support, but more disturbing mail came in, including a shocking number of letters from psychics who claimed to be in contact with John. He was trying to reach her, they said. Yoko had some investigated. Most were easily identified as frauds, but she spoke with and even met with a few of those who wrote.

Yoko took solace in the letters from fans (she wrote back to many), but there were many hate letters, too, and explicit threats. Those were turned over to Elliot Mintz, who forwarded them to Mahoney. They turned some over to law enforcement.

And the mail wasn't just letters—people sent drawings and collages. Elliot recalled, "One was just the barrel of a gun pointed at her saying, 'You're next,' signed 'the Mark David Chapman fan club.'"

In his book *We All Shine On*, Elliot wrote that the letters from that "fan club" were signed "Death to Ono." He reported that Yoko's security team started pinning the names and descriptions of the senders of threats on a bulletin board at Studio One and "imploring the staff to raise an alarm should any of them be spotted near the Dakota."

One day Mahoney had Yoko and Barbara Graustark, who was visiting, climb up a ladder and hide in a loft in a Dakota bedroom because he feared that someone had broken into the building. It was a false alarm, but the threats took a new ominous turn when Elliot, conducting an inventory, discovered that a cassette player of John's that had been near Yoko's bed was missing. This was the first inkling Yoko had of the ongoing thefts. Elliot soon discovered that much more than that cassette player was missing and informed Yoko. She had him tell Mahoney, who interrogated staffers and reported to Yoko that it had to be an inside job. This terrified her. After being bugged by the FBI during the 1970s, she was afraid that the apartment was now bugged "by her enemies," Elliot said. He arranged for it to be regularly "swept."

Yoko began to be suspicious of everyone. Mahoney wanted her to order lie-detector tests for the staff, but she thought it would crush morale. She agonized, torn between mistrust and the values by which she wanted to live.

The theft of John's possessions wasn't the only way people exploited his memory. Yoko soon heard about books in the works other than Green's. May

Pang was writing a memoir. Albert Goldman, known for salacious biographies, including one about Elvis Presley ("Elvis was a pervert, a voyeur," Goldman wrote), was writing about John.

It was all disheartening, but there was nothing Yoko could do.

Then she was shown a letter that took her breath away—it was from Mark David Chapman. John's killer had written her once before to apologize for murdering her husband. Now he said he wanted to get her permission to write a memoir—he promised he'd give the money to charity.

She burst into tears. Sam comforted her, reassured her that Chapman was legally barred from writing a book. But, as I witnessed, Yoko was inconsolable.

Two days after that, two men were stopped inside the Dakota. They said they had business with Yoko. When they were pressed for more information, they began to run. One got away, but the other was tackled by a bodyguard. Before he was taken away by police, the man shouted that he had come to "get" Yoko and Sean.

There were always bodyguards around—Yoko spent more than one million dollars on security the year after John died. The guards were constant reminders that her and Sean's lives could be in danger. Sean would remark on how scary it was to grow up with gun-carrying guards lurking nearby. As a child, he once reminded Yoko not to leave the house without a bodyguard because, he pointed out, if something happened to her, he would be an orphan.

DECEMBER 8 AGAIN. IT HAD been a year. On that first anniversary of John's death, Yoko cut off thirty inches of her hair. "In Japan, when a woman becomes a widow, she cuts her hair," she said.

She issued a statement announcing she would spend the day in seclusion. "I think of John's death as a war casualty," she said. "It is the war between the sane and the insane. All his life, John had fought the insanity within us and of the world. Ironically, he was killed by an insane act at the time he was enjoying the sanest moment of his life."

FRIENDS SUGGESTED YOKO MOVE OUT of the Dakota to get away from the fans, the security issues, and the place where her husband had been shot beside her. But, as she told me, "This is where John and I built a beautiful life for ourselves, and being here is almost like still being with John. There are still a lot of things from the life we had together that are unfinished. You just can't walk away from them."

Yoko attended to business. There was John's estate. There was the buying and selling of real estate and managing properties and investments. And there were court cases, including ones over the rights and royalties to Beatles songs.

Besides the business affairs, Yoko had been developing the *Milk and Honey* album, the follow-up to *Double Fantasy*—a continuation of the musical dialogue between her and John. It wasn't easy to get the record in shape. She and John had written and recorded the songs, but some weren't finished and none were polished. At one point, Yoko called Elton John and "urgently" asked him to come to the Dakota. Upon his arrival, she explained that she wanted him to help finish John's songs, but Elton declined. In his autobiography he wrote, "I thought it was too soon, the time wasn't right. Actually, I didn't think the time would ever be right. Just the thought of it freaked me out. . . . Yoko was insistent, but so was I. So it was a very uncomfortable meeting."

In the mixing booth, the engineer played John's voice in loops. "Again," she said. "Again." Over and over, John singing a song inspired by a Robert Browning poem that he'd written for her: "Grow old along with me / the best is yet to be."

She cycled from paralyzing depression to determination to get on with life, and she sometimes seemed lighter as she soldiered on. There were good times with Sam. Good times with friends. On June 14, 1982, with her bodyguards accompanying her, she marched in an anti-nuclear protest. As she walked, the crowd sang "Give Peace a Chance." She met with representatives of New York City to plan a memorial garden for John in Central Park that would be named Strawberry Fields. Ed Koch, the mayor, enthusiastically embraced the plan. She was at a reception with the mayor and others when an ensemble, meaning well, played the song "Woman." Hearing John's song, a love letter to her, she appeared stricken, but she held back tears.

Amid all this, Yoko decided on a title for a solo album she was working on: *It's Alright (I See Rainbows)*. If she said it, maybe it would come to be. She fully believed that we can create reality by picturing it, meditating on it, and saying it aloud to the universe. She was desperate to change the "negative energy" around her into "positive energy" and believed—*had to believe*—it was possible.

CHAPTER 25

THE ALBUM *IT'S ALRIGHT (I See Rainbows)* was released in December. As always, Yoko had worked obsessively on every aspect of the record. After laying down the basic tracks, she added percussion from around the world, synthesized cellos and horns and the sounds of toy ray guns and the ocean. She was creating, she said, a "positive prayer." It was about moving forward. She sang, "I know it's gonna be alright." The album was praised by many reviewers. This, *Season of Glass*, and "Thin Ice" were a kind of vindication.

The positive reviews were heartwarming, but Yoko's interviews to publicize the record caused some consternation on the home front—she never acknowledged Sam Havadtoy's existence. As far as the public knew, she was single, but the truth was that she had a new boyfriend. Sam was a fixture in her life. She relied on him. He helped with business and was a buffer when they were out, physically shielding her from paparazzi and rescuing her from persistent fans. "We had a full life together, but I didn't exist," Sam said. "Only John existed."

In some ways he was fine with hiding. "I really hated—and I still do hate—celeb life," he said. "So it was kind of a perfect match that I could be the little busybody businessman in the background, doing all the things and having kind of success and being proud of what I'm doing without being pushed in the limelight. So for me, that was perfect."

Nonetheless, sometimes he got fed up and they argued.

But mostly they got along. They frequently socialized, going out to lunch and dinner with friends. They went to the movies, museums, galleries, and the theater. They took long walks. She tried to carry on a normal life and sometimes she forgot about the betrayals and threats. As Jann Wenner observed, there were many times she was happy with Sam—but the respites didn't last.

MORE THAN TWO YEARS AFTER John's death, Sam, Elliot Mintz, and a handful of confidantes were still helping Yoko cope with what felt like a constant barrage. She felt under siege and petrified. She had moved to a bedroom in the Dakota that didn't face a neighboring apartment because she was afraid of a sniper.

There were more death threats. Elliot later admitted, "I carried a gun during that time. And [Dan] Mahoney of course was armed; and his two guys, who were always in the apartment, were armed. I mean, there were more guns in the kitchen than on a main street in any American city tonight—and that in the wake of Yoko's position on guns." There was a bomb scare one night. Mahoney moved Yoko and Sam into a hotel again, and she sent Sean to Bermuda with his nanny. What was a reasonable amount of fear? As Bob Gruen said, "You can't tell her not to worry after a man flew halfway around the world, camped out for a few days, then blew her husband away in front of her."

She had written the title song to the album *It's Alright* while hiding in the hotel. Yoko recalled that night: "I wrote the song 'It's Alright' while we were cooped up in the hotel room—as a prayer. Finally, I went to the studio despite the warning. I couldn't hide all my life."

There was also the unresolved issue of the thefts. Elliot and Sam continued investigating. They didn't know the culprit was Fred Seaman, but he had finally been fired when Yoko went into her private bathroom and discovered him taking a bath.

Seaman, no longer wanting to share his imagined riches with anyone, broke into "and ransacked" Bob Rosen's apartment and stole Rosen's manuscript, John's diaries, and other documents. Following the break-in, Rosen reached out to Jann Wenner at *Rolling Stone*, who advised him to contact Yoko. When he called the Dakota, he spoke to Sam. He explained that he'd been duped by Seaman and had thought he was working on a book with Yoko's blessing. He met Sam and a lawyer and, subsequently, Yoko herself.

When Yoko learned about Project Walrus, she was horrified. She had trusted Fred. And the extent of the thefts shocked her. Yoko cared more about getting the personal materials back safely—especially John's diaries—than about prosecuting Seaman, and she hesitated to bring in the police for fear Seaman would destroy the evidence.

The breaking point was when Yoko heard that Seaman had been given an advance to write a book about John. Sam finally called the police. Seaman was arrested. In April 1983, he pleaded guilty to second-degree larceny. A judge sentenced him to five years of probation and ordered him to return everything he'd stolen.

Seaman's plea required him not to reveal the contents of John's diaries, but that didn't stop him from talking about Yoko. One day outside the Dakota, I jumped in a taxi, and, bizarrely, Seaman was the driver. During the ride downtown, he called her "the black widow" and cast her as a drug addict who had been cheating on John. The hate he expressed was chilling.

Yoko finally received some welcome news that summer. Seaman's publisher dropped its plans to publish his book. However, the positive news was countered when Sam was told that Seaman had agreed to cooperate with Albert Goldman on his forthcoming biography of John, which was expected to be a hatchet job.

Seaman was just one of the people suggesting that they, and only they, had a special link to John and had somehow been ordained to tell his story. John Green's book was published in January 1983. In *Dakota Days*, Green described himself as Yoko and John's "marriage counselor and business advisor." He depicted Yoko as irrational, spiteful, paranoid, and scheming and John as self-obsessed, vindictive, and despairing. Green promoted his book at an event at which he read tarot cards for *Penthouse* "Pets" at a comedy club.

May Pang's book came out the same month. The book, entitled *Loving John*, included stories about John's out-of-control drinking and said he went back to Yoko because she had him hypnotized. She portrayed Yoko as cold, manipulative, and narcissistic.

The following month, *The Love You Make*, a book on the Beatles by Peter Brown, a former assistant, was published. It was another portrayal of Yoko as devious and calculating. "For God's sake, he was the best man at their wedding," Elliot said.

By coincidence, one day Brown was at the Russian Tea Room at the same time Yoko and Sam were having lunch there. Brown approached the table and greeted them. Sam barely acknowledged him, but Yoko was gracious. The book wasn't mentioned. When he left, Sam asked, "How can you be so civil to such uncivilized people?"

YOKO BARELY SLEPT. SHE WOULD tense when the old building creaked. One midnight I sat with her in apartment 72 in the room that doubled as both living room and kitchen. She sat on a couch slipcovered in denim fabric (denim was for winter, white linen for summer) with a throw pillow that read YOU CAN NEVER BE TOO THIN OR TOO RICH under framed photographs of Sean and John and Sean's scribblings and an ornate mirror, its frame studded with silver pineapples. Her white Persian cat, Sasha, slept on her lap. Yoko wore a light blue nightgown under an intricate *yukata* with oranges and golds. She inhaled from an ever-present cigarette and drank green tea. She sat cross-legged. There was a small stained-glass window in the door to the dining room. The night was quiet, but suddenly Yoko panicked: She thought she saw a face in the stained glass and was terrified. I checked for her, but no one was there. She had a security guard search the apartment.

She retired to her bedroom to try to sleep but gave up after fifteen minutes. Back in the kitchen, afraid, she sat up, alert, vigilant, on guard, constantly shuffling tarot cards through another sleepless night. Her mind was playing tricks on her, or she'd been visited by a ghost—she believed it was possible. Either way, she was terrified anew.

Her fear scared Sean too, as did the constant presence of gun-carrying bodyguards. For a while, a man who believed that Stephen King had killed John sat in his parked van outside the Dakota. Guards considered him potentially dangerous, but he hadn't broken any laws, so police couldn't make the man leave. When they walked Sean to school, the guards put him in a black bag and carried him past the van. His parents had gotten into bags for art's sake, but this terrified Sean.

ONE AFTERNOON, A MAN CALLED the building, said he was a pilot, claimed to be the reincarnation of John, and said if Yoko didn't marry him, he was going to crash a plane into the Dakota in order to kill her and Sean. Added to the other threats, it prompted Yoko to finally leave New York. *Milk and Honey* was nearly complete when she, Sam, and Sean flew to San Francisco, longing for a break from the stress and persistent sense of danger. She could complete the record there. My family lived near San Francisco, and Yoko had wonderful memories of the city from her time there with John and as a young girl. The air felt fresh, the fog invigorating.

She, Sean, and Sam stayed in a suite of rooms at the Fairmont Hotel, where Yoko had stayed as a child. They dined with us in Nob Hill restaurants, took drives to the wine country and West Marin. They visited Muir Woods and the Calistoga mud baths. Yoko and Sam began house-hunting in San Francisco and inquiring about schools.

She and Sam considered apartments in the Brocklebank, the setting of Alfred Hitchcock's film *Vertigo*, and a building across from the Mark Hopkins Hotel where Patty Hearst lived. Sam bought a small apartment down the street, across from Grace Cathedral, to use as an office and so they could use the building's swimming pool. Yoko asked the director of Sean's New York school to recommend one in San Francisco, and she was told about San Francisco Day School. Yoko met the head of school, Nancy Stearns. She and Stearns talked about John and cried together. Yoko enrolled Sean in second grade in the school. In spite of Sam's opposition, she insisted that a bodyguard be stationed on the first floor and accompany the class on field trips.

"The bodyguards didn't make it feel safer," Sam said. "It made it all worse."

They had moved to San Francisco to get away from the threats, but they followed the family across the country. Yoko had been told about a psychic in San Francisco, and she invited her to the hotel. The woman conducted a séance at which, Yoko claimed, John tried to warn her and make sure she had bodyguards for her and Sean. Yoko ramped up security.

Two or three days later, several police officers came to the Fairmont and told her they'd apprehended a sniper firing practice rounds out a window of an apartment. He claimed that Yoko was his target. The man was arrested with several guns, seven hundred rounds of ammunition, and books about Yoko and John.

One day Sean didn't show up for school. He and his family had returned to New York. He'd been enrolled for only two months.

SEAN TURNED EIGHT. AS FRIENDS and children arrived for his birthday party on October 9, 1983, the number of fans outside the Dakota grew in size. They held up signs with birthday wishes for John and Sean and, as always, sang John's songs. Upstairs, Yoko heard the familiar tunes and was pulled between celebrating her son and remembering her husband. The tension between those emotions was interrupted by the buzz of the apartment intercom. It was the doorman, calling to report that a man who had been asking for Yoko had somehow slipped past security and was in the building. A security guard caught the man as he stepped out of the elevator. He wanted an autograph. The guard explained that wasn't going to happen, escorted the intruder back downstairs, and warned him not to return.

As an adult, Sean would recall that in those days, he felt like he was "living in this very, very high-stakes world, almost like a thriller." And it wasn't only the break-ins, threats, thefts, and gun-toting bodyguards—or being put in a black bag on his way to school. He said he was living amid "the mystical, magical, spiritual stuff that got out of hand." One of the more heartbreaking experiences for both mother and son was when a distraught Yoko tried to get him to communicate with his father's ghost. She believed that as a child, he was closer to the spirit world. Sean, not wanting to disappoint her, answered yes or no to the questions she posed. He remembered this period with empathy, knowing "she was reacting to my dad having been murdered right in front of her, crazy amounts of criminal activity from her business associates, employees actually stealing from her, betrayals on levels that people can't even imagine."

The world, Sean knew, was chaotic and scary for her. "It had been true on one level when my dad was alive—they were followed by the FBI; Nixon was trying to deport them and their phones were tapped; there were screaming fans and weird people writing them disturbing letters—and then my dad was killed by a fan and it was even more chaotic and scary. I do think spirituality was something she clung to because it gave her a sense of control and some power during an overwhelming time."

It was hard for Sean, though. "It felt like she was dealing with trauma that she couldn't deal with by distracting herself with tarot and psychics. I didn't like seeing her that way. It felt like it came from a part of her that was out of control and overwhelmed."

CHAPTER 26

Yoko tried to carry on normally, often going through the motions. She and Sam spent relatively quiet days together. When they weren't working, they played chess, read, went out to lunch and dinner (La Goulue, Mr. Chow, the Russian Tea Room, and Il Mulino were favorite restaurants), and they socialized.

They attended and threw parties. She enjoyed being with artists and musicians. An array of rock stars paraded through the Dakota, including Ringo, David Bowie, and Elton John. Old friends came by: Cage and Merce Cunningham; Kate Millett. Yoko and Kate shared stories about the old days in the Village, and Yoko, supporting her old friend, bought a series of Millett's lithographs for far more than they were worth.

Sam had gotten the artist Victor Vasarely to represent Hungary in creating a painting for a book about Strawberry Fields, and he organized a birthday party for Vasarely at the Dakota. Fifty people came for a sit-down dinner. "You know the joke that if a bomb went off, the art world would die," Sam said. "I mean there was Jasper Johns, Andy Warhol, Louise Nevelson, Keith Haring, Basquiat . . . everyone was there."

Once Yoko held an impromptu dinner for Bob Dylan. Sam picked up Warhol beforehand. "We went in and it really was heavy-duty, everyone in a circle," Warhol reported in his diary. As always, guests were asked to take their shoes off. About Bowie, Warhol said, "I was disappointed, his suit was too modern." And Madonna, Warhol reported, "said she'd feel more comfortable with her top off than her shoes off."

Keith Haring couldn't help but be impressed. "When [Andy] brought me to Yoko's apartment the first time, it was incredible. You can't believe that you're there. The ultimate one was a dinner at Yoko's. I brought Madonna and the artist Martin Burgoyne. Andy was already there. Bob Dylan was there. David Bowie was there. And Iggy Pop. Just sort of in the kitchen."

Another star-studded party was held on October 9, 1984, Sean's ninth birthday. In Blake Gopnik's Andy Warhol biography, he identifies "the weird universe of celebrity friendship," and here was a microcosm of that universe, a seemingly random guest list that included Warhol, Haring, Walter Cronkite, Roberta Flack, Harry Nilsson, John Cage, Louise Nevelson, Kenny Scharf, and Steve Jobs. Guests took their shoes off (except for Warhol, who refused) and walked down the hallway past a sarcophagus encased in glass and Yoko's "Play It by Trust," the monochromatic chess set. A "Half a Painting" was mounted on the wall over "Wrapping Piece for London," a chair wrapped in white gauze. There was a Plexiglas column upon which were four silver spoons (the piece was titled "Three Spoons"). Another glass case contained four glass keys, her "Keys to Open the Skies."

Haring came with a large piece, the canvas still wet, a present for Sean. He'd painted Sean's face in the number 9. Warhol gave Sean a bracelet he'd made out of pennies and a spectacular painting of a heart-shaped candy box. Jobs lugged in a huge box containing a Macintosh computer. Before the night was over, Jobs taught Sean—and then Warhol, who'd been staring over their shoulders—how to use the Mac.

Down the hall to the right, in the evening light, was the White Room. Guests looking out the street-facing windows could see the park, a quilt of crystal and gray. There were three dozen white roses arranged in a glass vase atop the white piano on which John had written "Imagine."

The layout of the apartment remained largely the same as it was when

John was alive, but what had been Sean's playroom in 1980, dominated by a circus trampoline, had been returned to its original purpose as a dining room, where supper was served. The birthday cake, in the shape of a piano, had been sent by Elton John. Harry Nilsson led everyone in a song for Sean, a rousing "For He's a Jolly Good Fellow." When they finished, Sean told me, "If my dad were here, we'd sing, 'For they're jolly good fellows.'"

Yoko rarely allowed herself to cry those days, at least in public, but she couldn't help doing so then. She left the party so no one would see.

MILK AND HONEY HAD BEEN released early that year. To promote the record, Yoko granted an interview to Barbara Graustark for *People*. "By 4 a.m. her normal workday has already begun," Graustark reported. "Curled on a couch, her arm draped protectively around her son, she looks much the same as she did nearly two decades ago, when Lennon first brought her to the attention of the world. As Yoko approaches 51, Lady Clairol now washes away her gray, but her energy and slim figure remain those of a teenager. So does her Mona Lisa veneer—the flawless skin, the whisper-shy voice, an enigmatic smile."

About that smile, Graustark wrote, "Yoko smiles, but only when she means it. Her mother, the aloof heir to a Japanese banking fortune, warned her daughter never to smile in public. 'Smiles are for shopkeepers,' she said derisively—meaning those who need to ingratiate. So Yoko reserves smiles for her friends, hides insecurity behind dark glasses, and suffers the accusation of arrogance."

GRAUSTARK'S ARTICLE APPEARED TWO WEEKS after she accompanied Yoko, Sean, and a small entourage to Liverpool for Sean to see his father's childhood home for the first time. Sean was introduced to John's aunt Mimi, who had raised his father, and they visited places important in John's life—the home in which he'd grown up; the site of Strawberry Fields, the orphanage that inspired his song and John's grammar school.

But the trip was overwhelming because Yoko and Sean were dogged by paparazzi and tabloid journalists. A photographer climbed into their Liverpool hotel room window and was ejected by a security guard.

That year Yoko, Sam, and Sean also traveled to Japan, where Yoko saw Isoko for dinner one night at the Okura, her hotel in Tokyo. Yoko and her mother were civil, but they hardly spoke. Sam said, "It wasn't so much a love-hate relationship as a hate-hate relationship."

Among the places Yoko visited during that trip was Karuizawa. She took Sean and the rest of her entourage to the coffeehouse where she and John had spent those memorable afternoons, where John had marked a tree with a nail at Sean's height when they last visited together—Sean had been three or four years old.

Yoko wrote a story about returning to the coffeehouse. "It was as if time had stood still. There was the same stillness in the shop with only a few people sitting around. The scent of pine and aroma of good coffee was in the air. I had a cup of coffee and left.

"The owner came running after me and handed me a lighter. 'Your husband left this the last time he was here,' he said. I looked at him and the lighter. 'I'd like to return this to you.' I lit the lighter. The flame shot up, like it was alive."

THAT YEAR THERE WAS ANOTHER setback. In April 1984, Yoko lost a lawsuit brought by Jack Douglas, coproducer of *Double Fantasy* and *Milk and Honey*, over royalties that he was owed for those albums—according to the *New York Times*, she was ordered to pay him more than $2.5 million for *Double Fantasy* and an undetermined amount for *Milk and Honey*.

But there were positive events too. Sam had been working on a tribute album of Yoko's songs performed by other artists. It was a kind of birthday gift—the work on it had begun when she turned fifty in 1983.

Named after one of her *Double Fantasy* songs, the album—*Every Man Has a Woman*—was released in November 1984. It included recordings of Yoko's songs performed by Elvis Costello ("Thin Ice"), Roberta Flack (a reggae version of "Goodbye Sadness"), and Rosanne Cash's romantic "Nobody Sees Me Like You Do." Harry Nilsson contributed two songs, "Silver Horse" and an electrifying rendition of "Loneliness."

The title song was sung by John. He'd recorded a background vocal of the track for *Double Fantasy* that was remixed and brought up front. The final song on the record was Sean singing "It's Alright."

To celebrate the release, Sam threw a launch party at the Dakota. The album's musicians milled around. There was caviar and free-flowing champagne. The record blasted over the sound system. I was present, and Rosanne Cash told me, "This is surreal. To be here with Yoko Ono. I mean, *Yoko Ono*." Yoko hugged her. Harry Nilsson said, "With this record, maybe people will finally understand. John recognized her brilliance, but then she became Mrs. Lennon and that's all people saw."

Another project in the works at the time was a documentary, *Yoko Ono: Then and Now*, which Graustark wrote and directed and Sam coproduced. The film began with Yoko explaining why she always wore what had become her iconic sunglasses.

"The reason why I wear my sunglasses is that I feel more comfortable. I feel less exposed, and at this time I think I'm not really ready to emerge altogether. I feel as though the glasses protect me from revealing my emotions too much. Part of me feels very strange when I see a photo of me these days without the glasses on, because something's showing there that is still very sad."

There was an interview with McCartney in the film. "The problem in other people's eyes is that she's honest," he said. "The honesty is what hurts a lot of people, I think. I thought she was a hard woman. I don't think she is now; I think she's just the opposite. I think she's a very loving, caring woman. I thought she was pushy, which is wrong, I don't believe she is. She's just herself and she's determined more than some other people to be herself. Some people will just give in. She won't."

Every Man Has a Woman and the documentary were released in late 1984. Three singles from the album hit the *Billboard* charts, and the film aired to positive reviews. Referring to the two releases, Sam said, "I thought this would make people look at Yoko differently, but it didn't change an iota. People have their ideas, and they will not change. This is what she had to face all her life."

EVEN AS THE RECORD AND documentary came out, Yoko went back in the studio to record a new album, *Starpeace*, which was released on her fifty-second birthday, February 18, 1985. The title and eponymous song were a response to President Ronald Reagan's antiballistic-missile program, nicknamed Star Wars. Peaceniks like Yoko believed the program was an escalation of Cold War aggression.

The album hardly sold, but the single "Hell in Paradise" hit number twelve on the US dance charts. Later, a remix hit number one on the dance charts. The LP was dismissed as "60s hippie drivel" by the *Charlotte Observer* but received a rave review in the *New York Times*, which called it "the most balanced album Miss Ono has made."

In spite of the meager album sales, Yoko set out on a *Starpeace* world tour in 1986. The plan was to perform in forty-three cities in eleven countries. "The response of the audiences was phenomenal," said Graustark, who, with Jane Wenner, accompanied Yoko to Budapest and Vienna. Yoko gave her all to the audiences. In addition to the *Starpeace* songs, she performed older songs, including rockers like "Midsummer New York." She closed the set with "Imagine," and the applause was deafening. But many of the concerts, including those in Japan, were canceled due to poor ticket sales, and the album lost money.

"After *Starpeace* I was totally discouraged—not as a songwriter or composer, but by the fact that there was no kind of demand for what I was doing, to put it mildly!" she said. "I thought that it was just impractical for me to focus my energy on getting my music out. I had so many other responsibilities with business, and with issuing John's work. Forget Yoko Ono, there were lots of things I had to do as Yoko Ono Lennon."

CHAPTER 27

YOKO WAS COMPELLED TO KEEP John's legacy alive. She felt obligated—she owed it to fans, the world, and him. "I never even thought of the word *widow*. I thought I was a soldier. We were both fighting for freedom and justice and self-expression, and he just fell in the battlefield. That is how I thought of it. That I had to keep going," Yoko said.

She prepared for the opening of Strawberry Fields in Central Park. She had contributed one million dollars to create the memorial across from the Dakota. Strawberry Fields was to be a remembrance to John dedicated to peace. At its center was a mosaic, which was sent by the city of Naples, with the word *Imagine*. It was surrounded by benches, where visitors from around the world could gather to remember John.

"There are 150 trees, 5,000 shrubs and 20,000 perennials," Maureen Dowd wrote in the *New York Times*. "From the late Princess Grace of Monaco, there are dogwoods; from the Soviet Union, river birches; from the Canadians, maples, and from the Dutch, daffodil bulbs.

"And, to Miss Ono's delight, countries that are politically opposed have plants that are peacefully coexisting. Jordan's fothergilla grows beside Israel's cedar.

"The White House did not respond to Miss Ono's request, so the United States is not represented with a plant." (Later the United States came through.)

Yoko dedicated Strawberry Fields in the fall of 1985 on what would have been John's forty-fifth birthday—Sean turned ten that day. She had Julian fly in.

Things with Julian were better than they had been at any time before. Julian's relationship with Yoko had always been strained, and they wouldn't settle a lawsuit he brought contesting John's will until 1996, but she felt closer to him and championed his own efforts in music and art. He often stayed at the Dakota when he visited New York. In Cold Spring Harbor, he swam with Sean. They played video games and Julian taught Sean songs on the guitar.

Yoko began assembling albums of John's music to be released the next year. She called one *Live in New York City* and one *Menlove Ave.* after the Liverpool street on which John had lived when he was a child. The latter would be the third posthumous album. The songs were mostly outtakes and recordings made during rehearsals for John's *Rock 'n' Roll, Mind Games,* and *Walls and Bridges* albums. The front and back covers were images of John created by Andy Warhol from a photograph by Iain Macmillan.

From the start, critics charged Yoko with exploiting John for the money by releasing new (and, later, reissuing old) records. But David Geffen said, "She had her own reasons, and they weren't financial, I can assure you of that. She was determined to keep him relevant. She continually introduced him to new listeners and made sure no one forgets him." Jann Wenner pointed out that Paul McCartney was alive to do it for himself and the Beatles, but Yoko was left to protect John's place in the world.

In her role as manager of John's legacy, Yoko eventually released more than two dozen of his records—reissues, demos, remixes, collections, box sets. With every release, there were the inevitable snarky comments about her exploiting John, but the records were celebrated by fans, introduced John to new listeners, and ultimately did what she intended them to do: They kept John in the news, on the charts, and on the radio.

When she licensed "Instant Karma" for a Nike commercial in 1987, she responded to criticism by saying, "The way I see it is: I've got an access there for millions of people to hear 'Instant Karma'; and I got $800,000, which went to the United Negro College Fund. That's what I got for that song. You have a problem with that?"

I accompanied Yoko on her next major venture, a trip to Moscow in February 1987. She traveled to the USSR to attend Mikhail Gorbachev's International Forum for a Non-Nuclear World and for the Survival of Humanity—the Moscow peace forum. She arrived and checked in at the Cosmos Hotel along with Wenner and other friends, and the next day, dressed in fur (it was icy cold), she walked along the Arbat, the main boulevard in the center of the city. Recognizing Yoko, a group of students stopped and stared. There was a moment of disbelief followed by pandemonium. They gathered around Yoko and spontaneously began singing "Imagine."

On the third day of the conference, Yoko was told that Gorbachev and his wife, Raisa, were fans and wanted to meet her. She visited the Kremlin, where Gorbachev quoted "Imagine"—"Your husband's great song." Raisa Gorbachev sang a few bars of John's song "Woman." For the second time in two days, Yoko's eyes filled with tears.

IN SEPTEMBER 1988, THE IMPORTANCE of Yoko's work to secure John's image became apparent when the dreaded Albert Goldman book about John was published. Yoko had asked her friends not to speak to the author, but that might have backfired in one way—it meant he relied on people who had either limited knowledge of John's life (not that it stopped them from expounding on Yoko and John) or axes to grind.

The book was indeed a hatchet job—sensational, lie-filled, and racist. Goldman described Yoko as "simian-looking." He invented grotesque scenes: "John seizes Yoko by her great mop of hair and hauls her, screaming and scratching, to the stove, where he threatens to set her hair afire!" He wrote that the famous Annie Leibovitz cover of *Rolling Stone* "reduced the marriage of the rock world's most celebrated lovers to the image of an impassive bitch and her blindly sucking whelp." He wrote that John kicked Sean.

The book hit the *New York Times* bestseller list at number two, but it was denounced by countless reviewers. Paul McCartney called for a boycott and deemed the book "a piece of trash."

Yoko's response to the lies was mainly to ignore them and continue to spread the real story in interviews and let the music speak for itself, though she did address the Goldman book in an interview Elliot did that aired on Westwood One Radio. Sean was interviewed too. "It was a painful process," Elliot said. Yoko rebutted one lie after another. John was not "zonked out" on drugs for the last years of his life. Sean laughed when he was asked if his father had kicked him, as Goldman claimed he had; Sean emphasized that John was never once violent. Finally Yoko said, "I can't do this," and she stopped the interview.

And Goldman was just one of the authors who attempted to rewrite Yoko and John's history, inventing scurrilous stories, presumably to generate sensational headlines. Some accounts had Yoko and John heading toward divorce. Pang's had them getting back together after the lost weekend because Yoko hired someone to hypnotize John. However, these accounts were contradicted by people who actually knew Yoko and John and had spent time with them, all of whom drew the same conclusion: Yoko and John were devoted to each other and deeply in love.

ONE MORNING, AN ASSISTANT DISCOVERED notes to Yoko and a stranger's photograph on a dresser inside the apartment. Someone had broken in. Investigators determined that a man had climbed to the roof of the Dakota, fastened a rope, rappelled down, crawled along a ledge, and slipped into the apartment through an unlocked window in the dressing room. He was undetected by the security guards on duty. He left the messages for Yoko and fled, presumably by the same route. Dan Mahoney tracked the man down. "He wasn't dangerous; he was just a crazy fan." Locks on the windows were reinforced, and patrols were increased.

In its February 3, 1986, issue, *People* magazine reported on that "bizarre visitation" at the Dakota: "Last week a man broke into Yoko Ono's lavish New York apartment that she had shared with husband John Lennon before his murder in 1980. Yoko was asleep at the time, and the man, apparently deranged, left behind a picture and some notes. . . .

"But," the article continued, "even more strange has been the recent emergence of Yoko's shadowy former husband, Tony Cox, 49, with the first significant news in 14 years about his and Yoko's daughter, Kyoko."

The magazine contacted Yoko before the article came out, and when she learned what Kyoko had been through, she was horrified. In the article, Cox said that he and Kyoko, who was then twenty-two, had spent years as members of a religious cult called the Church of the Living Word, also known as the Walk.

Cox was granting the interview to promote *Vain Glory*, a documentary he'd made to expose the cult, which he said they had escaped in 1977. "Cox claims in *Vain Glory* that cult founder John Robert Stevens, in addition to praying for the deaths of political leaders, considered himself the earthly incarnation of Jesus Christ and practiced 'forehead bonding,' a form of mind control and hypnotism, with his disciples." Cox said that Kyoko helped him make the film but that she declined to go public.

Of Kyoko, Cox said, "Because of our life-style, she was taught with tutors, studied in foreign schools and has a conception of the world that's very mature for someone her age."

In the article, Cox said he harbored no ill will toward his ex-wife. "I don't have any bitterness toward Yoko. We both made terrible mistakes. Although [the Lennons] nearly destroyed me, at the same time she really had tremendous remorse, and when I found that out later, that changed my whole attitude. I really felt sorry for her. Regardless of how much I suffered, she was suffering also, and I'm genuinely aware of that."

The writer asked if there was a chance, then, for a reunion between mother and daughter? Tony said the decision was Kyoko's. "She's a completely independent individual."

People asked Yoko to respond to the article. She wrote an open letter to Kyoko, which the magazine published.

Dear Kyoko,

All these years there has not been one day I have not missed you. You are always in my heart. However, I will not make any attempt to find you now as I wish to respect your privacy. I wish you all the best in the world. If you ever wish to get in touch with me, know that I love you deeply and would be very happy to hear from you. But you should not feel guilty if you choose not to reach me. You have my respect, love and support forever.

Love, Mommy

The knowledge of what Kyoko had been through saddened Yoko, but she was glad of some news about her daughter. Real news. Over the years, many women claiming to be Kyoko had contacted Yoko. Elliot had been tasked with investigating them. They were all trying to con her. Yoko had come to expect disappointment, but each time, she couldn't help but hope.

ONE AFTERNOON, YOKO AND SAM were having lunch at Gino's, a restaurant on the Upper East Side, talking about her work. Sam made a suggestion that shocked her. He proposed she remake some of her early artworks in bronze. She was appalled—even angry. She saw his idea as a fundamental misunderstanding of her art, which was intentionally ethereal and ephemeral and unfinished. "I felt as though he said, why don't you stuff yourself in bronze, you know? And I was totally upset. And to my surprise, I was crying almost. I was in tears."

But afterward, she analyzed her reaction. "I realized that for something to move me so much that I would cry, there's something there. There seemed like a shimmering air in the sixties when I made these pieces, and now the air is bronzified. Now it's the eighties, and bronze is very eighties in a way—solidity, commodity, all of that. For someone who went through the sixties revolution, there has of course been an incredible change. . . . That freedom, all the hope and wishes are in some ways petrified." She became excited about re-creating some early works in bronze.

As Tony had once done, Sam took on the task of realizing Yoko's ideas—he oversaw the production of the bronze pieces. She chose the works to include, and he took them to a foundry, which created editions of nine each.

Around that time, she turned down the Pompidou Center, which had approached her to mount an exhibition. But when a curator at the Whitney Museum approached her and wanted to screen her films, Yoko agreed. After discussions with another Whitney curator, she also agreed to show the new bronze sculptures.

An exhibition of Yoko's work, *Yoko Ono: Objects, Films,* opened in early 1989, and it included the bronze versions of many of the instruction pieces she'd previously shown. There were bronze incarnations of "Painting to Be Stepped On" and "Painting to Hammer a Nail In." There was a bronzed "Play It by Trust" chess set and, on a pedestal, a bronzed apple on a stand. There was "Pointedness"—originally a white rubber ball and later a crystal ball displayed with the explanation "This sphere will be a sharp point when it gets to the far side of the room in your mind." Now it was bronze. Her ethereal glass "Keys to Open the Skies" was also cast in bronze. The whimsy and lightness of the original versions of the works were gone.

THE NEXT YEAR, SEAN TURNED fifteen. He had attended school at Ethical Culture, in Manhattan, and, for a year, at its Bronx campus, Fieldston, when he asked if he could transfer to boarding school in Europe. He hoped Yoko would allow him to live without the constant presence of bodyguards if he was outside the country. Guards had been a fixture in his life. Bodyguards taught him to ride a bike and they played baseball and soccer with him. Patrolling guards stood over the Cold Spring Harbor pool and watched as he played with friends. Once, Michael Jackson visited (Sean had appeared in Jackson's "Moonwalker" video two years earlier). The guards stood by while Sean and Michael ran around the yard hurling eggs at each other. Guards watched while Sean and Yoko played Ping-Pong. Guards walked Sean to school and were stationed outside it. They accompanied him whenever he went out. Guards were his friends, but he craved a "normal" life without them.

Yoko agreed that a boarding school in Europe would be safe, so he could live without guards, and he enrolled in Institut Le Rosey in Rolle, Switzerland, near Geneva. Sam told me, "Since he could get out twice a week, [Yoko and I] got a small apartment [in Geneva]—I mean, by our standards, it was a small apartment."

In Geneva, they finally had something like the normal life that Sam craved. He said, "It was one of my favorite times. I loved it because there was no security, no cook, nothing . . . I could take a basket and go shopping in Geneva, at the market, buy the food, bring it home, cook it, and we were kind of a normal family." Sean came home from school on Wednesday afternoons and for weekends. The apartment overlooked a square with, at its center, a huge chessboard painted on concrete and chess pieces a couple feet high. Yoko and Sam sat in a café on the square and watched the old men playing chess. They took long walks and went to the theater. When Sean came, they hung out in the square and a nearby park. "That was the best time," Sam said. "I loved that period."

Yoko and Sam kept the Geneva apartment while Sean attended Le Rosey, but, as Sam lamented, gradually they spent less time in Europe because Yoko wanted to be in New York to work.

YOKO HAD GATHERED SOME PRAISE and much criticism over the years for her music, especially what some described as her "caterwauling." A handful of critics praised Yoko's records, especially those released in the aftermath of John's death; she had fans among prominent rock critics. But at the time of their initial releases, her records were mostly dismissed or disdained.

However, by the late 1980s, a growing list of musicians acknowledged Yoko as groundbreaking and influential. John had always been her greatest fan, once asserting that her music was "as important as anything [the Beatles] ever did and as important as anything the Stones or Townshend ever did. . . . She makes music like you've never heard on earth. And when the musicians play with her, they're inspired out of their skulls."

In March 1992, Yoko released *Onobox*, a box set that included more than a hundred songs on six CDs. Some called it a vanity project, but it did exactly what she'd hoped it would: It made people look at her body of work anew.

A sticker on the box set asked listeners to "Smash your preconceptions!" The collection was the musical equivalent of an art retrospective that spanned her career to that point. It showed how much her work had evolved but also how consistent she'd been in the themes she'd tackled and styles she'd explored in albums from *Yoko Ono/Plastic Ono Band* through *Starpeace*. Disc 6 included *A Story*, the album she'd made during her separation from John that had never been released.

The six CDs contained both whimsy—lighthearted love songs—and political statements about feminism, sexism, class, violence, and peace. The songs were also forceful illustrations of the way Yoko channeled her emotions through her music.

The box set included her more traditionally structured songs, such as her forays into pop and rock. There were collages that mixed vocalizations, heavy breathing, and sound recordings. And there were the jams. The album earned a string of raves.

"The uniformly favorable reviews of *Onobox* have the whiff of apology, as though some critics feel ashamed of the way Yoko was maligned," wrote Rob Tannenbaum in *Newsday*. "Ironically, Yoko had the kind of career—protean, curious, funny, risky—that Beatles' fans expected but never got from George, Ringo, and Paul."

Entertainment Weekly gave the box set an A minus. A launch party for *Onobox* was held at Vrej Baghoomian Gallery in SoHo. Kim Gordon, Cyndi Lauper, and Joey Ramone were among the attendees. Lauper said, "Yoko was holding court, getting her due, and enjoying it; it was very satisfying for people who knew about all the years no one took her seriously."

CHAPTER 28

I N THE EARLY SUMMER OF 1994, an assistant buzzed Yoko and said that a person claiming to be a relative of hers had called. The person had refused to give her name but left a phone number. Yoko's first thought was that it could be Kyoko, but she knew it was most likely another impostor.

Yoko dialed the number and held her breath. "I was afraid to hope, but I did hope," she said.

Then she heard the voice on the phone. "Mom? It's Kyoko."

Yoko knew it was her daughter.

THE LITTLE YOKO KNEW ABOUT Kyoko's life since she'd disappeared came from the *People* article about Tony. She knew the broad strokes: Kyoko had escaped the cult in which she'd been raised, and her life had been turbulent since she'd last seen Yoko.

During the years Kyoko spent with both parents, Yoko was preoccupied with work, and Yoko's relationship with Tony was tumultuous. "I remember them separating many times," Kyoko said. "There was a lot of chaos around them." There was more chaos when her mother got together with John. Kyoko felt overwhelmed by the whirlwind around John. When she drove in cars with the two of them, it meant "being surrounded, people screaming. It was scary for a kid." She remembered being sneaked out the back door of a studio after a dance lesson because of the fans and paparazzi out front.

There had been good times with Yoko and John at Tittenhurst Park and in London, but her mother and John were mainly interested in each other and their work. Kyoko was often left with assistants and friends. Drugs were ubiquitous in that crowd. Bedtimes? Meals? No one paid attention. She was uncomfortable at the bed-in because people were yelling at her mother and John. She was bored in recording studios. And it was confusing when she was passed back and forth between her parents. When Yoko and Tony were in the same room, their encounters often devolved into arguments.

Kyoko had been kidnapped by a parent twice—by Yoko in Majorca and by Tony in Houston. She and her father went underground. She wanted to call her mother sometimes, but since Yoko had been awarded custody by the Texas court and Tony hadn't turned Kyoko over, there was a warrant out for his arrest. "I wanted to have a relationship with my mom, but I didn't want my dad to be put in jail."

Before Tony disappeared with Kyoko, he had raised her in a series of communes. For a brief time, he had lived with Kyoko in a UFO cult. That was followed by a commune run by a guru.

Around the time of the custody hearing in Houston, Tony had a religious conversion. He defied a court order, left Houston with Kyoko, and sought refuge in a church. Kyoko was eight when her father joined the Church of the Living Word, also known as the Walk. Tony and his second wife, Melinda, raised Kyoko in the Walk communities in Iowa and Southern California. When Tony and Melinda weren't getting along, the cult leader separated them and placed Kyoko in the care of her stepmother. Other than at church, she rarely saw her father for more than a year, during which time Tony became disillusioned with the cult leader and planned his escape.

The cult leader became suspicious of Tony and began to have Kyoko escorted to and from Walter Reed Junior High in North Hollywood, which she was attending under a fake name. Tony was afraid that the cult would take Kyoko away to keep him from leaving.

"He literally kidnapped me," Kyoko recalled. "I was sitting on the lawn at school, waiting for someone from the cult to pick us up to go home. My dad arrived and walked over and took me by the arm and dragged me into the car." It was the third kidnapping.

Tony took Kyoko to see Margaret Singer, a renowned psychologist who deprogrammed people who had been in cults; Patty Hearst had been a patient. "The thing the doctor said to me that was meaningful then was that there was a difference between a regular church and cult. She told me, 'You're in a cult. But it's okay to be a Christian.'"

As Kyoko explained, "Being a Christian helped me with my feelings of rejection I had from my family. I thought, 'Whatever else happens in the world, Jesus says I'm important, I'm valuable. Jesus still thinks it's good I was born.'"

After that, Tony moved frequently. He brought Kyoko to live in another Christian commune, this time in Berkeley, and from there they moved to Ashland, Oregon. Next they moved to Switzerland. When Tony returned to the United States to make a documentary about the Walk—he wanted to expose it—he offered to pay Kyoko to help him. She agreed. Her plan was to earn money for college. She saw college as a way to become independent and get back in touch with her mother "and not feel as if I was a burden on her like when I was a kid and they were fighting about who was going to take care of me." After college, she'd get a job and take care of herself. She couldn't be accused of wanting anything from Yoko.

She reached out to her mother once. Tony agreed when Kyoko wanted to call Yoko one Christmas. Sean remembered the moment. "I heard people saying, 'Kyoko's on the phone, Kyoko's on the phone!' I ran in to listen to my mother talk to her. I could only hear my mother's side of the conversation and I remember my mom saying, 'Mmm-hmmm.' 'Yeah.' 'That's interesting.' After a while, I heard my mom ask, 'So where are you?' and there was a click. I'm sure Tony hung up. Then my mom had tears in her eyes."

In 1980, with Tony, Kyoko had traveled across the United States, living in a van, stopping along the way to conduct interviews for the documentary. They were in Illinois when they heard that John had been shot. Kyoko was seventeen. She was devastated, and she and Tony thought about reaching out to Yoko, but Kyoko worried that it would be disturbing for Yoko to hear from Tony. "I didn't trust him to get back in touch with her and not get into a fight," she explained. "I thought it was probably the worst time in the world to have my mom have to hear from him." So instead, they sent condolences via telegram.

At eighteen, Kyoko enrolled in Wheaton College, in Illinois, where she majored in English literature. She went on to earn a master's degree in education at Colorado College and became a schoolteacher.

When Kyoko was twenty-eight, she married. She wanted to have children. The desire to be a mother made her want to reach out to her own mother. Also, she said, "I just felt terrible that she didn't know where I was. By then I had worked as a public-school teacher for six years. I also did a lot of work at homeless shelters and other distressed situations. I saw the need a mother has to be connected with her children, and I felt for my mom."

Kyoko still feared that Yoko—or, more likely, her lawyers—would have her father arrested if they found him through her. Her husband reassured her. "Your mom isn't going to have your dad arrested. You can totally get back in touch with her."

And so she called.

ON THE PHONE AFTER ALL those years, Yoko told Kyoko it was brave of her to call. She assured her daughter that she would not have had Tony arrested. Yoko said she was sorry that Kyoko had gone through so much. Then she invited Kyoko to come to New York.

"I had butterflies," Yoko told me. "I hung up the phone, and I think I was breathing hard and then I cried."

———

YOKO, SEAN, AND SAM MET Kyoko and her husband at the airport in New York. "I'll never forget when she walked off the plane," Sean said. "I knew it was her. We hugged."

"We went home and there was a lot of catching-up and a lot of crying. It was intense and beautiful," Sean continued. They traveled to the upstate New York farm for the Fourth of July. It was sometimes awkward at first, but Yoko and Kyoko were both thrilled to be together; there was joy and relief. But there were also years of pain to face. They had both suffered. Kyoko didn't know if Yoko could forgive her for taking so long to get back in touch. She feared the damage was irreparable, but Yoko made clear it wasn't. She said she understood. And as Kyoko felt guilty about Yoko's suffering, Yoko felt guilty about Kyoko's.

Over the years, Kyoko came to understand more about the reasons behind Yoko's reluctance to have a child and raise her. "I realized my mom felt super-anxious about being a good mother," Kyoko said. "I saw that a reason she had other people take care of me all those years ago was partly her insecurities. She felt almost everybody would be better than her as a mother, and that was sad."

Kyoko found joy in her new bond with Yoko. She said, "I went through a childhood when it was a battle. But now I cherish that I have my mother again. I think she feels that way too."

She did.

Yoko hadn't wanted a baby—she hadn't felt ready—but she fell in love with Kyoko. Losing her daughter had been another trauma. Now, as her friend Jon Hendricks observed, "When Kyoko came back, Yoko was the most whole since John was killed."

CHAPTER 29

AFTER THE *STARPEACE* ALBUM AND the poor ticket sales of the tour in 1985 and '86, Yoko had stepped away from making new music to focus on art, business, and the many projects meant to keep John's memory alive. But a combination of the positive reception of *Onobox* and Sean's encouragement drew her back to making new music. "I wanted her to make records more like the first *Plastic Ono Band*—that was my favorite Yoko record," Sean said. He knew that it wasn't popular but, he said, "I think her vocal technique was so primal and so expressive and beautiful and it moves me so much—I can't even describe it. Maybe because it's my mother's voice, but I love the *Plastic Ono* record. I wanted to hear Yoko wailing."

Kim Gordon said that "Sean was like a bridge from her to the outside world."

IT WAS NO SURPRISE THAT the son of Yoko and John had become a musician. When Sean was five, his mother put him on *Season of Glass*. She had featured him on other albums, including *It's Alright* and *Starpeace*. By the time he was a teenager, Sean was a virtuoso on guitar and piano and other instruments and had a singing voice reminiscent of his father's. Sonic Youth's Thurston Moore described him as "insanely gifted," saying, "There's a stigma when you're the 'son of,' but he'd developed into an exceptional artist in his own right."

Sean went on to collaborate with many musicians, including Lenny Kravitz, Adam Yauch of the Beastie Boys, and Les Claypool. He released several well-received solo albums and produced albums for a long and eclectic list of musicians. He played with his own and others' bands and with many incarnations of the Plastic Ono Band.

Initially, Sean saw music as a way of connecting with his father; music ended up connecting him with his mother too.

AFTER LE ROSEY, SEAN COMPLETED high school at Dalton in New York City. He moved downtown to a brownstone in the Village. He attended three semesters at Columbia University, where he studied anthropology, but he mainly focused on his passion: playing in his own and his friends' bands. He came by the Dakota for dinner with his mother once or twice a week.

Sometimes, while he and Yoko talked, Sean picked up one of his father's guitars and began noodling. When he played, Yoko sang. They had impromptu jam sessions. Once, Yoko heard a lick she liked and became excited. She asked him to bring the guitar into the White Room. She sat at the piano and they jammed. "It was a language my mother and I could speak together," Sean said. "There was a period I wished I had a conventional mother, someone less involved with her own life and art and more attuned to me, but when I was older, I realized how lucky I was."

He proposed a new record, a return to the free-form music of *Yoko Ono/ Plastic Ono Band*. "I kept saying, 'You should go back and make one of those wild punk records.' She thought it was a cool idea and we did it. . . . It was the funnest thing in the world," Sean said.

Like his father, Sean was one of Yoko's greatest fans and promoters. He said, "I hear [her vocalizations] as very much akin to when Jimi Hendrix plays with feedback and gets really out there and gets really deep and transcends the song and starts making emotional, expressive guttural sounds. I feel that that's what she does. I feel the emotion of her music in my stomach. It really moves me."

Together, they produced *Rising*, a phenomenal LP that was released on November 7, 1995. It had been a decade since *Starpeace*. Sean's band at the time, IMA, backed Yoko, and he served as guitarist and musical director for the record and subsequent tour.

Playing with Yoko meant playing with stellar musicians. "It didn't occur to me until later," he said. "Look at the bands Yoko played with. Her first record had Ringo as a drummer! Look at the musicians on *Fly* and *Approximately Infinite Universe*! Phil Spector coproduced *It's Alright*. She had the top engineers and producers on the planet. She worked with Jim Keltner on drums and Bernie Worrell, from Funkadelic, the greatest keyboard player ever. Now she's letting me, her teenage son, play and tour with her. Not a lot of people in her position would do that. It was very risky for her. I was simply lucky to have the opportunity to play with her then."

Yoko felt lucky too. She said, "I felt that Sean was very supportive of me, just like John. So there were no silly questions—you know, 'Why are you screaming, Yoko?'" Indeed, Sean once said, "I'm an expert in Yoko Ono's music, basically. So in the studio, when she'd say something like 'Make that guitar part more ocean-cricket,' I'd know exactly what she meant."

Reviewing *Rising* in *Rolling Stone*, David Fricke noticed the synchronicity between mother and son. He wrote, "Sean Lennon is the most sympathetic collaborator Ono has had since his father was killed." He called the record "a song cycle for the dying and the ones left behind—something that Ono personally knows something about."

The experience of making *Rising* was so positive that Yoko went out to tour again. She, Sean, and IMA performed in Europe, Japan, and throughout the United States. Venues sold out in many cities.

On the *Rising* tour stop in San Francisco in 1996, it was apparent how close she and Sean had become. They took long walks through the foggy city. They laughed together. They finished each other's sentences.

Onstage at the Great American Music Hall, Sean paid homage to his mom by vocalizing into the microphone à la Yoko, shyly at first, then louder and more confidently. The audience erupted in cheers. Yoko smiled at her son. There was pain expressed in the album they had made together, but there was also hope. The title track, "Rising," was all about building a life from the ashes, putting the pieces back together. Not alone, but together. "Have courage, have rage, we're rising."

Yoko was clearly feeling the power she expressed in "Rising."

"Finally things are a bit better," she told me. Then she said, "Thank you, thank you, thank you," the triple affirmation she often repeated—an expression of gratitude to the universe.

IN ADDITION TO THIS NEW MUSIC, Yoko also made new works of art. In 1997, she exhibited a piece that would be shown in galleries and museums over the following years. It was about the men in her life.

It had started with her relationship with her father, but Yoko felt the weight of a succession of other men judging, devaluing, and controlling her—or trying to. The oppression of women by men was the subject of many of her songs, films, writings, and artworks.

For the piece called "Vertical Memory," twenty-one photographs lined the gallery walls. They were identical: A man's face. Blurred. Yoko found photographs of John, Sean, and her father facing the same direction and merged the images. The photographs were accompanied by brief texts about men she'd encountered, beginning with the doctor present when she was born and through an "attendant" she envisioned would be with her at her death. Along the way was a succession of other men. They included her father—"I was two-and-a-half when I arrived in San Francisco on a liner to meet him for the first time. He came on board, kissed my mother, and then looked at me looking up at him."

There was also the doctor she saw as a child when the family evacuated to the countryside, the one who abused her. "He told me to close my eyes as he examined me. I felt very uncomfortable. Suddenly, warm, wet lips were pressed on my mouth. I froze."

There were more doctors, including one who "had one tooth missing and smelled of alcohol. He took my appendix out." Another was "a psychiatrist who told me my problem was that I was not dating."

Yoko combined some doctors. Doctor VII "performed a few abortions." And Doctor VIII "delivered my son and daughter."

The men who followed were artists and a priest who "was called in to perform the last rites and suggested I give my last confession. I refused."

The text for the final image, the "Attendant," read: "I saw a dark hole in a shape of an arch. I saw my body being slid into it. It looked like the arch I came out at birth, I thought. I asked where it was going to take me to. The guy stood there looking at me without saying a word, as I lay down. It all seemed very familiar. What percentage of my life did I take it lying down? That was the last question I asked in my mind."

YOKO CREATED MORE NEW WORK, some of which was shown the following year when she staged a pair of exhibitions that both opened on April 24, 1998, one at New York's Deitch Projects and the other at André Emmerich Gallery. At Emmerich, *En Trance* was what Jeffrey Deitch, the curator and gallerist, called "a compressed retrospective" that included works from the 1960s and, along a wall, an installation of "Vertical Memory." There was "Play It by Trust" and "Ceiling Painting (Yes)." There was a room dedicated to her delicate dot drawings. (Beginning in 1994, using a mechanical pencil, Yoko made hundreds of these "automatic" drawings. "The dots accumulated into a mass, and figures emerged from them," she explained.)

"Working with Yoko was unlike working with any other artist," said Deitch. "She doesn't just choose ten paintings and we hang them up. She creates a *gesamtkunstwerk*—a total concept of an immersive art experience."

As *En Trance* opened at Emmerich, an installation called *Ex It* opened at Deitch Projects in Soho. Here visitors walked into the cavernous gallery space and saw one hundred wooden coffins with trees growing out of them. Deitch said, "It was a haunted atmosphere dramatically combining a vision of death and rebirth."

Deitch described *Ex It* as "one of the most profound artistic experiences ever—to enter into that. Photos cannot capture it. People come in and it brings tears to their eyes. It induces deep emotional reactions."

But in spite of the power and profundity of these shows—and some positive reviews—the art world still looked askance at her. Deitch explained, "She was a celebrity, connected to John Lennon, and you couldn't take her seriously; that was the attitude." He said, "Even if there'd been no John Lennon, other factors were operative in the mid-nineties. Women weren't taken seriously. Asian women weren't taken seriously. American, German, and British men defined the art world." Gallerist Mary Boone, who also exhibited Yoko's work in the 1990s, said, "As a woman, she wasn't just dismissed. She was demonized."

However, these exhibitions plus the Whitney show sparked a reevaluation of Yoko's body of work.

THE NEXT EXHIBITION DID MORE for Yoko's reputation in the international art world than anything else so far. Yoko's life and work became an obsession of the curator Alexandra Munroe, who included Yoko in a groundbreaking group exhibition on postwar Japanese avant-garde art at the Yokohama Museum of Art in 1994 and then approached her about doing a major retrospective, which would be Yoko's first comprehensive survey. Eventually, the show was organized at the Japan Society Gallery in New York when Munroe became its director.

Munroe believed that Yoko's importance as a pioneer of conceptual art had never been acknowledged. She pointed out that Yoko hadn't been given credit as one of the first artists to conceive of "ultra-conceptual or dematerialized art." Instead, white men like Joseph Kosuth, Henry Flynt, John Baldessari, Lawrence Weiner, and Sol LeWitt had. "The omission is typical of the sexism Yoko experienced throughout her life."

In 1971, when *This Is Not Here* opened at the Everson Museum of Art in Syracuse, crowds were drawn to the show not by Yoko's work but by rumors of a Beatles reunion. The survey was largely ignored. The Whitney show—*Yoko Ono: Objects, Films*—and the recent exhibitions at Deitch, Emmerich, and several other galleries had received positive but muted attention. The exhibition that Munroe curated at the Japan Society was a sweeping retrospective that "caused the art world to look again and think again," Deitch said. Entitled *Yes Yoko Ono*, the show included Yoko's art from the late 1950s to 2000. People in the art world who'd ignored and dismissed her work took notice. The more than one hundred fifty works in *Yes Yoko Ono* showed how pioneering and influential she'd been.

With the help of Yoko's friend, the curator Jon Hendricks, and Karla Merrifield, Yoko's photo archivist, Munroe worked with Yoko to create an exhibition that included scores and instruction paintings, objects, film and video, political and advertising art, music, and sculpture and installations. Inevitably, there were pieces in the show that asked the audience to participate. For example, visitors could add their own wishes to "Wish Tree," a piece that would be installed in many of her exhibitions—people were asked to write their wishes and tie them to a tree branch. ("As a child in Japan," Yoko said, "I used to go to a temple and write out a wish on a piece of thin paper and tie it around the branch of a tree. Trees in temple courtyards were always filled with people's wish knots, which looked like white flowers blossoming from afar.") They could play the all-white chess set, "Play It by Trust," and navigate the Plexiglas "Amaze," first made in 1971. When participants reached the center of the maze, they came upon mirrored panels that concealed a toilet. Munroe recalled that the most popular piece in the exhibition was a phone installed on a gallery wall. It would occasionally ring, and a visitor would answer it. It was Yoko calling. She'd chat with whoever answered the phone.

The show opened with a party at the Japan Society Gallery on October 18, 2000, and the exhibition received praise from critics. Writing in the *Nation*, art critic Arthur C. Danto said, "Yoko Ono is really one of the most original artists of the last half-century. Her fame made her almost impossible to see. When she made the art for which her husband admired and loved her, it required a very developed avant-garde sensibility to see it as anything but ephemeral. The exhibition at the Japan Society makes it possible for those with patience and imagination to constitute her achievement in their minds, where it really belongs. It is an art as rewarding as it is demanding."

After closing at the Japan Society Gallery, *Yes* moved on to contemporary art museums in other cities, including the Walker Art Center in Minneapolis, the San Francisco Museum of Modern Art, and museums in several cities in Japan.

Yoko—as always traveling with an entourage that included assistants, security, a masseuse, various friends and family members (and lots of luggage, including a suitcase just for sunglasses, another for hats)—attended openings and parties. She participated in Q&As and onstage discussions at the museums. Yoko also staged events, such as breaking a vase and handing out shards to the audience. She said they'd meet in ten years and put the vase back together.

"She always had a reputation for being difficult, but it was as if she was going out of her way to be generous and cooperative," said Kyoko. "She realized she had to explain herself." She gave back-to-back interviews. She even followed photographer Bob Gruen's advice to smile more in photographs.

Fans camped out in hotel lobbies, and she patiently gave autographs and posed for photos. She enjoyed the attention and recognition. It was a triumph, a vindication.

YOKO SAVORED THE EXPERIENCE OF the Japan Society exhibition, but she still lived every day with the specter of John's death and, much as she resisted it, the circumstances of it.

She hated to think about John's killer, never mind talk about him. When journalists asked about him, she typically responded that she thought about John's life, not his death.

But that year Yoko faced a new and difficult challenge. In 1981, Mark David Chapman had been sentenced to twenty years to life in prison. Now, after serving twenty years of the sentence, he was up for parole. Yoko thought hard about what to write to the parole board. She read lines aloud to Sam and her friends. Her lawyer vetted drafts. She said it was the hardest letter she'd ever written.

"This is my reply to the petition of parole made by Mark David Chapman, from here on called 'the subject,'" she wrote. She didn't want to type his name. "It is not easy for me to write this letter to you since it is still painful for me to think of what happened that night and verbalize my thoughts logically."

She wrote about who John was and what he believed. Then she got personal. "For me, he was the other half of the sky. We were in love with each other like the most vehement of lovers to the last moment."

She talked about what Sean and Julian had lost, what the world had lost. And she expressed the pain she had felt and talked of how she tried to handle it.

She was afraid that if Chapman was released, it would bring back "the nightmare, the chaos and confusion" she and others had felt after his murder. She ended by saying, "Violence begets violence. If it is at all possible, I would like us to not create a situation which may bring further madness and tragedy to the world."

Chapman was denied parole—and, at the time of this writing, he has been denied parole every time he was up for it. Once Yoko was asked if she believed in forgiving him. Her interlocutor noted that Pope John Paul II had visited the jail of the man who'd tried to kill him and said he'd forgiven him. Yoko responded, "I'm not the pope."

CHAPTER 30

YOKO STILL THOUGHT OF HERSELF as John's wife even though she had been in a relationship with Sam Havadtoy for nearly twenty years. Like any couple, they had their squabbles, but it had gotten harder for Yoko to enjoy the positive aspects of the relationship. Sam was often angry about the presence of security guards, about the psychics Yoko consulted, about being—at least as far as the public knew—nonexistent.

The *New York Times* noted that he had been "described in news accounts as her boyfriend, companion, spokesman, partner, manager, assistant, business administrator and secret husband." Rumors (started by one of Sam's ex-lovers) had them married on a trip to Budapest.

A reporter once asked her about it.

"I am not married," she said.

Sam interjected, "That's a state of mind. We're happy. We're living together, boyfriend and girlfriend, yes."

But mostly Sam was hidden, and he was weary of being in "the shadow with John's ghost." Once, Sam made it onto her yearly Christmas card—but only dressed in a Santa suit.

Also, he felt Yoko didn't acknowledge how much he'd helped her with business and art. He complained that he got no credit. Sam recalled one afternoon in the mid-1990s when they were having lunch and he brought it up.

"What do you mean, I never give you credit?" she asked. "I just gave you credit."

Sam asked, "When?"

She said, "For the Whitney show."

"No, you didn't give me any credit," he said.

This upset Yoko. She said, "When we get home, I'll show it to you."

At home she pulled out the Whitney catalog. In it, she'd written about having lunch "with a friend" who suggested that she create bronze versions of her early artworks.

She said, "See?"

A friend.

Sam had provided support after John died. He'd sat with her. He'd comforted and reassured her when there were threats. He'd ventured out with her when she finally left the Dakota, shielding her from fans and paparazzi.

Increasingly over the years, Sam helped with business, negotiated deals, successfully recovered stolen valuables. He met with lawyers and businesspeople for her. He helped with court cases and managing the staff. He encouraged and even facilitated production of her art, like the bronzing of her work. He created the *Every Man* album. He arranged lunches and dinners and parties. He cared deeply about Sean and was good with him.

But the times she enjoyed his company were becoming fewer. He criticized her more. "Not only did the negative energy come from the outside world, but from in the house," she said. "I became one of those women afraid to express myself."

Yoko's survival tactic had always been to move on, and she decided to move on from Sam. When she finally took action, she did so swiftly and absolutely. Sam was away, and Yoko had the locks changed on the apartment doors. When she told him she was ending the relationship, he was deeply saddened. Sam later reflected on it. "For me, [this relationship] was the most incredible trip in my life. The problem is when things break down, people concentrate on the bad. And so did I at first. I mean, I'm not unusual in that sense. But as time went by . . . when I turned sixty is when I realized how lucky I was."

He continued, "I had somebody who loved me for years and years. I have a child—not a blood child, but a child—out of that relationship, Sean, who I will love until the day I die. This is something that is irreplaceable."

AFTER THE BREAKUP, SAM MOVED to England and then back to Hungary. He'd begun painting in the 1980s, but in Europe he became a full-time artist, showing his work across the Continent. He had well-reviewed exhibitions in Milan, Budapest, Warsaw, Rome, Bucharest, and Brussels. A set of bronze doors he made commemorating a papal visit to Milan is on permanent display in Monza, Italy. He created seventy paintings for his seventieth birthday in 2022. "He's authentic," Arturo Schwarz, an Italian art historian and curator, told the *New York Times*. "A real artist must be faithful to his inner self, and his art is very personal."

Meanwhile, Yoko landed firmly on her feet. She was relieved to be on her own again. "Some loneliness is fine," she said. "I'm used to loneliness. It's better than not being able to breathe."

SAM'S ABSENCE MIGHT HAVE BEEN a relief, but he had helped her in many ways, including protecting her from some of those who tried to exploit her. "Yoko was very smart, but she could be gullible, because she still tended to trust people," Sam said. She once described herself as being in a "typical widow situation. When the husband is not around, it's easier to rip off widows."

The first person to take advantage of her after John's death was Fred Seaman. He'd brazenly stolen from Yoko when she was in mourning, declared himself John's biographer, spread misinformation about Yoko, and pleaded guilty to second-degree larceny for his theft of materials, and decades later, Seaman was still trying to profit off his former employers.

Earlier, Seaman's publisher had backed out of a book deal, but another publisher signed on. Though he was legally barred from including anything from John's diaries, Seaman released a book called *The Last Days of John Lennon: A Personal Memoir*. The *Library Journal* described the book as "a sad portrait of a tormented man." Yoko sued Seaman for violating his confidentiality agreement. She also sued to get back hundreds of photographs of her, John, and Sean that Seaman hadn't returned and to secure her copyright to the photos. Yoko prevailed; Seaman settled the suit. He agreed never to exploit Yoko and John again. He also agreed not to republish his book, and he abandoned a copyright claim to the photos he'd taken when he worked for the couple.

The *New York Post* described Seaman sitting in the courtroom the day of the settlement "with his head bowed" as his "humbling" apology was read "in a devastating finale to his sleazy career as an opportunist who lied to the Lennons about his intentions and began stealing by the truckload the moment John Lennon died." Yoko and Sean were present.

The *Post* reported that Seaman approached Sean at the courthouse and presented him with a gift: the Japanese edition of his book—the very book Yoko had never wanted to see the light of day.

"Taken by surprise, Lennon politely attempted to make small talk with his dad's onetime 'man Friday' Frederic Seaman before telling him of the anguish Seaman had caused his mom and himself, from the time he was a boy.

'You were the closest of family—I felt so betrayed by you, more than anyone,' the soft-spoken Lennon said.

"He then added, with a slight smile, 'This will be the best book I'll ever burn.'"

Left: An undated family portrait taken in San Francisco shows Yoko with her parents, Eisuke and Isoko. They were cold and distant; Yoko never got the love and support she needed from them. © *Yoko Ono*

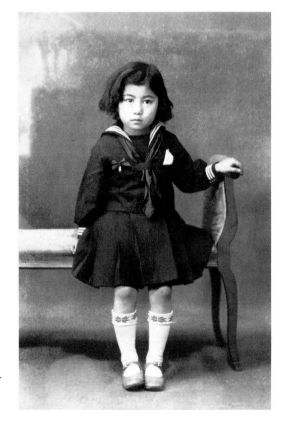

Right: Yoko won a scholastic medal at her elite private school in Tokyo in 1937. As she grew older, she attended schools in Japan and the United States. She felt bifurcated, alienated in both countries. © *Yoko Ono*.

Right: Yoko playing the family piano in Tokyo in 1949. Her father, a pianist who gave up a career in music to become a banker, pressured her to play. She was desperate to please him, but she never could. © *Yoko Ono*

Below: After dropping out of university in Tokyo, Yoko (center) enrolled at Sarah Lawrence College in Bronxville, New York, where she was introduced to avant-garde music and art. This photo was taken at the school circa 1955. *Courtesy Sarah Lawrence College Archives; photo by Frank Horch.*

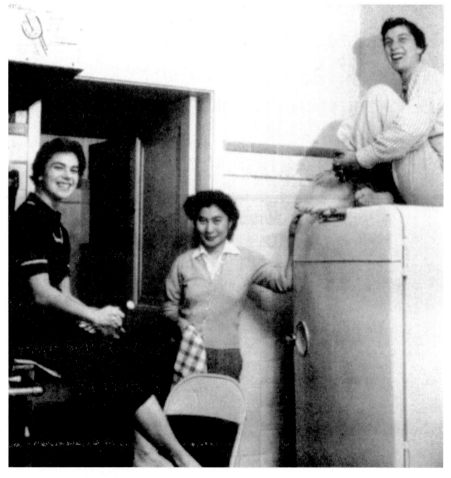

```
SECRET PIECE

Decide on one note that you want to play.
Play it with the following accompaniment:

        The woods from 5 a.m. to 8 a.m.
        in summer.

(The above is the later revision of the
following original.)
```

```
1953  summer
```

Below: Yoko met her first husband, Toshi Ichiyanagi (at keyboard), in Japan and then again in New York. They married despite her parents' vehement objections. She often performed with Toshi, including at her Chambers Street Loft in New York in 1961. *Photo by Minoru Niizuma* © *Yoko Ono*

Above: Yoko was influenced by avant-garde composer John Cage (at keyboard), with whom she performed his "Music Walk" during his 1962 tour of Japan. *Photo by Yasuhiro Yoshioka, courtesy of Yoko Ono.*

Below: After divorcing Toshi, Yoko married Tony Cox (left), a filmmaker from New York, in Tokyo. They worked together on many artworks, including her irreverent and lauded film *No. 4 (Bottoms)* in 1966. *Photo by Graham Keen / TopFoto*

Right: On March 21, 1965, Yoko performed "Cut Piece," hailed by critics, feminists, and others and one of her most influential works of art, at Carnegie Recital Hall in New York. *Photograph by Minoru Niizuma © Yoko Ono*

Below: For Yoko's "Ceiling Painting," visitors to the Indica Gallery in London climbed a ladder and looked through a magnifying glass at the ceiling and saw the tiny word *yes*. The night before the 1966 opening, John Lennon visited the gallery and was entranced by the piece. *Photo by Graham Keen / TopFoto*

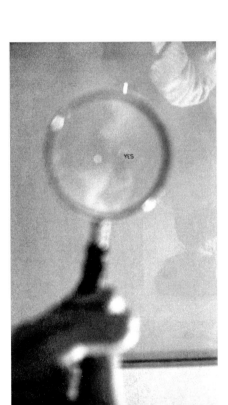

Right: Yoko's "Apple" was a sculpture about the cycle of life: the apple would rot and eventually disintegrate. Horrifying Yoko, John took a bite of the apple the first time she exhibited the work in 1966. *Trinity Mirror / Mirrorpix / Alamy Stock Photo*

Left: Yoko and John were married in Gibraltar, off the coast of Spain, on March 20, 1969. "We knew that we shouldn't need a marriage license or anything, but I did feel sentimental about our relationship," she said. "I wanted to be able to commit myself ritually to John." *Photo by David Nutter © Yoko Ono Lennon*

Right: War was raging in Vietnam. Yoko and John knew their marriage would be big news, so they decided to use their honeymoon to protest the war and create an event to get the word "peace" on the front pages of newspapers. They staged two Bed-ins for Peace, including one at The Queen Elizabeth Hotel in Montreal, Canada, in 1969. *Photo by Ivor Sharp © Yoko Ono Lennon*

Above: Though it was initially credited only to John, Yoko cowrote the song "Imagine." In the video for the song, Yoko joined John at a white piano at their estate at Tittenhurst Park, in 1971. © *Yoko Ono Lennon*

Below: Yoko and John inspired each other when they created far-out music, Yoko vocalizing—warbling, moaning, screaming—while he played guitar. Here they are at Butterfly Studios in New York on April 4, 1972, rehearsing for a concert. © *Bob Gruen*

Above: After several miscarriages, Yoko and John were elated when they had a child—a son, Sean Taro Ono Lennon—on October 9, 1975. Here all three are together in their Dakota apartment in New York. Sean is two months old. © *Bob Gruen*

Left: After a five-year break from recording, Yoko and John went back into the studio to record the album *Double Fantasy*. Soon after the record's release, they posed in front of the the Dakota in New York on November 21, 1980—weeks before he was murdered. *Photo by Allan Tannenbaum/ Getty Images*

Left: After the shooting, Yoko was rushed to Roosevelt Hospital, where John was pronounced dead. She was decimated. Aided by David Geffen and a police officer, she left the hospital and returned to the Dakota that night, December 8, 1980. *AP Photo/Lyndon Fox.*

Right: Yoko returned to the recording studio soon after John's murder. For the cover of the album *Season of Glass*, she photographed his glasses, splattered with his blood, at the Dakota in April 1981. © *Bob Gruen*

Left: Yoko was asked to change the *Season of Glass* cover, but she refused. The cover, like the album itself, reflected her pain and rage. Later, she would use the cover photograph in anti-gun campaigns. *Photo by Yoko Ono © Yoko Ono*

Above: Yoko was criticized for making a record so soon after John's murder, but it was part of her grieving process. "They thought she should be in mourning," Sean Lennon said. "But that was her mourning." She recorded *Season of Glass* at the Hit Factory in New York in April 1981. © *Bob Gruen*

Below: Yoko said that music was her salvation when John died. Even when she could barely get out of bed, she went to the studio to record. This photo was also taken at the Hit Factory in April 1981. © *Bob Gruen*

Right: Though she never got over John's death, Yoko slowly healed. Two years later, in November 1982, she sits at the white piano in her Dakota apartment. © *Bob Gruen*

Below: Yoko's album *Starpeace* was a response to President Ronald Reagan's anti-ballistic missile program, nicknamed "Star Wars." She believed the program was an escalation of Cold War aggression. In February 1986, Yoko—here with ten-year-old Sean looking on—rehearses in New York with her band for a *Starpeace* world tour. © *Bob Gruen*

Right: Yoko had a tumultuous relationship with Paul McCartney, but later in life they became friends. She attended the MusiCares Person of the Year Gala honoring Paul at the Los Angeles Convention Center, in Los Angeles, on February 10, 2012. *Photo by Kevin Mazur/WireImage*

Left: Yoko filled in for John alongside Ringo Starr and George Harrison when the Beatles were inducted into the Rock and Roll Hall of Fame at the Waldorf-Astoria Hotel in New York on January 20, 1988. *Photo by Michael E. Ach/Newsday RM via Getty Images*

Below left: Yoko was friends with Sam Havadtoy, a decorator who became an artist, before they became a couple; their relationship lasted twenty years. On April 1, 1987, they attended the Andy Warhol memorial at the Diamond Horseshoe restaurant in New York. *Photo by Ron Galella, Ltd./Ron Galella Collection via Getty Images*

Below right: Julian Lennon's relationship with Yoko had always been strained, but she felt closer to him as time went on, and she championed his efforts in music and art. She attended the opening of his "Timeless" photo exhibition at the Morrison Hotel Gallery, New York, September 16, 2010. *Photo © 2010 Wendell Teodoro*

Above: Like his father, Sean Lennon was one of Yoko's greatest fans and promotors. They connected through music and frequently performed together, such as at a gig at the Bowery Ballroom, in New York, on September 15, 2013. © *Bob Gruen*

Right: When Yoko gave birth to a daughter in 1963, she was unprepared to be a mother, but when she lost Kyoko, she pined for her. When they reunited, she was "the most whole since John was killed," according to a friend. Yoko and Kyoko Ono went out to lunch in New York on October 3, 2001. *Photo by Arnaldo Magnani/Getty Images*

Below: Yoko was an unconventional mother to her children Kyoko and Sean, but she cherished them. Here, the family gathers at Yoko's seventy-eighth birthday party at Dominion, in New York City, February 18, 2011. © *Bob Gruen*

Above left: If there is one art project that fully embodied Yoko's message, on a large scale for posterity, it is the Imagine Peace Tower—a tower of light on an island in Iceland dedicated to John.
2024 webcam image © Yoko Ono

Above right: Yoko's "To See the Sky" was a spiral staircase that led to a skylight. The piece was shown around the world, including at an installation at Faurschou in Beijing, 2015. *Artwork © Yoko Ono. Courtesy of Faurschou. Photo by Jonathan Leijonhufvud.*

Left: Yoko thought deeply about her relationship with her mother. She created a series of art pieces devoted to Isoko—and all mothers—called "My Mommy Is Beautiful." Visitors to museums were invited to contribute to the piece. One iteration was an installation at the Crystal Bridges Museum of American Art, Arkansas, in 2024. *Courtesy of Yoko Ono.*

Right: For Yoko's "Ex It," visitors walked into a cavernous gallery space and saw a sea of wooden coffins with trees growing out of them, a vision of death and rebirth. The piece was re-created at Faurschou in New York, in 2023. *Artwork © Yoko Ono. Courtesy of Faurschou. Photo by Sean Davidson.*

Above: Even as Yoko approached eighty years old, she didn't slow down. Here she dances at her seventy-ninth birthday party at Le Poisson Rouge in New York, February 18, 2012. © *Bob Gruen*

Below: Yoko was "out there on the edge of experimental music," David Byrne said. Her voice communicated the sound of childbirth, of rage, of terror—but also ecstasy. She performed at Háskólabíó in Reykjavík, Iceland, on October 9, 2010. © *Bob Gruen*

Yoko often said that her goal after John's murder was surviving. But she did more than survive. She created a body of work that edified and inspired. She's pictured here at her installation "En Trance" at the Louisiana Museum of Modern Art, Humlebaek, Denmark, 2013. *Photo by Bjarke Ørsted © Yoko Ono*

THE SEAMAN ORDEAL WAS SETTLED—or so Yoko thought. In 2020, he gave an interview in which he spoke about Yoko and John and said he hoped to republish his book. Yoko's attorneys sued again. It was reported that another deal was reached that the court signed off on in January 2021. According to the reporting, Seaman agreed to acknowledge that he'd violated the earlier agreement and said he would never again speak publicly about or write about Yoko, John, or Sean.

IN 2006, FOUR YEARS AFTER what Yoko thought was a final settlement of the Seaman case, there was a fresh assault from another man she'd trusted.

For almost a decade, Yoko's driver had been Koral Karsan, from Turkey. I was often in the back seat of the car with her when Karsan drove. He was always impeccably dressed and always professional. He was solicitous, addressing her as "Miss Ono," and seemed fiercely protective of her.

It was unusual when, on the anniversary of John's death in 2006, Karsan asked to meet with Yoko. At the Dakota, Karsan claimed he had installed a tape recorder and cameras in the car. In a letter he'd written, he threatened to publish books "using information obtained from ten years of listening to you as well as pictures taken with hidden cameras and literally thousands of hours of recordings I have been compiling since 1996. Within these tapes, there are recordings . . . that will quite frankly, astound the world."

In the letter, Karsan accused Yoko of "systematic and continuous physical and psychological abuse" that "has caused me to become a different person, stripped of any kind of dignity and self-respect." He said that if she wanted the "pictures, recordings, e-mails, conversations, and memories to vanish from the face of the earth and never hear from me again," she had to pay him two million dollars.

Karsan left. Yoko was stunned. She gave the letter to Dan Mahoney. He and Jonas Herbsman, Yoko's longtime personal lawyer, called the police.

In a subsequent interview recorded by the NYPD, Herbsman told Karsan that Yoko wasn't going to pay him, and Karsan threatened to kill her, her family, and himself.

Karsan was arrested and charged with extortion. In court on December 14, 2006, the prosecutor said Karsan claimed he had people "on standby" ready to kill Yoko, according to the *New York Times*. A judge ordered him jailed until he could post bail. Ultimately Karsan took a plea deal, admitting to attempted grand larceny. He agreed to return items he'd stolen and was ordered to immediately return to Turkey. No tapes or pictures were ever discovered, suggesting that Karsan had been bluffing when he said he'd recorded and filmed her.

It shook Yoko—the ordeal was draining and scary. And it wasn't over. A decade later, in 2017, police in Berlin contacted Herbsman to report that eighty-six items belonging to Yoko had been found in storage facilities of a German auction house that had gone bankrupt. When the man who had sold them to the auction house was arrested, he confessed that the items, including eyeglasses and John's diaries, had come to him through Karsan.

They would eventually be returned to Yoko, but she'd endured another terrifying betrayal.

CHAPTER 31

IN 2003, YOKO CELEBRATED A milestone birthday: she turned seventy. Sean threw a party at Mr. Chow. There were two hundred guests, among them Lou Reed, Susan Sontag, and members of the B-52's. A huge photo of Yoko and John hung on one wall. On another was a "War Is Over (If You Want It)" banner. *Bottoms* was projected on another wall. A "Painting to Be Stepped On," a huge canvas, served as a dance floor—"Everyone was doing the 'Painting to Be Stepped On,'" Sean said—and people were encouraged to get into bags. There were "Add Color Paintings" as you walked in. As party favors, every guest was given a copy of *Grapefruit* and a "Box of Smile."

At the time she said, "I just want to say to the people who have not yet reached this age . . . and most of the fans of John Lennon and John and Yoko are younger than me . . . I want to tell them, it's fine. It's ok. You shouldn't be scared of it. In fact, it gets better."

YOKO ATTENDED OPENINGS OF THE touring *Yes Yoko Ono* show and exhibited and performed around the world. In the fall of 2003, she traveled to Paris to perform "Cut Piece" for the first time in almost forty years. She explained, "'Cut Piece' is my hope for world peace." She said she wanted to show that it was "a time where we need to trust each other." She told Reuters, "When I first performed this piece in 1964, I did it out of rage and anger. This time, I do it for you with love for the world."

At this performance of "Cut Piece," she asked the people who did the cutting to send the fragments of her clothes—she wore a dress by the fashion designer John Galliano—to loved ones. Friends insisted that Yoko have a bodyguard standing by, but she said no. "Cut Piece" was about trust; she said that having a bodyguard would imply she didn't trust the audience. "That's not right," she said.

It was significant that Yoko was doing "Cut Piece" at the age of seventy. It was one of her oldest and most famous pieces. It was also a piece that had gotten her in trouble with her parents back in the 1960s when she performed it in Japan. The scars left by her parents had marred her own ability to parent and form connections with people throughout her lifetime, at least before she met John. Yoko's feelings about her father mellowed when he returned to Tokyo after the war, but it took longer for her to express affection for her mother. Yoko thought deeply about her relationship with Isoko. Maybe it was easier to love the idea of a mother—a *conceptual* one—than the reality of the one who hurt her. Whatever allowed her feelings to change, the turnabout was dramatic. In 1997, she created the first in a series of pieces devoted to Isoko—and all mothers—called *My Mommy Is Beautiful.* (Like many of Yoko's works, it had multiple titles and many iterations. The first version was called *Mommy Was Beautiful.* It morphed to *My Mummy Was Beautiful* and then to *My Mommy Is Beautiful.*)

Isoko died in 1999. About a decade later, Yoko wrote a poem that accompanied a version of the piece:

Mommy, I'm sorry.
How did I know
you were suffering silently?
Your touch, your warm voice and your smile

Will always be with me.
This is a tribute to you and
all mothers of the world
from each of your children.
We love you!

In 2004, Yoko presented *My Mummy Was Beautiful* in Liverpool. To open the exhibition, in September of that year, she traveled to that city, landing at John Lennon Airport, which she'd christened in 2001. The occasion was the Liverpool Biennial. A Tate Liverpool gallery featured a "participation wall" on which people were encouraged to share stories about their mothers. It was accompanied by massive images of a woman's breast and vulva. Banners and posters with the same images were placed around the city, including in front of a church and at the airport. Some people found the images scandalous. A headline in the *Independent*: "Lennon's Sister Calls for Yoko's 'Offensive' Art to Be Torn Down." (Julia Baird was John's half sister.)

Yoko was genuinely stunned by the response. "I didn't understand the reaction at all," she said in 2006. "I was very shocked, because when I thought of the idea, I thought of covering the city of Liverpool with all these beautiful elements of my mother, or motherhood, and I thought it was my way of saying thank you to Liverpool." She was surprised the images were criticized. "They were meant to be innocent, not shocking," she said, "attempting to replicate the experience of a baby looking up at its mother's body."

Yoko went on to present other versions of *My Mommy Is Beautiful* that were less controversial. In 2011, she spoke at the United Nations on the first International Widows Day. An enormous image of Isoko with Yoko as a young girl was projected on the wall of the UN, and she invited people to upload images of and messages to their mothers to *My Mommy Is Beautiful* social media groups.

In 2017, Yoko exhibited a *My Mommy Is Beautiful* wall in the lobby of the Smithsonian's Hirschhorn Museum and Sculpture Garden in Washington, DC, which described the piece as "a living shrine, of sorts, to matriarchy."

Yoko had a huge blank canvas attached to the wall of a gallery. Visitors were invited to write memories on strips of paper and tape them onto the canvas.

After two months, visitors had added more than twenty thousand messages to or about their mothers to the canvas. In *Smithsonian Insider*, Emily Karcher Schmitt wrote, "At a distance, the little strips of paper and tape on the *My Mommy Is Beautiful* wall could be sprinkles on a cake or an Impressionist snowfall. But up close, the complicated intensity of motherhood and the child's reaction, one by one, slips out—each revealing one tiny piece of an intricate puzzle."

"The power of this piece is in its wide range of responses, from sweet to devastating to angry," said Connor Monahan, Yoko's studio director. "Just like Yoko's feelings toward her mother."

Thousands more people followed these instructions. A celebration of mothers had evolved from Yoko's difficult relationship with Isoko.

THE *MY MOMMY IS BEAUTIFUL* installations were the latest of Yoko's feminist artworks, and feminist themes were at the center of *Blueprint for a Sunrise,* Yoko's first album with new material after 1995's *Rising,* beginning with its cover, designed by Sean. On the jacket, Yoko was depicted in the red headdress and ceremonial robe of the dowager empress of China, Tz'u-hsi—the first "Dragon Lady." In the liner notes, Yoko wrote that the name was "specially coined for her by the British Press at the time, fueling Britain's then colonialism. She died disgraced and brokenhearted." The album's theme was the suffering of women. She wrote, "Sometimes, I wake up in the middle of the night hearing thousands of women screaming."

DURING HER SEVENTIES AND EIGHTIES, Yoko continued making feminist works that invited women to participate. One work she exhibited was a stunning project called *Arising*, shown in cities around the world, initially at the 2013 Venice Biennale and later, in 2016, at Iceland's Reykjavik Art Museum and in 2019 in Montreal's PHI Foundation. To prepare for the exhibits, she asked "women of all ages, from all countries of the world" to "send a testament of harm done to you, for being a woman." She asked women to also send photographs of their eyes.

Arising took different forms in different cities but all the installations included a wall covered with sheets of paper with women's responses to Yoko's instructions—their memories of pain—below the photographs of the authors' eyes. Below are submissions from the *Arising* exhibition in the Vancouver Art Gallery in 2022:

> Sexually molested as a child, sexually molested as an adult.
>
> Raped at 14, raped at 26, raped at 42 . . . finding relief in ageing, maybe someday I'll be safe.
>
> Finally, after 25 years of marriage, I left the abusive marriage.
>
> Being told . . . that I deserved to get raped . . . because nobody would want me as I was poor, stupid, fat and ugly . . . that I was a drunken Indian and I was a girl.
>
> Thrown down the stairs and then beaten for trying to protect my child from my husband. It made me stronger.

Some women addressed the men who harmed them: "When you pinned me down and touched me, I learned to leave my body." "I tell you NO . . . No, I am too drunk to have sex with you. It DOESN'T deter you." And "I understand that you are married and had a daughter. I want to know how you'd feel if someone did to her what you did to me at the young age of 11."

As early as 2002 Yoko had been encouraging women to come forward and providing them with safe and sacred spaces to express that they'd been harmed and to raise their voices together. Later *Arising* took its rightful place as part of the #MeToo movement. Indeed, in the Vancouver *Arising* installation, one woman wrote *#MeToo* five hundred times.

IN 1971, YOKO HAD HELD an exhibition at New York's Museum of Modern Art, but not because she'd been invited. That was her infamous guerrilla Museum of Modern (F)Art event.

Forty-four years after the unauthorized show, the MoMA opened an actual, officially sanctioned exhibition with the same title as the one in 1971—*Yoko Ono: One Woman Show*—but with the dates *1960–1971* added. The show opened in May 2015 in a sixth-floor MoMA gallery. More than one hundred pieces were exhibited. There were paintings, films, the anti-war campaigns, interactive installations, and performances. The film of "Cut Piece" was shown and a gallery was devoted to *Grapefruit*. The pages of the book ran along a wall. The instructions in *Grapefruit* were shown near the pieces based on them.

In his review of the MoMA exhibition in the *New York Times*, Holland Cotter retold Yoko's history up to her marrying John, continuing, "In a larger way, though, her position as his wife obscured her independent career. Worse, it left her a natural target for the misogyny and racism that she had always battled. Her subsequent roles, honorably assumed, as celebrity-widow and political spokeswoman have tended to blunt the edge and limit the variety of new art she's made in recent decades and set a '60s aura around it."

But Cotter said that "this impression [was] neatly countered" by the newest piece in the exhibition, titled "To See the Sky." Cotter described the piece and the experience of interacting with it:

> It's a free-standing steel spiral staircase that leads upward toward something I had never noticed before: a clear glass skylight piercing the museum's sixth-floor gallery ceiling. The sky, limitless and shifting, source of nurture and destruction, has been a central image in Ms. Ono's art all along. Viewed through the gallery skylight, it makes an attractive goal for a climb.
>
> But as you reach the top of the staircase, something unnerving happens. The structure starts to wobble and sway, like a ship on a moody sea. Looking skyward becomes hard; your gut tells you to focus on where your feet are.

Even when you've come back down, it takes a minute to find your land legs. So, just when you thought you were in for a bit of transcendence, free and clear, you've been given a wake-up poke, a little slap of fear, a reminder that looking for light is perilous; danger is always near; which is the message that this imaginative, tough-minded and still underestimated artist has been delivering for years.

CHAPTER 32

A S A LONGTIME FAN OF Yoko's music, the musician Thurston Moore was angered when a review of the Japan Society exhibition that lauded her artwork said, in essence, as he recalled, "the less we can talk about the screaming and shouting the better." "I was like 'No, no, no, no!'" Moore said, "Yoko has a very innate sense of music and music theory. It's not like she's just shouting and blathering. It's so outside the sensibility of art criticism, they can't see the music as being as important as the visual art, as the performance work. I took offense at that. Her musical output has always been discounted in relationship to her art, but they are utterly intertwined."

By the early 2000s, Yoko's art career had found solid footing, but even after the positive critical reception of *Onobox* and *Rising*, the mainstream music audience ignored her new albums. She once said she didn't aspire to be a pop star, but that was disingenuous. She believed pop music was "the people's form," and she wanted to communicate with the people, not just with appreciators of the experimental and avant-garde. Indeed, artist Pipilotti Rist said, "Pop media and fine art were always divided. Yoko was a bridge in both directions."

Perhaps as a way of bridging the gap, Yoko focused on two very different spheres of music during her seventies and eighties, efforts that were remarkably successful. As a result, she became an unlikely chart-topping phenomenon in the dance-music world while also creating some of her most far-out music yet in collaboration with cutting-edge artists from diverse genres.

Few would have predicted that Yoko would become a dance-club diva. She initially resisted allowing others to remix her songs, but she relented in 2001 when a group of young producers called the Orange Factory approached her. They remixed "Open Your Box," the song from the *Fly* album, with its original scandalous lyrics and created a pounding track that took off in clubs.

Later, an influential DJ, Danny Tenaglia, remixed "Walking on Thin Ice," combining Yoko's vocals with "elements of post-disco and electronic music," generating more buzz. Other DJs also remixed "Thin Ice," propelling it to the top of dance charts. John once predicted that the song would be Yoko's first number-one record and it was. Tenaglia's remix of "Thin Ice" hit number one on the *Billboard* dance chart in 2003 (another "Thin Ice" remix hit number one in 2013).

"She was beyond thrilled," said Tenaglia. Yoko took him up on his invitation to appear at clubs in New York and Miami where he was DJing. He introduced her to the crowd, and she performed the song live. "She gets on the mic and starts singing—utilizing her voice in the unique way she does—and people went nuts," Tenaglia said.

In 2007, Yoko's success in clubs led her to release a pair of albums of dance remixes of her songs, ranging from tracks on *Yoko Ono/Plastic Ono Band* through her recent albums. For *Yes, I'm a Witch* and *Open Your Box*, renowned DJs and producers created new or modified original tracks for Yoko's vocals.

From *Open Your Box*, "You're the One" was released as a single and reached number two on the *Billboard* Hot Dance Club Play chart in the United States. In August 2008, a remix of "Give Peace a Chance" hit number one. That hit was especially meaningful to Yoko. "It brought the kids our message," she said. "They were all singing along with us on 'Give Peace a Chance.' John would have loved it."

Another renowned producer and DJ, Superchumbo, created dance versions of "Kiss Kiss Kiss," "Thin Ice," "I'm Moving On," and "Hell in Paradise." Another DJ produced a version of "Every Man Has a Woman Who Loves

Him," this one titled, "Everyman Everywoman," with lyrics Yoko revised to include same-sex couples.

With these and other remixes of her songs rising to the top of dance charts worldwide, Yoko was introduced to a new audience. Her move into the dance-music scene might have seemed unlikely. However, her artistic evolution had always been marked by a willingness to experiment with new forms and to collaborate. By 2018, she had thirteen number-one dance hits. At eighty-three years old, Yoko hit number eleven on *Billboard*'s "Greatest of All Time Dance Club Artists."

WHILE THE POPULAR SUCCESS IN clubs and on the dance charts was gratifying (and fun) for Yoko, her main interest as a composer and performer was still her nonmainstream work, and during these decades, she created radical new music in collaboration with musicians whom she'd inspired, from Kim Gordon and Thurston Moore of Sonic Youth to the B-52's to Wu-Tang Clan's RZA. In 2002, she joined the B-52's in New York for their twenty-fifth-anniversary concerts, performing "Rock Lobster" with the band. John had recognized Yoko's influence on "Rock Lobster" when he heard the song in 1980.

Yoko also found kindred spirits—and new collaborators—in Gordon and Moore, both when they were together in Sonic Youth and after, when she worked with them as solo artists.

Moore contributed to a 1996 album of remixes of songs from *Rising*, performing the title track, which he built around Yoko's breathing. The following year, Moore and Gordon made a record of Sonic Youth doing covers of pieces by twentieth-century composers and chose Yoko's "Voice Piece for Soprano." They had their daughter, Coco, who was four years old, perform the piece. As Gordon recalled, "She stood in front of the microphone, and we said, 'Okay, pretend you are screaming at a wall,' 'Pretend you are screaming at the sky . . .' It was great having a child do it, because there is such a child energy to Yoko's music."

A remarkable and unexpected collaboration occurred in 2010, when RZA of Wu-Tang Clan participated with Yoko in an extraordinary event at the Orpheum Theater in Los Angeles. RZA, who knew Sean, turned out to be a fan of his mother. When he was young, "crate-digging" at used-record stores, RZA happened to pick up a copy of *Yoko Ono/Plastic Ono Band* and was, he said, "blown away." He sampled her voice and music; the first song he sampled was "Greenfield Morning I Pushed an Empty Baby Carriage All Over the City." Sean told Yoko about it and she invited RZA to perform with her, suggesting they do an art piece to accompany a concert.

RZA remembered that she proposed performing one of her early works, "Play It by Trust." He described the experience of playing on the all-white chess set onstage with Yoko as "definitely trippy, fun, beautiful." After a while, the band started playing, and soon there was an all-out jam. RZA said, "It was historic. It was like a bridge between generations."

There were many other bridges between generations—and genres—when Yoko collaborated with other musicians. Sean said he never had to sell artists on Yoko's music. "In my generation, the generation that would birth grunge, we all loved her. The Melvins loved her. Mike D was down. Kurt Cobain and Nirvana loved her. Courtney Love loved her. Bands like Redd Kross had side projects like the Tater Totz that were Yoko Ono tribute bands. The B-52's loved her. The avant-garde work was loved by the coolest people on the planet." Kate Pierson of the B-52's said, "When she sings simple songs, her voice could be so, so soft and enchanting and it draws you in. And then she, on the other hand, has these blasting vocalizations that just kind of send out a message to the aliens. It makes the earth shake when she does her vocalizations."

YOKO'S SEVENTY-SEVENTH BIRTHDAY, IN 2010, was celebrated with a star-studded concert at the Brooklyn Academy of Music Howard Gilman Opera House. Sean organized the concert and led the Plastic Ono Band that included Eric Clapton, Klaus Voormann, and Jim Keltner; they were joined by special guests Kim Gordon, Bette Midler, Thurston Moore, Paul Simon, and others. Yoko opened the show by singing "It Happened" a cappella. Bette Midler sang "Yes, I'm Your Angel." Paul Simon and his son Harper Simon sang her "Silver Horse" and John's "Hold On." There were rocking jams. While Clapton played lead guitar on the Beatles' "Yer Blues," Yoko was onstage—in a bag. Gordon and Moore joined Yoko on "Mulberry." The crowd sang Yoko "Happy Birthday." Then the show ended when the Plastic Ono Band played "Give Peace a Chance." The audience, flashing peace signs, sang along.

Madeline Bocaro was at the show and wrote: "If suffering produces the best art, then all that this woman has endured in her life has led her to this moment— the accumulation of all the hardship, sadness and loss—and the expulsion of it all in her music. Nobody sings the blues like Yoko. . . . [At] the end of each song, she instantly purges the pain, revels in the wild applause and still seems amazed (after being conditioned by years of indifference) that people actually love her now!"

YOKO STROVE TO INVENT NEW ways to communicate throughout her life, including when it came to her political messages. The bed-in was a new way for artists to engage in politics. At the time Yoko and John created them, billboards and ads in newspapers were a new way to advocate for a cause. And when the internet became available, Yoko quickly took to it. "The computer is my favorite invention," she said in 2009.

The internet, social media, and smartphones were ideal mediums for Yoko's art and political action. The technologies were like blank canvases and had the potential to reach many millions of people around the world. Many of her major installations in the past had asked people to connect with her and one another by contributing their wishes (for example, "Wish Tree") and stories (as in My Mommy Is Beautiful and Arising). She sent instruction postcards and asked people to send her photographs of their eyes and smiles. Technology allowed her to include far more people in these events. The audience didn't have to come to galleries or museums to participate in her work.

In 1967 she had proposed the *Smiles Film* in *Grapefruit*:

My ultimate goal in film-making is to make a film which includes a smiling face snap of every single human being in the world. Of course, I cannot go around the whole world and take the shots myself. I need cooperation from something like the post offices of the world. If anybody would drop a snapshot of themselves and their families to the post office of their town, or allow themselves to be photographed by the nearest photographic studio, this would be soon accomplished.

Of course, the film would need constant adding of footage. Probably no-one would like to see the whole film at once, so you can keep it in a library or something, and when you want to see some particular town's people's smiling faces you can go and check that section of the film. We can also arrange it with a television network so that whenever you want to see faces of a particular location in the world, all you have to do is to press a button and there it is.

This instruction reads like a longing for the functionality of the internet. In 2012, she created Smilesfilm.com online.

Dear Friends,

Our smiles change moods and opinions as they radiate positive energy out into the world, creating joy, healing and peace, changing the Universe for the better.

People from cities and countries around the world can freely upload their smiles from their camera, phone, tablet or computer—to the world and its people.

Each time we add our smiles to #smilesfilm, we are creating our future, together.

Give us a smile!
I love you!

Yoko also put up a website for the *My Mommy Is Beautiful* project, asking people to go to MyMommyIsBeautiful.com, "a virtual blank canvas." She was "inviting all people to make an accolade to their mothers, publicly probably for the first time, and share their love for her with us all." She asked people to upload photos and messages to Facebook, Instagram, and Twitter.

Over the years, Yoko embraced technology in other ways. She created online events like happenings from the 1960s. Once again she had been ahead of her time when, back in 1996, she posted an instruction online every day for a hundred days. More than half a century later, many of her early instruction pieces read like tweets to be shared. She joined Twitter in 2008 and by 2024 had 4.4 million followers. Twitter (now X) and other platforms—Facebook and Instagram in particular—allowed her to share instructions, poems, photographs, announcements of events, and promotions for her and John's records. She engaged in online dialogues with fans, answering their questions.

Yoko also turned to social media to push political messages. She posted about peace, feminism, climate change, gun control, and many other issues. She was as fearless online as she was onstage. In November 2016, three days after Donald Trump was elected president, she tweeted: "Dear Friends, I would like to share this message with you as my response to @realDonaldTrump. Love, Yoko." It was a nineteen-second audio clip of her screaming.

YOKO'S ADVOCACY FOR PEACE AND her other political campaigns were often criticized as naive and ineffective. One problem with the criticisms of Yoko was that she was an artist and not a politician. The artist Ai Weiwei said, "All art activities can be understood as naive, of course, because what really dominates the world is power and profit-oriented economic discourse. This naivety is apparently one of her attributes."

To the charge that his mother was naive, Sean responded, "I think her naïveté was hard won. She survived World War Two and the assassination of her husband. So the truth is she *wasn't* naive. In spite of that, she chose to remain hopeful and optimistic and childlike in her appreciation of the beauty of the universe."

Yoko said, "Most people say, 'Oh, you're so optimistic. I mean, what's wrong with you?' I'm not really that optimistic. I am trying to make us survive. And in the course of survival, we don't have the luxury to be negative. That's a luxury that we can't afford."

IF THERE WAS ONE PROJECT that fully embodied her message on a large scale for posterity, it was the Imagine Peace Tower—a tower of light on an island in Iceland dedicated to John.

Yoko dedicated the site in October 2006 on what would have been John's sixty-sixth birthday. At a ceremony in Reykjavík announcing the project, she told the story of how, forty years earlier, John had invited her to lunch at his house after meeting her at the Indica Gallery. He had asked her about building a lighthouse in his garden, the lighthouse she described in "Ono's Sales List." She told him it was conceptual but said, "I'm convinced that one day it could be built."

The Imagine Peace Tower was installed on Viðey Island, reachable from Reykjavík by ferry. It has as its base a stone wishing well from which fifteen searchlights project a beam of light skyward. It shoots up as high as thirteen thousand feet.

Inscribed on the wishing well are the words *Imagine Peace* in twenty-four languages.

On October 9, 2007, again on John's birthday, the Imagine Peace Tower was unveiled. Sean, Ringo Starr, Olivia Harrison, and her son Dhani Harrison attended with Yoko. (The Harrisons stood in for George, who had died in 2001.)

"Some of us are here physically, some are joining us in spirit," Yoko said in a statement.

> Some of us are imprisoned, tortured, maimed, and silenced, but they are also here today with us. Some of us have passed away before being able to enjoy a new age of love and peace.
>
> But we are all here today standing together with hope.
>
> The light is the light of wisdom, healing, and empowerment.
>
> Even in the moments of confusion, fear, and the darkness of your souls, hold the light in your hearts, and you will know that you are not alone, that we are all together in seeing the light of peace.

Since then, the Imagine Peace Tower has been lit every year from John's birthday, October 9, through December 8, the date he was shot, and on other occasions.

CHAPTER 33

YOKO WAS ON TOUR IN Europe on her eightieth birthday in February 2013. In Berlin the night before her birthday, she performed for a sold-out audience, backed by the Plastic Ono Band (Sean served as bandleader). Guests that night included Peaches, Michael Stipe, Rufus Wainwright, and Martha Wainwright. The set list ranged in tone—a plaintive "It Happened," electric "Thin Ice," cheeky "Yes, I'm a Witch," and exuberant and pleading "Give Peace a Chance." Yoko performed a triumphant scream. And she danced. "Wildly," Peaches said.

Articles about Yoko's birthday appeared in newspapers around the world. The *Houston Press* ran a piece titled "Yoko Ono Turns 80, Still Weird as Hell," but a more nuanced article by Jon Wiener ran in March in the *Nation*. "She's done more in the last year than most of us do in a decade," Wiener wrote. He listed the whirlwind of art shows, music, and political activity.

Most of those who interviewed Yoko in this period rhapsodized about her extraordinary energy and appearance for her age. The *Financial Times* profiled her: "Knocking on 80, she still has the nimble appearance of someone for whom the word 'elfin' was coined; a clear complexion and, when the trademark shades on the end of her nose are removed, a gaze merry and friendly."

"I know you're not supposed to show your legs at my age," she told the

Times of London. "I don't know how long I've got, so I'm just going for it. I thought I better just do what I want to do."

In June of her eightieth year, Yoko danced onstage in London at Meltdown, an annual artist-curated music festival. She'd been asked to be the guest curator that year. The acts Yoko selected to perform were an eclectic mix that ranged from Iggy Pop and the Stooges to Savages. Patti Smith and Kim Gordon performed, as did Thurston Moore, Boy George, Pussy Riot, Siouxsie Sioux, Marianne Faithfull, and Peaches. In addition to musical performances, there were installations, art performances, and panel discussions with feminist artists, including the Guerrilla Girls; Laura Bates, the founder of the Everyday Sexism Project; and members of Pussy Riot. There were screenings of Yoko's films and Yoko asked Peaches to perform "Cut Piece."

Performing "Cut Piece" was, for Peaches, "transformative." She said, "The first thing you realize is that 'Cut Piece' is completely timeless." After ninety minutes, her clothes had been snipped away—she was nude. "It was scary, but it felt powerful to sit there." Yoko came onto the stage, put a ring on Peaches's finger, and kissed her hand. Peaches cried.

The success of Meltdown proved that Yoko at eighty was as relevant as she'd ever been. And more proof came that September when she released a new album, titled *Take Me to the Land of Hell*. "People tell me this kind of music is young people's music, and I tell them, 'I was doing this kind of music before you were born,'" Yoko said.

The record was produced by Sean and featured a stellar (and, once again, eclectic) lineup of musicians, among them Mike D and Ad-Rock of the Beastie Boys, Questlove, and the Tune-Yards' Merrill Garbus.

Yoko's eightieth year was also marked by the publication of a new book, *Acorn*, a kind of sequel to *Grapefruit*, which had been published fifty years earlier. *Acorn* was another book of instructional poems and included Yoko's mesmeric three-dimensional dot drawings. The *Los Angeles Times* said, "As always with Ono, the playfulness disguises a deeper purpose, which has to do with being present, with seeing things in a different way."

Acorn contained a number of "Sky Pieces," a reminder of how central the image of the sky had been for Yoko's entire life. For her, the sky represented safety, hope, freedom, and peace. She had a trompe l'oeil sky painted on the ceiling in her office. There was that line in "Imagine": "Above us only sky." There were many other pieces turning the viewer's gaze skyward over the years, including the Imagine Peace Tower, which shot its beam of light upward in tribute to John. In 2018, Yoko created mosaic murals of the sky on the walls of the Seventy-Second Street subway station in New York City under the Dakota.

In *Acorn*, the instruction to "Sky Piece VIII" read:

Sit under a blue sky.
Keep your head open
and empty.
Let ideas come into you.
Cherish them.

FOR ALL THE PRIDE AND dignity that Yoko found through her own work, decades after losing John, she was still tied to the Beatles. She often represented John at Beatles-related events and announcements.

Yoko filled in for John alongside Paul, Ringo, and Olivia Harrison in June 2006, in Las Vegas for the opening of Cirque du Soleil's Beatles "Love" show. (Sean and Cynthia and Julian Lennon were there too.) A couple of years later, she joined Paul, Ringo, and Olivia onstage again at a Microsoft event to launch the Beatles: Rock Band video game. She remained involved with the surviving Beatles (and Olivia) as they dealt with new and old business. Working with the three wasn't without challenges, but it became easier over time. Yoko was fond of Olivia Harrison, remained close to Ringo, and had a genuine rapprochement with Paul. "Time does heal," she said.

Yoko and Paul had indeed come far in a relationship that had been contentious at the start, with Paul glaring at Yoko as he sang, "Get back to where you once belonged."

The resentment and backbiting had percolated since the beginning of Yoko and John's romance. When Paul admitted he didn't like Yoko "at first," John said it was too late. But things shifted. Over the years, there had been many friendly visits.

Recently, Paul had begun to show his respect for Yoko publicly, including in a 2012 interview with David Frost in which he confirmed that she hadn't broken up the Beatles.

The following year in a *Rolling Stone* profile, he admiringly said, "She's badass."

BY YOKO'S EIGHTH DECADE, SHE and Paul were closer than they'd ever been. Her affection for him was genuine, not manufactured for the press. Nevertheless, Yoko and Paul's relationship continued to be the subject of speculation. Interviewers invariably asked her about Paul (and he was asked about her), just as they invariably asked about her breaking up the Beatles—a subject that reared its head again in 2021.

Beginning in November, amid the COVID pandemic and lockdown, the Peter Jackson–directed documentary *The Beatles: Get Back* streamed on television, riveting housebound audiences. The film covered the writing and recording of the songs that made up the *Let It Be* album. Jackson relied on footage and audio recordings made for Michael Lindsay-Hogg's 1970 *Let It Be* documentary. The three-part movie showed the group's creative process and countered the often-told story of the dreariness and tension that characterized the making of the album. In that regard, it countered John's experience of the record's production, which, he said in a 1970 interview, was "the most miserable session on Earth."

The director of the film also sought to put to rest the enduring myth that Yoko had broken up the Beatles by intruding as the band made *Let It Be*. "She never has opinions about the stuff they're doing," Jackson told *60 Minutes*. "She's a very benign presence and she doesn't interfere in the slightest."

"The World Owes Yoko an Apology!" trumpeted a headline in the *Guardian*.

But in fact, *The Beatles: Get Back* didn't put the nattering to rest. Her innocuous but constant presence invited people to project their own inclinations onto her. She was there to support John, as the artist Takashi Murakami saw it. "She is always at John's side as the group plays, making you wonder, 'Why is this person here?'" he said. "In the documentary, John Lennon pulls himself together at one point and starts facing his creative challenges. My takeaway was that Yoko Ono was the compassionate soul that helped him during those times." Indeed, Yoko was there because John wanted her there—he would have said he needed her there. As I noted earlier, if she hadn't accompanied him, he might not have shown up at all.

FOR MANY PEOPLE, YOKO WAS still known mainly as the wife and then the widow of John Lennon. As such, she had endured a lifetime of sexism and racism—she'd been denigrated and loathed. But she'd also, by some, been admired.

The critic Lindsay Zoladz wrote, "I have always been drawn to the women who can arouse this kind of vitriol. The kind of hate that seems too big and billowing to be directed at just one woman, the kind that seems like a person or an entire society is vomiting out all its misogyny onto one convenient scapegoat. At some point . . . I started to see this position of feminine abjectness as a kind of superpower. A position from which a woman could offend far more deeply than a man."

Rather than ignoring the haters, Yoko provoked them. "Yes, I'm a witch," she sang. "I'm a bitch. I don't care what you say." Yoko once said, "I get thank-you notes from Asian women sometimes for standing up. In my day, Madame Butterfly—that image—was the Asian women's image. Now it's a little bit different."

Yet the tired myth that she had broken up the Beatles persisted. In 2022, I caught a glimpse of an old station wagon with a bumper sticker reading

STILL PISSED AT YOKO. In December 2023, Taylor Swift's boyfriend's football team suffered a series of losses, and Swift was blamed; newspapers around the world reported that fans charged Swift with "Yoko Ono–ing" the Kansas City Chiefs—destroying the team by seducing Travis Kelce as Yoko destroyed the Beatles by seducing John Lennon. But a sign of a shift, at least in the art world, had come years earlier when the artist David Horvitz released a T-shirt that went viral. It read JOHN LENNON BROKE UP FLUXUS.

IN 2016, JUST BEFORE HER eighty-third birthday, Yoko was hospitalized. It was rumored that she'd had a stroke. Elliot and Sean both rushed to correct the false reports. Sean tweeted, "Hey guys it was only rumors from press: was NOT a stroke, just dehydration/tired. She is FINE." A second tweet read "Only stroke @yokoono had was a Stroke of Genius! :-) She's really fine. Thanks for all the well wishes! Big Love, Sean."

Elliot confirmed that she had flu-like symptoms. "Dehydration and feeling tired would fall under the umbrella of the flu," he said.

Whether it was the flu or another illness, Yoko appeared frailer when she went out in public after that. In September 2016, she made a rare public appearance. Dane Worthington, the caretaker who had become Sean's nanny and, later, an assistant, escorted her to Strawberry Fields. Fans gathered around, sang "Imagine," and took photos and videos. Yoko insisted on walking, but she was shaky and weak. She and Dane went slowly, sitting on benches to rest on the way back to the Dakota. The next time pictures of her visiting Strawberry Fields appeared in the papers, in April 2017, she was in a wheelchair accompanied by an assistant, an aide, and a security guard.

Yoko once publicly acknowledged she was sick—"I've learned a lot from having this illness," she said in 2017. "I'm very thankful that I went through this"—but she never specified what illness it was. Yoko lived one of the most public lives of anyone in history, but she stopped granting interviews, and her family wanted to protect her privacy as she entered the twilight of her life. They declined to comment on her health.

Yoko was slowing down, but only comparatively. Six months after the hospital stay, she attended Sean's concert with Les Claypool at Irving Plaza in New York City. An assistant helped Yoko onstage, and she was handed a microphone. While the band played the Primus song "Southbound Pachyderm," Yoko let loose. Bob Gruen was at the concert. "She was sitting in the wheelchair in the balcony, watching the whole show. Then she came out on stage and she [seemed] kind of frail, you know, but then she took the microphone and *wow!*" Les Claypool told Sean, "Your mom . . . I mean that was the wildest thing I ever heard."

ONE OF THE MOST SIGNIFICANT events of Yoko's life occurred later in 2017. Sean helped her on the stage to accept the National Music Publishers Association's Centennial Song Award for "Imagine." It had become one of the most important songs ever recorded. *Rolling Stone* described "Imagine" as "an enduring hymn of solace and promise that has carried us through extreme grief, from the shock of Lennon's own death in 1980 to the unspeakable horror of September 11th. It is now impossible to imagine a world without 'Imagine,' and we need it more than he ever dreamed."

It wasn't John's song alone, as he had said multiple times, and at the 2017 award ceremony, the head of the NMPA, David Israelite, made it official. "While things may have been different in 1971, today I am glad to say things have changed," he said. "So tonight, it is my distinct honor to correct the record some forty-eight years later and recognize Yoko Ono as a cowriter of the NMPA Centennial Song 'Imagine' and to present Yoko Ono with this well-deserved credit," he said.

Patti Smith, accompanied on piano by her daughter Jesse, sang "Imagine" and thanked Yoko and John.

Yoko once said that "Imagine" was her and John's most significant contribution to the world. "Imagine" is Yoko's philosophy and central to her own legacy and her joint legacy with John. It's an expression of their partnership and shared mission. That Yoko finally received the credit John said she deserved was significant for rock-and-roll history, but it was also meaningful in another way, because "Imagine" synthesized the belief system that was then and had always been central to Yoko's life and work—the basis of her conceptual art and thinking and, indeed, her survival.

Sean once spoke about "Imagine" as a bookend to the childhood trauma that both his parents experienced. About Yoko, he said, "You can find a direct link—that's not even subjective, that's clear and true—from the trauma she went through in World War Two, the experience she had almost starving with my uncle Kei and aunt Setsuko and having to make Kei stop crying by imagining food, and how that led her to be a conceptual artist, and how her conceptual art led my dad to write the song 'Imagine' with her. It's pretty amazing."

Ultimately, Sean said, "It's one of my mom's most powerful talents: that she has this ability to overcome difficulty with positive thinking. She really wanted to teach the world to do that. She taught my dad to do that. It's not going to stop a moving train or a bullet. But I think there's something profound about it. And I think it affected the world."

IN 2020, IT WAS MADE public that Sean was taking over the family's business interests. He took Yoko's place working with Apple and running his parents' publishing companies, licensing operations, and other businesses. Sean, who was assisted by Jonas Herbsman and Yoko's staff, would also be managing the ongoing promotion of his mother's and father's work.

Sean was taking on a formidable responsibility. In 2024, Yoko's estate was rumored to be valued at $500 million with her art collection alone worth more than $100 million. John was perpetually on the *Forbes* list of the highest-paid dead celebrities. In 2023, the income was reported to be $22 million. (In 2007, it was $44 million, second to Elvis Presley.) Yoko made money but gave it away too; she donated to a long list of international and domestic charities, focusing on issues like childhood hunger, homelessness, education, and, of course, peace. Her Spirit Foundation built over one hundred schools in Africa and Asia. In 2002, she established the LennonOno Grant for Peace, an award given to artists creating "positive social change."

WHEN THE WORLD LOCKED DOWN because of the COVID pandemic, Yoko moved from the Dakota to her farm in upstate New York. It was safe, private, and bucolic on six hundred meandering acres of fields and forests. Yoko leaving the Dakota was big news for New Yorkers, who had felt her presence on the Upper West Side for fifty years. She had stayed in the city after losing her husband in front of her home, had weaved through fans, and heard John's songs played every October 9 and December 8. In the *New York Times*, Anna Kodé observed, "The thought of New York without Ms. Ono is a New York with a little less magic."

Sean and his girlfriend, Charlotte Kemp Muhl, stayed on the farm with Yoko during the lockdown and most evenings had dinner with her. This continued even after things opened up again whenever Sean was at the upstate residence.

Yoko hadn't seen herself as having the skills or temperament to be a mother or a grandmother, but at this stage of her life, she took obvious pleasure from having her family around. Kyoko, who often visited the farm, reflected about her mother: "She literally believed she could change the world, and my mom did . . . now she is able to be quiet—listen to the wind and watch the sky." Still the sky.

With Sean at her side and regular visits from Kyoko and her children, Yoko, who has spent her life advocating for peace, may finally have some herself. "She is very happy, in a happy place," Kyoko said. "This is well deserved and genuine peacefulness."

IN HER SONG "WILL I," a clock ticks. Then Yoko speaks. She asks:

Will I miss the skies?

Will I miss the clouds?

Will I miss the ocean?

Will I miss the bay?

Will I miss the sunrise?

Will I miss the moon?

Will I miss the mountains?

Will I miss the trees?

Will I miss the city lights?

Will I miss the snow?

Will I miss the laughter?

Will I miss the jokes?

Will I miss touch?

Will I miss love?

Will I miss you?

Will I?

Will I?

EPILOGUE

Everything in the Universe Is Unfinished

FROM YOKO'S EARLIEST DAYS AS an artist, much of her work—visual art and musical compositions—was unfinished: An instruction to be followed. A painting to be stepped on. A dress to be cut. A wish to be written. She handed her work off to her audience to complete.

The work remained unfinished even in her ninth decade. Projects on multiple fronts were ongoing, including art exhibitions and her campaign for peace. There was also the continued promotion of both Yoko's and John's work, which Sean oversaw; he wanted to keep them relevant and continue to spread their message. An animated short film he co-executive-produced and cowrote, *War Is Over! Inspired by the Music of John and Yoko*, won an Academy Award in 2024, and Sean launched a website for Nutopia, a virtual version of the conceptual country Yoko and John created—everyone can become a citizen.

Although overseeing his parents' legacies and business took up a good chunk of his time, Sean remained a musician at heart. Through the early 2020s, he produced albums and videos and performed on others' records. He collaborated with Les Claypool on a Claypool Lennon Delirium tour that continued through late 2023. In 2024, he released a new album, *Asterisms*, an instrumental record that bridged jazz, rock, and electronic music—

"a beautiful and exploratory instrumental project by one of the most creative and versatile musicians, composers, producers and songwriters working today," according to *Tinnitist*.

It was a challenge for Sean to balance his responsibilities running "the family business" with producing, recording, and performing—the other family business—a balance his mother had also struggled to achieve. "I feel like as my responsibilities expand, so do my abilities," Sean said. "That's what you want in life, to be growing."

Around this time, Kyoko was living in the western United States. She'd retired from teaching and was working as an artist, and she changed the name she used to Kyoko Ono. "I used Cox for years; it's not like I'm trying to hide the fact that my dad was Tony Cox. I just want to focus on the current time of paving this precious relationship with my mother."

Kyoko worked in photography and ceramics, tracing her interest in photography to the Polaroid camera Yoko had given her when she was six years old.

Yoko projects were still being released and more were in the works. In 2022, Ben Gibbard, from the band Death Cab for Cutie, organized a Yoko tribute album. The record, *Ocean Child: Songs of Yoko Ono*, was, according to the *Guardian*, "intended to demonstrate the breadth, charm and brilliance of her output." On the album, released on Sean's Chimera label, David Byrne, the Flaming Lips, US Girls, Sudan Archives, and Japanese Breakfast covered her songs. Byrne chose to record "Who Has Seen the Wind" with the band Yo La Tengo. "The song was so Yoko," Byrne said, "saying that there's this invisible force—whether it's love between people or the wind. It's completely invisible and yet has a huge effect."

Exhibitions of Yoko's art, some in the works for years, continued to be mounted. In 2023, Yoko was one of four women in the group show *Out of Bounds: Japanese Women Artists in Fluxus* at the Japan Society in New York. In February 2024, a major retrospective, *Yoko Ono: Music of the Mind*, opened in London at the Tate Modern. It was the largest Yoko Ono exhibition ever, with more than two hundred works of art. As Yoko always aspired to do, this exhibition handed some of her work to others to finish. People got in bags, hammered in nails, watered a canvas, played the "Play It by Trust" chess set, added color to "Add Colour (Refugee Boat)," wrote down memories about their mothers, and shared their wishes.

YOKO OFTEN SAID THAT HER goal after John's murder was surviving. But she did more than survive. She fought her melancholia, loneliness, and fear and experienced moments of great joy. She used the traumas in her life—her childhood interrupted by war, losing Kyoko, John's death—to create work that edified, enlightened, and inspired. Yoko imagined a better world—and she worked to create one.

ACKNOWLEDGMENTS

I would like to thank Yoko Ono for her friendship and support. She continues to inspire me.

This book couldn't have been written without the help of Sean Lennon, who granted hours of interviews about his mother and spoke with insight, honesty, and love. He also helped by encouraging others to give interviews and by granting me permission to use photographs, his parents' song lyrics and writings, and more. I'm indebted to him and to his sister, Kyoko Ono, who was also gracious, kind, and candid when she spoke about her life and her mother.

My special thanks go to Jonas Herbsman, who helped at every stage, and Elliot Mintz, Yagi Takako, Karla Merrifield, and Bob Gruen.

Among the many who granted interviews or helped in other ways, I wish to thank the following: Erica Abeel, Bruce Altshuler, Laurie Anderson, Eleanor Antin, Ei Arakawa, Elizabeth Beier, Fred Bernstein, Madeline Bocaro, Mary Boone, David Byrne, Jung Hee Choi, Alan Clayson, Kevin Concannon, Ray Connolly, Caroline Coon, Tony Cox, Corrie Deeb, Jeffrey Deitch, Richelle DeLora, Gina Devincenzi, Jack Douglas, John Dunbar, Anat Ebgi, David Geffen, Barry Golson, Beate Gordon, Kim Gordon, Barbara Graustark, Jim Harithas, Sam Havadtoy, Jon Hendricks, Simon Hilton, Reiko

Kaga, Tony King, Donald Kirk, Alison Knowles, Jutta Koether, Cyndi Lauper, Julian Lennon, Mark Lewisohn, Michael Lindsay-Hogg, Dan Mahoney, Fiona Maynard, Barry McGee, Barry Miles, Kate Millett, Connor Monahan, Thurston Moore, Alexandra Munroe, Takashi Murakami, David Newgarden, Hans Ulrich Obrist, Akiko Ono, Kei and Masako Ono, Kousuke Ono, Tad (Tadahiko) Ono, Yugo Ono, Catherine Opie, Peaches, Jeffrey Perkins, Kate Pierson, Keiko Yasuda Prater, Eva Prinz, Craig Pyes, Stephen Randall, Dan Richter, Jill Richter, Pipilotti Rist, Geraldo Rivera, Betty Rollin, David Ross, RZA, Sara Seagull, Vicki Sheff-Cahan, Nancy Simon Stearns, Kristine Stiles, Danny Tenaglia, Reiko Tomii, Klaus Voormann, Rebecca Warfield, Koichi Watari, Ai Weiwei, Jann Wenner, Jon Wiener, Mel Woody, Dane Worthington, Midori Yamamura, Tadanori Yokoo, Midori Yoshimoto, and La Monte Young.

At CAA, as always, I'm grateful to Amanda Urban for her guidance, wisdom, and friendship. Also at CAA, in London, I extend my thanks to Helen Manders and Peppa Mignone.

At the Steven Barclay Agency, thank you to Eliza Fischer and my dear friend Steven Barclay. For legal advice, I'd like to thank John Pelosi. For their legal review of the book, thanks to Edward Klaris and Mariella Salazar.

At Simon & Schuster, thank you to the wonderful Suzanne Baboneau in the UK and, in New York, Tzipora Chein, and production editor Jonathan Evans. Also at Simon & Schuster, thank you to publicist Cat Boyd, marketing manager Ingrid Carabulea, and the book's designers Jackie Seow and Wendy Blum. In Canada, thank you to publicist Lisa Wray. In addition, thank you to the book's wondrous copyeditor, Tracy Roe.

Thank you to Andy Young, who fact-checked the book; Frederick T. Courtright, who helped with permissions; and photo researcher Denise Bosco, who gathered and secured the rights to the photographs. Others who helped include researchers Mariel Brunman, Anna Guth, and Theodora Walsh. Thanks also to Chip Madinger and Scott Raile, coauthors of *Lennonology: Strange Days Indeed*, who vetted the Yoko and John years.

Once again I've been blessed to have Eamon Dolan as my editor. He believed in this book from the beginning—and in me. I can never fully express my affection for Eamon and my gratitude for his vision, wisdom, support, patience, and awe-inspiring talent as an editor.

Hilary Liftin, a gifted and conscientious collaborator, also worked with me on multiple drafts of the book and occasionally served as wrangler and therapist. Thank you, Hilary.

Finally, I would like to thank my family: Daisy, Jasper, and Nic Sheff and Karen Barbour. They offered their tireless support, read and reread the manuscript, and provided insightful criticism and suggestions. You are everything to me.

NOTES

AUTHOR'S NOTE

ix *Portions of this book:* As noted, portions of this book were previously published in the following magazine articles and book: David Sheff, "The *Playboy* Interview with John Lennon and Yoko Ono," *Playboy* (January 1981); Vicki Sheff and David Sheff, "The Betrayal of John Lennon," *Playboy* (March 1984); David Sheff, "The Night Steve Jobs Met Andy Warhol," *Playboy* (January/February 2012); David Sheff, "Yoko Ono: How She Is Holding Up," *People*, January 12, 1981, https://people.com/archive /cover-story-checking-in-with-yoko-vol-15-no-1/; David Sheff, "Yoko and Sean: Starting Over," *People*, December 13, 1982, https://people.com/archive/cover-story -yoko-and-sean-starting-over-vol-18-no-24/; David Sheff, *All We Are Saying: The Last Major Interview with John Lennon and Yoko Ono,* rev. ed. (New York: St. Martin's Griffin, 2020). The interview was previously published as *The Playboy Interviews with John Lennon and Yoko Ono* (New York: Playboy Press, 1981).

PROLOGUE

xv *"The atmosphere changed":* Ellen Papazian, "Oh Yoko! 20 Ways of Looking at an Art-World Icon," *Bitch* (November 17, 2009).

xvi *"It's very delicate":* A video of the New York performance of "Cut Piece" is online at, among other places, https://vimeo.com/106706806.

xvi *"Yoko made a slight gesture":* Papazian, "Oh Yoko!"

xvi *"It was an extremely dangerous piece":* Ibid.

xvi *"one of the twenty-five most influential works of American":* Zoë Lescaze et al., "The 25 Most Influential Works of American Protest Art Since World War II," *New York Times,* October 15, 2020, https://www.nytimes.com/2020/10/15/t-magazine/most -influential-protest-art.html.

xvii *"All of us are in a bag":* David Sheff, *All We Are Saying: The Last Major Interview with John Lennon and Yoko Ono,* rev. ed. (New York: St. Martin's Griffin, 2020).

xvii *"Yoko had this revolutionary idea":* Author interview with Laurie Anderson, October 16, 2022.

xvii *"She is a conceptual artist":* Author assistant's interview with Reiko Tomii, December 13, 2022.

xviii *Yoko was sick with a fever:* Austin Allen, "'My Beautiful Never-Nevers': Yoko Ono's Poetry Revisited," *Los Angeles Review of Books*, April 4, 2022, https://lareviewof books.org/article/my-beautiful-never-nevers-yoko-onos-poetry-revisited/. Her fever was also referred to in Louis Menand, "Yoko Ono's Art of Defiance," *New Yorker*, June 13, 2022, https://www.newyorker.com/magazine/2022/06/20/yoko -onos-art-of-defiance.

xviii *"We were starving":* Yoko Ono, interview with Michael Kimmelman, *TimesTalks*, October 5, 2012, https://www.youtube.com/watch?v=0WIosw1gv50.

xviii *"Lying on our backs":* Alexandra Munroe, "Spirit of Yes: The Art and Life of Yoko Ono," in *Yes Yoko Ono*, eds. Alexandra Munroe and Jon Hendricks (New York: Harry N. Abrams, 2000); excerpt at https://web.archive.org/web/20160307183246 /http://www.alexandramunroe.com/spirit-of-yes-the-art-and-life-of-yoko-ono-2/.

xviii *"We made those menus":* Author interview with Keisuke Ono, June 16, 2022.

xviii *"Canonized":* Lescaze et al., "The 25 Most Influential Works."

xix *"I felt kind of like I was praying":* Yoko Ono, "Just Me," *Bungei Shunju* (September 1974), published in Japan as *Yoko Ono, Just Me!* (Tokyo: Kodansha, 1990).

xix *"I get into a trance":* Yoko Ono speaking about "Cut Piece," Museum of Modern Art, https://www.moma.org/audio/playlist/15/373.

INTRODUCTION

xxi *"wondrous mystic prince":* David Sheff, *All We Are Saying: The Last Major Interview with John Lennon and Yoko Ono*, rev. ed. (New York: St. Martin's Griffin, 2020).

xxi *"ugly Jap":* Yoko speaking at the First International Feminist Conference, Harvard University, Cambridge, MA, June 1–4, 1973, reprinted in an introduction to her song "Coffin Car" on the 1973 album *Feeling the Space*.

xxii "Bitch *was how Yoko was referred to":* Author interview with Klaus Voormann, June 2, 2022.

xxii *"We were not too keen on it at all":* Paul McCartney, interviewed by Terry Gross, *Fresh Air*, NPR, November 3, 2021, https://www.npr.org/2021/11/03/1051809546 /paul-mccartney-didnt-break-up-the-beatles.

xxii *"one of the most controversial ladies":* Ariella Budick, "Yoko Ono: One Woman Show 1960–1971, MoMA, New York—Review," *Financial Times*, May 25, 2015, https:// www.ft.com/content/52a8cf6e-fd79-11e4-9e96-00144feabdc0.

xxii *"Meghan Markle's treatment":* Author interview with Ray Connolly, July 27, 2022.

xxiii *"She is a painter, poet, sculptor":* Author email interview with Hans Ulrich Obrist, October 10, 2024.

xxiii *"I'd been told about this 'event'":* Sheff, *All We Are Saying*.

xxiv *"That's why they couldn't take Van Gogh":* Jann Wenner, "*Rolling Stone* Interview," *Rolling Stone*, December 1970, https://www.johnlennon.com/music/interviews /rolling-stone-interview-1970/.

xxiv *"The actual peace event":* Anthony Fawcett, *John Lennon: One Day at a Time* (New York: Grove Press, 1976); excerpt at https://www.imaginepeace.com/archives/15702.

xxv *"There was very much a sense":* Author interview with Barbara Graustark, October 9, 2023.

xxv *"Is there any contemporary art style":* Jonathan Jones, "Yoko Ono Show at Guggen-heim Shines Light on Pioneering Conceptual Artist," *Guardian*, March 13, 2014,

https://www.theguardian.com/artanddesign/2014/mar/13/yoko-ono-guggen
heim-bilbao-conceptual-influence.

xxv   *"The Conceptual Art Pioneer"*: Caroline Roux, "Yoko Ono, Tate Modern Review—
the Conceptual Art Pioneer Gets Her Due," *Financial Times*, February 13, 2024,
https://www.ft.com/content/015b77ad-f3e0-450e-bef2-f7b213ed9e60.

xxv   *"first female punk rocker"*: Kurt Cobain, interviewed by Cake Nunez and Al Kowalewski,
Flipside (May 1992), https://www.livenirvana.com/interviews/9203akcn/#gsc.tab=0.

xxv   *"She was one of the first"*: Yoko Ono, ed., *Memories of John Lennon* (New York: Harper-
Collins, 2005).

xxv   *Miley Cyrus:* "Why Miley Cyrus Got a Note from Yoko Ono Tattooed on Her Back,"
The Howard Stern Show, December 3, 2020.

xxv   *"Yoko is still one of the most"*: Peter Piatkowski, "Why Yoko Ono's Music Matters,"
Pop Matters, May 4, 2021, https://www.popmatters.com/why-yoko-onos-music
-matters#:~:text=As%20Kim%20Gordon%20once%20declared,so%20ahead%20
of%20her%20time.%E2%80%9D.

xxvi *"neo-disco queen"*: Jason Farago, "Hearing Yoko Ono All Over Again," *New York
Times,* June 25, 2015, https://www.nytimes.com/2015/06/28/arts/music/hearing
-yoko-ono-all-over-again.html.

xxvi *"People were focusing on the Beatles"*: Author interview with David Byrne, October 10,
2022.

xxvi *"Before there was Bono"*: Rich Thomas, "My Philosophy: Yoko Ono," *Magnetic,*
June 2, 2011, https://magneticmag.com/2011/06/my-philosophy-yoko-ono/.

xxvi *"She broke the freakin' mold"*: Author interview with Cyndi Lauper, January 24, 2023.

xxvi *"She's the teacher"*: Sheff, *All We Are Saying.*

xxvii *"Yoko's coming out of a hybrid"*: Amei Wallach, "The Widow Peaks," *New York Times,*
September 24, 2000, https://archive.nytimes.com/www.nytimes.com/library/magazine
/home/20000924mag-ono.html.

xxviii *"Imagine six apartments"*: Elton John, *Me* (New York: Henry Holt, 2019).

xxviii *"It is nice to keep oneself small"*: Yoko Ono, "To the Wesleyan People," January 23,
1966, https://www.flickr.com/photos/yokoonoofficial/2892207133.

xxix *"People like Carter"*: David Sheff, "The *Playboy* Interview with John Lennon and
Yoko Ono," *Playboy* (January 1981), https://www.playboy.com/magazine/articles
/1981/01/playboy-interview-john-lennon-and-yoko-ono/.

xxix *"This is a very important time"*: Sheff, *All We Are Saying.*

PART ONE: ABOVE US ONLY SKY

CHAPTER 1

3   *"My parents were close with each other"*: Betty Rollin, "Top Pop Merger: Lennon and
Ono, Inc.," *Look,* March 18, 1969.

3   *"I adored my mother"*: Chrissy Iley, "Yoko Ono: 'John's Affair Wasn't Hurtful to Me. I
Needed a Rest. I Needed Space,'" *Telegraph,* March 26, 2012, https://www.telegraph
.co.uk/culture/photography/9160041/Yoko-Ono-Johns-affair-wasnt-hurtful-to-me.
-I-needed-a-rest.-I-needed-space.html.

3   *"I'm glad that my mother"*: John Lennon and Yoko Ono, *John and Yoko/Plastic Ono
Band* (London: Thames and Hudson, 2020).

4 *"My mother used to"*: Ibid.

4 *richest man in Japan:* "Zenshiro Yasuda, 60, Japanese Financier," obituary, *New York Times*, October 9, 1937, https://www.nytimes.com/1937/10/09/archives/zenshiro -yasuda-60-japanese-financier-head-of-eight-banks-is.html.

4 *a patron:* Akiko Ono, email to the author, August 18, 2023.

4 *a "modern girl":* Alexandra Munroe, "Spirit of Yes: The Art and Life of Yoko Ono," in *Yes Yoko Ono,* eds. Alexandra Munroe and Jon Hendricks (New York: Harry N. Abrams, 2000); excerpt at https://web.archive.org/web/20160307183246/http://www .alexandramunroe.com/spirit-of-yes-the-art-and-life-of-yoko-ono-2/.

5 *impoverished samurai:* Ibid. and email to the author from Yugo Ono, Yoko's cousin, who is writing a history of the Ono family.

5 *"Grandmother told me":* Akiko Ono, email to the author, June 4, 2022.

5 *Isoko's family was Buddhist:* Lindsay Zoladz, "Yoko Ono and the Myth That Deserves to Die," *Vulture*, May 13, 2015, https://www.vulture.com/2015/05/yoko-ono-one -woman-show.html.

6 *"say good night":* Barbara Graustark, "The Lost 1981 Yoko Ono Interview," *Rolling Stone*, October 1, 1981, https://www.rollingstone.com/music/music-features/yoko -ono-cover-story-john-lennon-death-1234681088/.

6 *"She never spent so much time":* Lennon and Ono, *John and Yoko.*

6 *"didn't really want to admit":* Charles McCarry, "John Rennon's Excrusive Gloupie," *Esquire*, December 1970, https://classic.esquire.com/article/1970/12/1/john-ren nons-excrusive-gloupie.

6 *They were not to rock Yoko:* Yoko Ono, "Just Me," *Bungei Shunju* (September 1974), published in Japan as *Yoko Ono, Just Me!* (Tokyo: Kodansha, 1990).

6 *"My mother was germophobic":* Ibid.

7 *"I think my hands actually shrunk":* Lennon and Ono, *John and Yoko.*

8 *"I would go to see a film":* Jieun Rhee, "Performing the Other: Yoko Ono's 'Cut Piece,'" *Art History* 28 (February 2005), https://www.academia.edu/73702682/Per forming_the_Other_Yoko_Onos_Cut_Piece.

8 *"It didn't occur to me":* Craig McLean, "Yoko Ono: Back to Where She Once Belonged," *Times Online*, March 6, 2010.

8 *"My mother felt":* Yoko Ono, interview with Michael Kimmelman, *TimesTalks*, October 5, 2012, https://www.youtube.com/watch?v=0WIosw1gv50.

CHAPTER 2

11 *"Only a few months":* Jieun Rhee, "Performing the Other: Yoko Ono's 'Cut Piece,'" *Art History* 28 (February 2005), https://www.academia.edu/73702682/Performing _the_Other_Yoko_Onos_Cut_Piece.

11 *"Before leaving":* "Defining Moments: Yoko Ono," *Defining Moments*, BBC News, July 13, 2003, http://news.bbc.co.uk/1/hi/world/asia-pacific/3058721.stm.

12 *Yoko's high fever:* Austin Allen, "'My Beautiful Never-Nevers': Yoko Ono's Poetry Revisited," *Los Angeles Review of Books*, April 4, 2022, https://lareviewofbooks.org/article /my-beautiful-never-nevers-yoko-onos-poetry-revisited/. Her fever is also referred to in Louis Menand, "Yoko Ono's Art of Defiance," *New Yorker*, June 13, 2022, https:// www.newyorker.com/magazine/2022/06/20/yoko-onos-art-of-defiance.

12 *watched Tokyo burn:* Menand, "Yoko Ono's Art of Defiance."

12 *"gave us a hard time":* Paula Devlin, "Go Yoko," *Vogue,* June 8, 2012, https://www
.imaginepeace.com/archives/17770.

12 *an American spy:* Yoko Ono, "When Molecules Rise, They Converge," sleeve notes
on *Rising,* 1995, https://www.imaginepeace.com/archives/12042/comment-page-1.

12 *"being stoned by the village kids":* Ibid.

12 *"I filled my knapsack":* Nell Beram and Carolyn Boriss-Krimsky, *Yoko Ono: Collector
of Skies* (New York: Amulet Books, 2013).

13 *"Eat this imaginary apple":* Author interview with Keisuke Ono, June 16, 2022.

13 *"It did fill her up":* Ibid.

13 *diagnosed with pleurisy:* Ono, "When Molecules Rise."

13 *abused by a doctor:* Ibid.

13 *kissing her:* Yoko refers to being kissed on the mouth in the text for "Vertical Memory"; see https://www.flickr.com/photos/mickeyono2005/5578886898.

13 *As many as 140,000:* Alex Wellerstein, "Counting the Dead at Hiroshima and Nagasaki," *Bulletin of the Atomic Scientists,* August 4, 2020, https://thebulletin.org/2020
/08/counting-the-dead-at-hiroshima-and-nagasaki/.

13 *"was hopeless":* Author interview with Masako Ono, June 16, 2022.

14 *"Tokyo, this is Tokyo":* Simon Schama, "Interview with Yoko Ono," *Financial Times,*
June 1, 2012, https://www.ft.com/content/eca25228-a9eb-11e1-9772-00144feabdc0.

14 *"I saw this tall, handsome man":* Setsuko Ono, interview for *Family History: Yoko
Ono,* NHK Television, 2017.

14 *Bank of Tokyo:* Alexandra Munroe, "Spirit of Yes: The Art and Life of Yoko Ono,"
in *Yes Yoko Ono,* eds. Alexandra Munroe and Jon Hendricks (New York: Harry N.
Abrams, 2000); excerpt at https://web.archive.org/web/20160307183246/http:/www
.alexandramunroe.com/spirit-of-yes-the-art-and-life-of-yoko-ono-2/.

14 *"My father had a huge desk":* Yoko Ono, "Feeling the Space," *New York Times,* August 24,
1973, https://www.nytimes.com/1973/08/24/archives/feeling-the-space.html.

14 *"He was going somewhere":* Caroline Coon, "In Defense of Yoko Ono," Yahoo! Entertainment, July 2, 2012, https://www.yahoo.com/entertainment/rock-backpages
-flashback-defense-yoko-ono-1974-132405253.html.

15 *"My God, if I didn't count them":* Jonathan Cott, "Yoko Ono and Her Sixteen-Track
Voice," *Rolling Stone,* March 18, 1971, https://www.rollingstone.com/music/music
-news/yoko-ono-and-her-sixteen-track-voice-237782/.

15 *multiple attempts as a teenager:* Barbara Graustark, "The Lost 1981 Yoko Ono Interview," *Rolling Stone,* October 1, 1981, https://www.rollingstone.com/music/music
-features/yoko-ono-cover-story-john-lennon-death-1234681088/. Yoko also talks
about her suicide attempts in John Doran, "Yoko Ono's Quiet Revolution Has Not
Always Been So Quiet," *Stool Pigeon,* September 2009, https://www.flickr.com
/photos/yokoonoofficial/3943436576.

15 *she compared to Eton:* Charles McCarry, "John Rennon's Excrusive Gloupie," *Esquire,*
December 1970, https://classic.esquire.com/article/1970/12/1/john-rennons-excru
sive-gloupie.

16 *"My father was listening very carefully":* Melody Sumner et al., eds., *The Guests Go In
to Supper* (New York: Burning Books, 1986).

16 *"also because he knew":* Author interview with Keisuke Ono, June 16, 2022.

CHAPTER 3

17   *"Well, Yoko, you're too opinionated"*: Caroline Coon, "In Defense of Yoko Ono," Yahoo! Entertainment, July 2, 2012, https://www.yahoo.com/entertainment/rock-backpages-flashback-defense-yoko-ono-1974-132405253.html.

18   *"teaches you that you have the right"*: "Notable Alumni," Sarah Lawrence College, https://www.sarahlawrence.edu/about/notable-alumni/, accessed June 24, 2024.

18   *"with framed photographs of their horses"*: Author interview with Betty Rollin, November 24, 2021.

18   *"[The school] attracted a certain artistic, high-strung nonconformist"*: Author interview with Erica Abeel, November 22, 2021.

19   *"Mel had started dating Yoko"*: Heather Clark, *Red Comet: The Short Life and Blazing Art of Sylvia Plath* (New York: Knopf, 2020).

19   *"I danced with Yoko"*: Author assistant's interview with Mel Woody, August 31, 2022.

20   *"I was writing in the style"*: Paul Zollo, "A Conversation with Yoko," *American Songwriter* (1992), updated August 2, 2021, https://americansongwriter.com/a-conversation-with-yoko/.

20   *"If you wished"*: Hans Ulrich Obrist, "Mix a Building and the Wind: An Interview with Yoko Ono," 2001, https://www.imaginepeace.com/archives/2678/comment-page-1.

21   *"The grapefruit, a citrus hybrid"*: Christophe Cherix, "Yoko Ono's Lightning Years," in *Yoko Ono: One Woman Show, 1960–1971*, exhibition catalog, ed. Klaus Biesenbach and Christophe Cherix (Museum of Modern Art, 2015), https://www.moma.org/momaorg/shared/pdfs/docs/publication_pdf/3218/MoMA_YokoOno_PREVIEW.pdf.

22   *"I was doing all that"*: Jonathan Cott, "Yoko Ono and Her Sixteen-Track Voice," *Rolling Stone,* March 18, 1971, https://www.rollingstone.com/music/music-news/yoko-ono-and-her-sixteen-track-voice-237782/.

22   *"We'd often go into the city"*: Frank Alagno, "Expatriate Dream: A Woman's Journey in the 50's," *Metropolitan Spirit,* 2022, https://www.themetropolitanspirit.com/fiction.html.

22   *"Whenever I wrote a poem"*: Cott, "Yoko Ono and Her Sixteen-Track Voice."

22   feeling *"asphyxiated"*: Paola Genone, "Yoko On Yes," *Madame Figaro,* February 14, 2016, https://madame.lefigaro.fr/celebrites/yoko-ono-au-musee-dart-contemporain-de-lyon-050216-112319.

CHAPTER 4

24   *"because of social pressure"*: Author interview with Beate Gordon, 1983.

24   *waitressed and sometimes cooked*: Hendrick Hertzberg, "John and Yoko Take Manhattan," *New Yorker,* January 1, 1972, https://www.newyorker.com/magazine/2022/08/29/john-and-yoko-take-manhattan.

24   *she was fired*: Ibid.

25   *lighting matches*: Jonathan Cott, "Yoko Ono and Her Sixteen-Track Voice," *Rolling Stone,* March 18, 1971, https://www.rollingstone.com/music/music-news/yoko-ono-and-her-sixteen-track-voice-237782/.

25   *"I couldn't figure out"*: Ibid.

26 *"It has been called 'the Silent Piece'"*: Alex Ross, "John Cage's Art of Noise," *New Yorker*, September 27, 2010, https://www.newyorker.com/magazine/2010/10/04/searching-for-silence#:~:text=He%20was%20performing%20"4%2733,outside%20during%20the%20first%20movement.

26 *"What Cage gave me"*: Hans Ulrich Obrist, "Mix a Building and the Wind: An Interview with Yoko Ono," 2001, https://www.imaginepeace.com/archives/2678/comment-page-1.

27 *"under candlelight"*: Mark Kemp, "Yoko Ono Reconsidered," *Option* (July 1992), https://beatpatrol.wordpress.com/2014/12/28/mark-kemp-yoko-ono-reconsidered-1992/.

27 *"A 'stepping painting'"*: Madeline Bocaro, *In Your Mind: The Infinite Universe of Yoko Ono* (New York: Conceptual Books, 2016).

28 *The sound of her moving hair*: Cott, "Yoko Ono and Her Sixteen-Track Voice."

29 *"chick who owns this loft"*: Midori Yoshimoto, *Into Performance: Japanese Women Artists in New York* (Piscataway, NJ: Rutgers University Press, 2005); excerpt at https://www.academia.edu/15515816/Yoko_Ono_One_Woman_Show_1960_1971.

29 *"Women in art were only known"*: Caroline Coon, "In Defense of Yoko Ono," Yahoo! Entertainment, July 2, 2012, https://www.yahoo.com/entertainment/rock-backpages-flashback-defense-yoko-ono-1974-132405253.html.

29 *"Yoko became an important person"*: Paul Taylor, "Yoko Ono's New Bronze Age at the Whitney," *New York Times*, February 5, 1989, https://www.nytimes.com/1989/02/05/arts/art-yoko-ono-s-new-bronze-age-at-the-whitney.html.

30 *"for instance, by laughing aloud"*: *Yoko Ono: One Woman Show, 1960–1971*, exhibition catalog, ed. Klaus Biesenbach and Christophe Cherix (Museum of Modern Art, 2015), https://www.moma.org/momaorg/shared/pdfs/docs/publication_pdf/3218/MoMA_YokoOno_PREVIEW.pdf.

30 *"My music is performed"*: Yoko Ono, "9 Concert Pieces for John Cage, December 15, 1966," in *Yes Yoko Ono*, eds. Alexandra Munroe and Jon Hendricks (New York: Harry N. Abrams, 2000).

CHAPTER 5

34 *"actually worked to my advantage"*: Yoko Ono, "Summer of 1961," in *Yoko Ono: One Woman Show, 1960–1971*, exhibition catalog, ed. Klaus Biesenbach and Christophe Cherix (Museum of Modern Art, 2015), https://www.moma.org/momaorg/shared/pdfs/docs/publication_pdf/3218/MoMA_YokoOno_PREVIEW.pdf.

34 *The exhibition was important*: Ibid.

34 *"with a pair of"*: Ibid.

35 *"It had many meanings"*: Ibid.

35 *"Purge the world of"*: Clive Phillpot, "Fluxus: Magazines, Manifestos, Multum in Parvo," https://georgemaciunas.com/about/cv/manifesto-i/.

35 *"You have no idea"*: Author interview with Alexandra Munroe, September 16, 2022.

36 *299-seat*: *Yoko Ono: One Woman Show*.

36 *"Whenever I go to a toilet"*: Jonathan Cott, "Yoko Ono and Her Sixteen-Track Voice," *Rolling Stone*, March 18, 1971, https://www.rollingstone.com/music/music-news/yoko-ono-and-her-sixteen-track-voice-237782/.

36 *"big moment for me"*: Ibid.

36   *"One thing you can surely say"*: Andy Rich, "Far-Out Music Is Played at Carnegie," *New York Times*, November 25, 1961, https://www.nytimes.com/1961/11/25 /archives/farout-music-is-played-at-carnegie.html.

37   *"Ono, I assume it was Ono"*: Jill Johnston, "Life and Art," *Village Voice*, December 7, 1961.

37   *"When I performed at Carnegie Recital"*: Madeline Bocaro, *In Your Mind: The Infinite Universe of Yoko Ono* (New York: Conceptual Books, 2016).

37   *"There's one particular kabuki singing style"*: Robert Palmer refers to his interview in his liner notes for *Onobox*; see https://www.johnlennon.com/music/with-yoko-ono/onobox/.

37   *"Hers was a voice from another world"*: Author interview with Laurie Anderson, October 16, 2022.

38   *"Like Fluxus, Gutai"*: Louis Menand, "Yoko Ono's Art of Defiance," *New Yorker*, June 13, 2022, https://www.newyorker.com/magazine/2022/06/20/yoko-onos-art-of-defiance.

38   *"working out their dissatisfaction"*: Author interview with Tadanori Yokoo, June 16, 2022.

39   *"Since the event I had put on"*: Yoko Ono, "Just Me," *Bungei Shunju* (September 1974), published in Japan as *Yoko Ono, Just Me!* (Tokyo: Kodansha, 1990).

39   *"She gently, almost imperceptibly"*: Jason Farago, "Hearing Yoko Ono All Over Again," *New York Times*, June 25, 2015, https://www.nytimes.com/2015/06/28/arts /music/hearing-yoko-ono-all-over-again.html.

39   *"The audience became exhausted"*: Yoko Ono, "Just Me."

39   *"What a strange artist"*: Glenn D. Lowry, "Forward," in *Yoko Ono: One Woman Show*.

39   *"don't see any originality"*: Jieun Rhee, "Performing the Other: Yoko Ono's 'Cut Piece,'" *Art History* 28 (February 2005), https://www.academia.edu/73702682/Per forming_the_Other_Yoko_Onos_Cut_Piece.

40   *"women wearing pants"*: Jon Weiner, "Yoko Floating Alone," *Mother Jones*, June 1984.

40   *"vocal lines that pirouette"*: Seth Colter Walls, "Give Yoko Ono a Chance," *Slate*, September 26, 2012, https://www.slate.com/blogs/browbeat/2012/09/26/yoko kimthurston_and_john_cage_shock_yoko_ono_has_been_making_interesting _music_for_50_years_.html.

40   *"Jon Keji shokku"*: Zachary Woolfe, "John Cage Shock: When Japan Fell for Cage and Vice Versa," *New York Times*, September 23, 2023, https://www.nytimes.com/2023 /09/23/arts/music/john-cage-japan-society.html.

40   *"on its ear"*: Mark Swed, "A Dean of Japanese Music Talks Boundaries, John Cage, and Yoko Ono," *Los Angeles Times*, May 15, 2015, https://www.latimes.com/enter tainment/arts/la-ca-cm-toshi-ichiyanagi-profile-20150517-column.html.

40   *"Who was I"*: Alexandra Munroe, "Spirit of Yes: The Art and Life of Yoko Ono," in *Yes Yoko Ono*, eds. Alexandra Munroe and Jon Hendricks (New York: Harry N. Abrams, 2000); excerpt at https://web.archive.org/web/20160307183246/http://www .alexandramunroe.com/spirit-of-yes-the-art-and-life-of-yoko-ono-2/.

41   *"almost unconsciously"*: Yoko Ono, "Just Me."

41   *she took a handful of pills*: Ibid.

CHAPTER 6

43   *"I was a beat"*: Jim Calio, "Yoko Ono's Ex-Husband, Tony Cox, Reveals His Strange Life Since Fleeing with Their Daughter 14 Years Ago," *People*, February 3, 1986, https://people.com/archive/yoko-onos-ex-husband-tony-cox-reveals-his-strange -life-since-fleeing-with-their-daughter-14-years-ago-vol-25-no-5/.

43 *Tony traveled:* Tony Cox, letter to the author, July 12, 2022.

43 *"He was dedicated":* Yoko Ono, "Just Me," *Bungei Shunju* (September 1974), published in Japan as *Yoko Ono, Just Me!* (Tokyo: Kodansha, 1990).

43 *"He could convince":* Author interview with Jeffrey Perkins, July 15, 2022.

44 *"We were treated badly":* Cox, letter.

44 *"The forerunners of what we now call hippies":* Yoko Ono, "Just Me."

44 *"I was still struggling":* Barbara Graustark, "The Lost 1981 Yoko Ono Interview," *Rolling Stone*, October 1, 1981, https://www.rollingstone.com/music/music-features /yoko-ono-cover-story-john-lennon-death-1234681088/.

44 *"I wasn't particularly taking care of her":* David Sheff, *All We Are Saying: The Last Major Interview with John Lennon and Yoko Ono*, rev. ed. (New York: St. Martin's Griffin, 2020).

44 *"The time that I decided":* John Doran, "Yoko Ono: Naked Ambition," *Stool Pigeon*, October 2009, https://www.rocksbackpages.com/Library/Article/yoko-ono-naked -ambition.

45 *"We took a drive out to the country":* Perkins, interview.

46 *"Grapefruit was like a cure":* Jonathan Cott, "Yoko Ono and Her Sixteen-Track Voice," *Rolling Stone*, March 18, 1971, https://www.rollingstone.com/music/music -news/yoko-ono-and-her-sixteen-track-voice-237782/.

47 *"served as a kind of portable museum":* Christophe Cherix, "Yoko Ono's Lightning Years," in *Yoko Ono: One Woman Show, 1960–1971*, exhibition catalog, ed. Klaus Biesenbach and Christophe Cherix (Museum of Modern Art, 2015), https://www .moma.org/momaorg/shared/pdfs/docs/publication_pdf/3218/MoMA_YokoOno _PREVIEW.pdf.

47 *"When I left home at 17":* Cyndi Lauper, JohnLennon.com, https://www.johnlennon .com/music/with-yoko-ono/walking-on-thin-ice/, accessed on September 30, 2024.

47 *"He argued":* Author interview with Dan Richter, June 6, 2022.

48 *"By being in a bag":* Yoko Ono, "Bag Piece (1964), performed during *Perpetual Fluxfest*, Cinematheque, New York, June 27, 1965," Museum of Modern Art, https:// www.moma.org/audio/playlist/15/374.

CHAPTER 7

49 *"I just had to rescue myself":* Craig McLean, "Yoko Ono: Back to Where She Once Belonged," *Times Online*, March 6, 2010.

49 *"Tony yelled":* Author interview with Jeffrey Perkins, July 15, 2022.

49 *"Yoko used to call me":* Author interview with Beate Gordon, 1983.

50 *"drive him nuts":* Perkins, interview.

50 *two hundred shares:* Paul Taylor, "Yoko Ono's New Bronze Age at the Whitney," *New York Times*, February 5, 1989, https://www.nytimes.com/1989/02/05/arts/art-yoko -ono-s-new-bronze-age-at-the-whitney.html.

51 *"As the flame burns down":* Chrissie Iles, "Erotic Conceptualism: The Films of Yoko Ono," in *Yes Yoko Ono*, eds. Alexandra Munroe and Jon Hendricks (New York: Harry N. Abrams, 2000).

51 *became known as:* Many of Yoko's films and other works had multiple names; some changed over time, and many pieces shared the same name.

51 *"What initially inspired":* Yoko Ono, "Just Me," *Bungei Shunju* (September 1974), published in Japan as *Yoko Ono, Just Me!* (Tokyo: Kodansha, 1990).

52 *"there were four pyramids"*: Author interview with Jill Richter, September 21, 2022.

52 *a manifesto*: Kristine Stiles, "Synopsis of the Destruction in Art Symposium and Its Theoretical Significance," *The Act* (Spring 1987), https://monoskop.org/images/c/c9 /Stiles_Kristine_1987_Synopsis_of_the_Destruction_in_Art_Symposium_and_Its _Theoretical_Significance.pdf.

53 *"could not have been more poignant"*: Kristine Stiles, "Destruction in Art," in *Yes Yoko Ono*.

53 *"Four or five very hot-blooded"*: Yoko Ono, "The Making of 'Imagine,'" Imaginejohn yoko.com, https://imaginejohnyoko.com/the-films/.

53 *"She gave what can only be described"*: Cornelius Cardew, *Cornelius Cardew: A Reader*, ed. Edwin Prévost (Harlow, England: Copula, 2006).

54 *"He wanted it to be both of us"*: Betty Rollin, "Top Pop Merger: Lennon and Ono, Inc.," *Look*, March 18, 1969.

54 *"If parents don't stay"*: Yoko Ono, "Just Me."

54 *"I held Kyoko in my arms"*: Ibid.

55 *"very acidy afternoon"*: Kate Bernard, "Playing to the Gallery," *Guardian*, November 4, 2006, https://www.theguardian.com/artanddesign/2006/nov/05/art1.

55 *"Other galleries . . . it was dull"*: Author interview with John Dunbar, October 25, 2022.

PART TWO: THE BALLAD OF YOKO AND JOHN

CHAPTER 8

60 *"Once I give the instruction"*: Christophe Cherix, *Yoko Ono: One Woman Show*, Museum of Modern Art, https://www.moma.org/audio/playlist/15/379.

60 *"You are supposed to mend"*: Yoko Ono, instruction for "Mend Piece for John" from 1967; see https://x.com/yokoono/status/1711064035951595849.

60 *"I lost her twice"*: David Sheff, *All We Are Saying: The Last Major Interview with John Lennon and Yoko Ono*, rev. ed. (New York: St. Martin's Griffin, 2020).

61 *"I was crying for help"*: Ibid.

61 *John took Dunbar up on the invitation*: Author interview with John Dunbar, October 5, 2022.

61 *"The place wasn't really opened"*: The story of Yoko and John's meeting at Indica has been told many times. This is from Sheff, *All We Are Saying*.

62 *"It's so symbolic"*: Betty Rollin, "Top Pop Merger: Lennon and Ono, Inc.," *Look*, March 18, 1969.

62 *"Let him hammer"*: Sheff, *All We Are Saying*.

63 *"It's absolutely not true"*: Dunbar, interview.

63 *"She didn't understand"*: Author interview with Dan Richter, June 6, 2022.

63 *"I had heard about the Beatles"*: John Lennon and Yoko Ono, *Imagine John Yoko*, limited ed. (London: Thames and Hudson, 2018).

64 *"[In] the crowd I was in"*: Andrew Smith, "Just Imagine: Yoko Ono," *Observer Music Monthly*, November 4, 2001.

64 *"By the time I met John"*: Caroline Coon, "In Defense of Yoko Ono," Yahoo! Entertainment, July 2, 2012, https://www.yahoo.com/entertainment/rock-backpages -flashback-defense-yoko-ono-1974-132405253.html.

64 *"[The show] was a lot of fun"*: Dunbar, interview.

64 *"It was pretty good"*: Paul Zollo, "A Conversation with Yoko," *American Songwriter* (1992), updated August 2, 2021, https://americansongwriter.com/a-conversation -with-yoko/.

65 *"I sort of looked away"*: Jann Wenner, "Lennon Remembers," *Rolling Stone,* February 1, 1971, https://www.rollingstone.com/music/music-news/lennon-remem bers-part-two-187100/.

65 *"I used to read it"*: Ibid.

65 *"If you do some of the things"*: Alan Smith, "John Lennon & Yoko Ono: Doing the Rounds for Publicity," *NME,* July 31, 1971.

65 *"Nothing about bottoms is aggressive"*: Yoko Ono, "Just Me," *Bungei Shunju* (September 1974), published in Japan as *Yoko Ono, Just Me!* (Tokyo: Kodansha, 1990).

65 *"It wasn't just put together"*: Scott MacDonald, "Yoko Ono: Ideas on Film," *Film Quarterly* (Fall 1989), https://womenfilmeditors.princeton.edu/assets/pdfs/ONO _Ideas_on_Film_MacDonald.pdf.

65 *"In 50 years or so"*: Yoko Ono, "On *Film No. 4* (in Taking the Bottoms of 365 Saints of Our Time)," in *Thirteen Film Scores by Yoko Ono 1968* (self-published, 1968); excerpt at https://www.degruyter.com/document/doi/10.1525/9780520957411-097/pdf.

66 *"Miss Yoko Ono's bottom"*: "No to Miss Ono," *Evening Standard,* April 17, 1967, https://www.royalalberthall.com/about-the-hall/news/2017/april/boxing-bottoms -pop-music-and-elephants-banned-at-the-royal-albert-hall/.

66 *"many happy endings"*: Jonathan Cott, "Yoko Ono and Her Sixteen-Track Voice," *Rolling Stone,* March 18, 1971, https://www.rollingstone.com/music/music-news /yoko-ono-and-her-sixteen-track-voice-237782/.

66 *fifty years later*: Lydia Smith, "Boxing, Bottoms, Pop Music and Elephants: Banned at the Royal Albert Hall," Royal Albert Hall, April 10, 2017, https://www.royalalber thall.com/about-the-hall/news/2017/april/boxing-bottoms-pop-music-and-ele phants-banned-at-the-royal-albert-hall/.

66 *"When the audience discovered"*: Yoko Ono, ed., *Memories of John Lennon* (New York: HarperCollins, 2005).

67 *"In London, everybody was talking"*: Melody Sumner et al., eds., *The Guests Go In to Supper* (New York: Burning Books, 1986).

67 *"One morning at breakfast"*: Cynthia Lennon, *John: A Biography* (London: Hodder and Stoughton, 2012).

67 *"as important as Sgt. Pepper"*: Wenner, "Lennon Remembers."

67 *"Cards kept coming through the door"*: Philip Norman, *John Lennon: The Life* (New York: HarperCollins, 2008).

67 *"There were times"*: Yoko Ono, "John Lennon Remembered by Yoko: 'We Were in Love Desperately,'" *Uncut* (September 2003), https://www.uncut.co.uk/features /john-lennon-remembered-by-yoko-ono-we-were-in-love-desperately-71166/.

CHAPTER 9

69 *"I said, 'It's very sweet'"*: Yoko Ono, "John Lennon Remembered by Yoko: 'We Were in Love Desperately,'" *Uncut* (September 2003), https://www.uncut.co.uk/features /john-lennon-remembered-by-yoko-ono-we-were-in-love-desperately-71166/.

70 *"I realized that there was a half-empty space"*: Yoko Ono, 2002; posted on Twitter on July 5, 2020, https://x.com/yokoono/status/1279822492744499201.

70 *"There was something sad"*: Jon Wiener, "Yoko Floating Alone," *Mother Jones*, June 1984.

70 *"Well, why don't you"*: Yoko Ono, "John Lennon Remembered by Yoko."

70 *"I just thought"*: Ibid.

70 *"totally on the same wavelength"*: Philip Norman, *John Lennon: The Life* (New York: HarperCollins, 2008).

71 *"too uptight"*: Jann Wenner, "Lennon Remembers," *Rolling Stone*, February 1, 1971, https://www.rollingstone.com/music/music-news/lennon-remembers-part-two -187100/.

71 *"Like the half-destroyed room at its heart"*: Jonathan Jones, "Yoko Ono Show at Guggenheim Shines Light on Pioneering Conceptual Artist," *Guardian*, March 13, 2014, https://www.theguardian.com/artanddesign/2014/mar/13/yoko-ono-guggen heim-bilbao-conceptual-influence.

71 *"Ornette told me"*: Miya Masaoka, "Unfinished Music: An Interview with Yoko Ono," *San Francisco Bay Guardian*, August 27, 1997, http://miyamasaoka.com/writ ings-by-miya-masaoka/1997/unfinished-music/.

71 *"Listen, if your band is willing"*: Melody Sumner et al., eds., *The Guests Go In to Supper* (New York: Burning Books, 1986).

72 *"When I said the piece had to be mine"*: Masaoka, "Unfinished Music."

72 *"Okay. I'll go back"*: Yoko Ono, radio interview by Jody Denberg, 1977, https://every thing2.com/user/pingouin/writeups/aos?showwidget=showCs510422.

72 *"some sort of kooky girl"*: Sumner et al., *The Guests Go In to Supper*.

72 *It was a set of written instructions*: John Lennon and Yoko Ono, *John and Yoko/Plastic Ono Band* (London: Thames and Hudson, 2020).

72 *"Now, I'm not a fan"*: S. Victor Aaron, "WTF?! Wednesdays: Yoko Ono with Ornette Coleman, 'AOS' (1968)," *Something Else Reviews*, July 31, 2013, https://somethingelse reviews.com/2013/07/31/wtf-wednesdays-yoko-ono-with-ornette-coleman-aos-1968/.

73 *"John was becoming increasingly cold"*: Cynthia Lennon, *John: A Biography* (London: Hodder and Stoughton, 2012).

73 *"trying to reach God"*: David Sheff, *All We Are Saying: The Last Major Interview with John Lennon and Yoko Ono,* rev. ed. (St. Martin's Griffin: New York, 2020).

73 *"I'm a cloud"*: Betty Rollin, "Top Pop Merger: Lennon and Ono, Inc.," *Look*, March 18, 1969.

74 *"all this far-out stuff"*: Lennon and Ono, *John and Yoko*.

74 *"She was doing her funny voices"*: Sheff, *All We Are Saying*.

74 *"Yoko and I were on the same wavelength"*: Ray Coleman, *Lennon: The Definitive Biography* (New York: Harper Perennial, 1992).

74 *"He's changed everything"*: Richard Williams, "John and Yoko Interview," *Melody Maker*, December 20, 1969.

CHAPTER 10

75 *Yoko said that wasn't true*: Yoko Ono, *Desert Island Discs*, BBC Radio, June 10, 2007, https://www.bbc.co.uk/sounds/play/b007nc7n.

75 *"We both knew this was it"*: Philip Norman, *John Lennon: The Life* (New York: HarperCollins, 2008).

75 *"They never thought about the other side of it"*: *The Real Yoko Ono* (documentary), part 3 of 6, 2001.

76 *"The other Beatles were pissed off"*: Barry Miles, email to the author, January 9, 2023.

76 *"When John hitched up with Yoko"*: John Lennon and Yoko Ono, *Imagine*, 1972; script available at http://www.script-o-rama.com/movie_scripts/i/imagine-john-len non-script-transcript.html.

76 *"The Beatles had developed"*: Ray Connolly, *Being John Lennon* (London: Pegasus, 2018).

76 *"I was just living"*: Paul Zollo, "A Conversation with Yoko," *American Songwriter* (1992), updated August 2, 2021, https://americansongwriter.com/a-conversation -with-yoko/.

77 *he had Yoko sing a line*: "The Continuing Story of Bungalow Bill," *The Beatles Bible*, https://www.beatlesbible.com/songs/the-continuing-story-of-bungalow-bill/#:~:text =The%20most%20notable%20feature%20of,her%20shaky%20grasp%20of%20mel ody, accessed August 12, 2024.

77 *"Take 18 was different"*: Mark Lewisohn, *The Beatles Recording Sessions* (New York: Harmony Books, 1988).

77 *"was unbending"*: Connolly, *Being John Lennon*.

77 *"Once I heard her stuff"*: David Sheff, *All We Are Saying: The Last Major Interview with John Lennon and Yoko Ono*, rev. ed. (New York: St. Martin's Griffin, 2020).

77 *"She's a musician"*: Zollo, "A Conversation with Yoko."

78 *"Our sculpture is two acorns"*: Yoko Ono, posted on Twitter, April 22, 2022, https://x .com/johnlennon/status/1517509093069660161.

78 *Hecklers yelled*: Philip Norman, *John Lennon: The Life* (New York: HarperCollins, 2008).

78 *"At that time Yoko was on the scene"*: Author interview with Ray Connolly, July 27, 2022.

79 *"'You and your Jap bastard'"*: Maurice Hindle et al., "Interview with John Lennon," *Unit*, January 1969, https://filmboards.com/t/John-Lennon/Lennon-on-Lennon -3342040/.

79 *"Two of us against the world"*: Barbara Graustark, "The Lost 1981 Yoko Ono Inter-view," *Rolling Stone*, October 1, 1981, https://www.rollingstone.com/music/music -features/yoko-ono-cover-story-john-lennon-death-1234681088/.

79 *"girl with kaleidoscope eyes"*: Sheff, *All We Are Saying*.

79 *"the fulfillment of my whole life"*: Ibid.

79 *"We saw each other's"*: Barbara Graustark, *Yoko Ono: Then and Now* (documentary), 1984.

79 *"I always had this dream"*: John Lennon and Yoko Ono, interview by Peter McCabe and Robert Schonfeld, *Penthouse*, September 5, 1971, http://www.beatlesinter views.org/db1971.0905.beatles.html.

80 *"I was thinking that Jimi Hendrix"*: Connolly, *Being John Lennon*.

81 *"I did not give any instructions"*: Hans Ulrich Obrist, "Mix a Building and the Wind: An Interview with Yoko Ono," 2001, https://www.imaginepeace.com/archives/2678 /comment-page-1.

81   *"When we shot the picture"*: Yoko Ono, "Just Me," *Bungei Shunju* (September 1974), published in Japan as *Yoko Ono, Just Me!* (Tokyo: Kodansha, 1990).

82   *"We were mainly concerned"*: Jonathan Cott, "John Lennon: The *Rolling Stone* Interview," *Rolling Stone*, November 23, 1968, https://www.imaginepeace.com/archives/7636#:~:text=Yoko%3A%20The%20films%20SMILE%20and,once%20in%20a%20billion%20years.

83   *"The girl in the film did not know"*: Scott MacDonald, "Yoko Ono: Ideas on Film," *A Critical Cinema*, May 1, 1989, https://womenfilmeditors.princeton.edu/assets/pdfs/ONO_Ideas_on_Film_MacDonald.pdf.

83   *"The cameraman doesn't say anything"*: Yoko Ono, interview with Michael Kimmelman, *TimesTalks,* October 5, 2012, https://www.youtube.com/watch?v=0WIosw1gv50.

CHAPTER 11

85   *The musician James Taylor*: Jenny Stevens, "'I Was a Bad Influence on the Beatles,'" *Guardian*, February 17, 2020, https://www.theguardian.com/music/2020/feb/17/james-taylor-i-was-a-bad-influence-on-the-beatles-lennon-love-and-a-life-in-song.

86   *"He doesn't even say hello"*: Jann Wenner, "Lennon Remembers," *Rolling Stone*, January 21, 1972, https://www.rollingstone.com/music/music-news/lennon-remembers-part-one-186693/.

86   *"Sometimes they seemed fine"*: Author interview with Dan Richter, June 6, 2022.

86   *"breakup film"*: Rob Sheffield, "The Long, Winding, and Weird Legacy of the Beatles' Notorious 'Let It Be' Movie," *Rolling Stone*, April 18, 2024, https://www.rollingstone.com/music/music-features/beatles-let-it-be-movie-peter-jackson-1235006477/.

86   *"dimly lit portrayal"*: David Remnick, "Paul McCartney Doesn't Really Want to Stop the Show," *New Yorker*, October 18, 2021, https://www.newyorker.com/magazine/2021/10/18/paul-mccartney-doesnt-really-want-to-stop-the-show.

86   *"They were all in different stages of ennui"*: Author interview with Michael Lindsay-Hogg, October 10, 2022.

87   *"So for the first time"*: Ibid.

87   *"They loved playing together"*: Ibid.

87   *"We probably do need a central daddy figure"*: *The Beatles: Get Back,* directed by Peter Jackson (Disney, 2021), https://brianhassett.com/2021/12/the-beatles-get-back-time-coded-and-annotated/.

87   *"difficult [writing songs] with Yoko there"*: Ibid.

87   *"The only thing about being in"*: Betty Rollin, "Top Pop Merger: Lennon and Ono, Inc.," *Look*, March 18, 1969.

88   *John had suggested:* Melody Sumner et al., eds., *The Guests Go In to Supper* (New York: Burning Books, 1986), https://www.imaginepeace.com/archives/2577.

88   *"I'd never really wanted to be married"*: Philip Norman, *John Lennon: The Life* (New York: HarperCollins, 2008).

88   *"Because we're romantic"*: David Sheff, *All We Are Saying: The Last Major Interview with John Lennon and Yoko Ono,* rev. ed. (New York: St. Martin's Griffin, 2020).

88   *"We knew that we shouldn't"*: Caroline Coon, "In Defense of Yoko Ono," Yahoo!

Entertainment, July 2, 2012, https://www.yahoo.com/entertainment/rock-backpages -flashback-defense-yoko-ono-1974-132405253.html.

89 *"came directly from Yoko"*: Anthony Fawcett, *John Lennon: One Day at a Time* (New York: Grove Press, 1976); excerpt at https://www.imaginepeace.com/archives/15702.

89 *"For us, it was the only way"*: Ibid.

89 *"We're going to stay in bed"*: "Almanac: John and Yoko's 'Bed-In for Peace,'" *Sunday Morning,* CBS, March 25, 2018, https://www.cbsnews.com/news/almanac-john-len non-yoko-ono-bed-in-for-peace/.

89 *"There we were"*: *The Beatles Anthology* (San Francisco: Chronicle Books, 2002).

90 *"It's the best idea we've had yet"*: Fawcett, *John Lennon.*

90 *"Yoko and I are quite willing"*: Ibid.

90 *"If people did interviews"*: John Lennon and Yoko Ono, *The David Frost Show,* aired June 14, 1969, https://www.beatlesbible.com/1969/06/14/television-john-lennon -yoko-ono-david-frost-show/,

91 *"I think that everybody owes"*: Ritchie Yorke, "Lennon-Ono Bed-in: 40th Anniversary," *Globe and Mail,* May 22, 2009, https://www.theglobeandmail.com/arts/lennon -ono-bed-in-40th-anniversary/article4275217/.

92 *"Good God"*: "John Lennon Blows His Top at Al Capp (Montreal, 1969)," https:// www.youtube.com/watch?v=iYxFO8o-t2E; see also https://newenglandhistorical society.com/al-capp-meet-john-yoko-doesnt-go-well/.

92 *"'Give Peace a Chance' is basically John's"*: Jordan Potter, "Yoko Ono Discusses Her Favourite John Lennon Peace Songs," *Far Out,* March 20, 2023, https://faroutmaga zine.co.uk/yoko-ono-john-lennon-peace-songs/#.

92 *"I didn't write it with Paul"*: Sheff, *All We Are Saying.*

93 *"He put a few plastic objects together"*: John Lennon and Yoko Ono, *John and Yoko/ Plastic Ono Band* (London: Thames and Hudson, 2020).

93 *"It wasn't just John and Yoko"*: Yoko Ono's preface in ibid.

CHAPTER 12

95 *"Actually, they weren't babysitters"*: Author interview with Kyoko Ono, May 11, 2022.

96 *"So sitting at the [mixing] board"*: Helen Brown, "'John Wanted the Beatles Over With—So He Used Yoko to Do It': Lennon's Former Assistant Tells All," *Telegraph,* January 3, 2023, https://www.telegraph.co.uk/music/interviews/john-wanted-beat les-used-yoko-do-lennons-former-assistant/.

96 *"It felt weird"*: Kenneth Womack, "In 1969 the Fifth Beatle Was Heroin: John Lennon's Addiction Took Its Toll on the Band," *Salon,* February 15, 2019, https://www .salon.com/2019/02/15/in-1969-the-fifth-beatle-was-heroin-john-lennons-addic tion-took-its-toll-on-the-band/.

96 *"When we were on it"*: Glenn Plaskin, "Yoko Ono, a Decade After the 'Horrible Thing,'" *Los Angeles Times,* May 6, 1990, https://www.latimes.com/archives/la-xpm -1990-05-06-ca-245-story.html.

96 *"We just went straight cold turkey"*: Womack, "In 1969 the Fifth Beatle."

97 *During the flight*: Author interview with Klaus Voormann, June 2, 2022.

97 *"enraging people"*: Ibid.

97 *"Now Yoko is going to do her thing"*: Mal Evans, JohnLennon.com, https://www
.johnlennon.com/music/albums/live-peace-in-toronto/, accessed August 13, 2024.

98 *"People were just open-mouthed"*: Alexis Petridis, "'We Were Lucky People Didn't
Throw Tomatoes': Klaus Voormann on His Beatles and Plastic Ono Days," *Guardian*,
November 4, 2020, https://www.theguardian.com/music/2020/nov/04/klaus-voor
mann-beatles-plastic-ono-fab-four-moptops-revolver.

98 *"one of the fuckin' best"*: Jann Wenner, "Lennon Remembers," *Rolling Stone*, January 21, 1972, https://www.rollingstone.com/music/music-news/lennon-remem
bers-part-one-186693/.

98 *"The buzz"*: *The Beatles Anthology* (San Francisco: Chronicle Books, 2002).

98 *booed throughout the performance:* Ritchie Yorke, "John, Yoko, and Eric Clapton
Kick Up Their Blue Suede Shoes," *Rolling Stone*, October 18,1969, http://www.rocks
backpages.com/Library/Article/john-yoko-and-eric-clapton-kick-up-their-blue
-suede-shoes.

98 *"I'm sure some people booed"*: Interview, Voormann.

99 *"You don't seem to understand"*: Philip Norman, *John Lennon: The Life* (New York:
HarperCollins, 2008).

99 *"Before he was with Yoko"*: *John and Yoko: Above Us Only Sky*, directed by Michael
Epstein (2018).

99 *"You know the song"*: David Sheff, *All We Are Saying: The Last Major Interview with
John Lennon and Yoko Ono*, rev. ed. (New York: St. Martin's Griffin, 2020).

100 *"Side two, alas"*: Vladimir Bogdanov, Chris Woodstra, and Stephen Thomas Erlew-
ine, eds., *All Music Guide to Rock* (Lanham, MD: Backbeat Books, 2002).

100 *"It was like our sharing our wedding"*: "UK Album Release: Wedding Album by John
& Yoko," *The Beatles Bible*, November 14, 1969, https://www.beatlesbible.com/1969
/11/14/uk-lp-release-wedding-album-john-lennon-yoko-ono/.

100 *"I am returning this MBE"*: John's letter is posted online at https://x.com/johnlennon
/status/934468232827867136?lang=en.

101 *"That was actually one of the better times"*: Kyoko Ono, interview.

101 *"We believe"*: See, among other sources, Yoko Ono, "John Lennon Remembered by
Yoko: 'We Were in Love Desperately,'" *Uncut* (September 2003), https://www.uncut
.co.uk/features/john-lennon-remembered-by-yoko-ono-we-were-in-love-desper
ately-71166/.

101 *"Many toilet walls"*: Alan Travis, "Lennon's Art Showed a Sick Mind, Said Yard,"
Guardian, January 26, 2001, https://www.theguardian.com/uk/2001/jan/26/freedom
ofinformation.thebeatles.

101 *"I was only thinking about"*: Jon Wiener, "Yoko Ono Floating Alone," *Mother Jones*,
June 1984.

102 *"Within hours"*: Ray Connolly, *Being John Lennon* (London: Pegasus, 2018).

103 *"in bad shape"*: Randall Roberts, "How Intense Psychotherapy and a Bel-Air Love
Nest Led to John Lennon's Classic Debut Album," *Los Angeles Times*, April 26, 2021,
https://www.latimes.com/entertainment-arts/music/story/2021-04-26/john-lennon
-plastic-ono-band-yoko-primal-scream-reissue.

103 *"John had about as much pain"*: Arthur Janov, interview by John Harris, *Mojo* (2000),
https://tittenhurstlennon.blogspot.com/2009/07/arthur-janov-interview-about
-john.html.

103 *"I think in fact"*: Primal Center, https://primaltherapy.net/primal-therapy-and-john -lennon, accessed October 2, 2024.

103 *"They cut the therapy off"*: Janov, interview.

CHAPTER 13

105 *"Klaus and Ringo"*: Jonathan Cott, "Yoko Ono and Her Sixteen-Track Voice," *Rolling Stone*, March 18, 1971, https://www.rollingstone.com/music/music-news/yoko-ono -and-her-sixteen-track-voice-237782/.

105 *"Her record was fun"*: John Lennon and Yoko Ono, *John and Yoko/Plastic Ono Band* (London: Thames and Hudson, 2020).

105 *"If you were drowning"*: Cott, "Yoko Ono and Her Sixteen-Track Voice."

106 *"I never will forget"*: Yoko Ono, liner notes to the *London Jam* CD in *Onobox* (1992).

106 *"Well, you make your own dream"*: David Sheff, *All We Are Saying: The Last Major Interview with John Lennon and Yoko Ono*, rev. ed. (New York: St. Martin's Griffin, 2020).

107 *"Wide swaths"*: Marissa Lorusso, "Turning the Tables: The 150 Greatest Albums Made by Women," *NPR Music*, July 24, 2017, https://www.npr.org/2017/07/24 /538387823/turning-the-tables-150-greatest-albums-made-by-women.

107 *"Her image stands"*: Amanda Hess, "The Sublime Spectacle of Yoko Ono Disrupting the Beatles," *New York Times*, December 8, 2021, https://www.nytimes.com/2021/12 /08/arts/music/yoko-ono-beatles-get-back.html.

108 *"John Rennon's"*: Charles McCarry, "John Rennon's Excrusive Gloupie," *Esquire*, December 1970, https://classic.esquire.com/article/1970/12/1/john-rennons-excru sive-gloupie.

108 *"when I thought about that joke"*: Cott, "Yoko Ono and Her Sixteen-Track Voice."

108 *"manifesto . . . where bodily reparation"*: Matt McKinzie, "Defragmenting Bodies: Yoko Ono's 'Fly' at 50," *Pop Matters*, April 22, 2020, https://www.popmatters.com /yoko-ono-fly-2645758379.html.

109 *"There's all sorts of levels"*: Yoko Ono and John Lennon, *The Dick Cavett Show*, ABC, aired May 11, 1972.

109 *"I wasn't man enough to let her have credit for it"*: Sheff, *All We Are Saying*.

109 *"If it had been Bowie"*: Andy Peebles, "Interview with John Lennon," BBC Radio, December 6, 1980, https://www.npr.org/2017/06/17/533368546/yoko-ono-joins -john-lennon-with-credit-line-for-writing-imagine.

110 *"The song 'Imagine' could"*: Callum Crumlish, "John Lennon: 'Imagine Could Never Have Happened Without Yoko Ono,'" *Daily Express*, October 10, 2021, https://www .express.co.uk/entertainment/music/1488230/john-lennon-imagine-yoko-ono -anniversary.

110 *"In many countries"*: Joe Taysom, "The Misunderstood Meaning of Iconic John Len-non Song 'Imagine,'" *Far Out*, December 14, 2020, https://faroutmagazine.co.uk /john-lennon-imagine-real-meaning-communism/.

110 *"is the Buddhist core"*: David Fricke, "'Imagine': The Anthem of 2001," *Rolling Stone*, January 27, 2001, https://www.rollingstone.com/music/music-news/imagine-the -anthem-of-2001-83559/.

110 *"Anti-religious"*: "500 Greatest Albums List (2003)," *Rolling Stone*, May 31, 2009,

https://www.rollingstone.com/music/music-lists/500-greatest-albums-of-all
-time-156826/john-lennon-imagine-2-159074/.

110 *"greatest musical gift"*: "500 Greatest Songs of All Time (2004)," *Rolling Stone*, December 11, 2003, https://www.rollingstone.com/music/music-lists/500-greatest
-songs-of-all-time-151127/john-lennon-imagine-38368/.

110 *"I feel in the big picture"*: *John and Yoko: Above Us Only Sky*, directed by Michael Epstein (2018).

CHAPTER 14

111 *More than fifty years later:* Author interview with Kyoko Ono, May 11, 2022.

112 *"We would argue, of course"*: Yoko Ono, "Behind the Music: Jealous Guy," Imagine-JohnYoko.com, https://www.imaginejohnyoko.com/behind-the-music-jealous-guy/, accessed April 12, 2024.

112 *"a joy to write and a joy to sing"*: John Lennon, *Crawdaddy*, December 5, 1971.

112 Plastic Ono *"with chocolate coating"*: David Sheff, *All We Are Saying: The Last Major Interview with John Lennon and Yoko Ono*, rev. ed. (New York: St. Martin's Griffin, 2020).

112 *"a masterpiece of"*: Alexis Petridis, "Yoko Ono: Her 20 Greatest Songs—Ranked," *Guardian*, November 9, 2023, https://www.theguardian.com/culture/2023/nov/09
/yoko-ono-her-20-greatest-songs-ranked?CMP=Share_iOSApp_Other.

113 *"fearlessly confronts"*: Matt McKinzie, "Defragmenting Bodies: Yoko Ono's 'Fly' at 50," *Pop Matters*, April 22, 2020, https://www.popmatters.com/yoko-ono-fly
-2645758379.html.

113 *"you'll hear not only the B-52's"*: Peter Occhiogrosso, "Yoko Ono: Here's the Best of Me," *Soho News*, December 3, 1980, https://www.peterocchiogrosso.com/_files/ugd
/d28fff_be28e76c24b54aa9aafc024ed7d85af6.pdf.

113 *"distasteful"*: "Power to the People," *The Beatles Bible*, https://www.beatlesbible.com
/people/john-lennon/songs/power-to-the-people/, last updated March 3, 2023.

113 *"Hi! My name is John"*: Yoko Ono, *Grapefruit* (New York: Simon and Schuster, 2000).

114 *"In England I'm regarded"*: "The Spirit of John Lennon," Absoluteelsewhere.net, 1971, https://history3.absoluteelsewhere.net/July/july19.html#:~:text=1971%2D%2
DA%20press%20conference,guy%20who%20won%20the%20pools.

114 *"We wanted to make a surrealistic film"*: Scott MacDonald, "Yoko Ono: Ideas on Film," *Film Quarterly* (Fall 1989), https://womenfilmeditors.princeton.edu/assets
/pdfs/ONO_Ideas_on_Film_MacDonald.pdf.

115 *"a hilarious game"*: Blake Gopnik, *Warhol* (New York: HarperCollins, 2020).

115 *"Look, the whole museum is yours"*: John Lennon and Yoko Ono, *Imagine John Yoko*, limited ed. (London: Thames and Hudson, 2018).

116 *The first time*: Emily Wasserman, " 'This Is Not Here' (A Report on the Yoko Ono Retrospective at Syracuse)," *Artforum* 10 (January 1972), https://www.artforum
.com/features/this-is-not-here-a-report-on-the-yoko-ono-retrospective-at-syra
cuse-210172/.

116 *"The idea came to me"*: Connor Monahan, studio director for Yoko Ono, email to the author, August 13, 2024.

116 *"I think it was the same expression"*: Lennon and Ono, *Imagine John and Yoko*.

116 *"In this show here I'd like"*: Steve Aminoff, "Mr. and Mrs. John Lennon in Syracuse," *Albany Student Press*, October 12, 1971, https://archives.albany.edu/downloads /7h149q29s?locale=en.

117 *"It's important to consider how radical that was"*: Lennon and Ono, *Imagine John and Yoko.*

117 *"Then when word started filtering out"*: Author interview with David Ross, August 11, 2022.

118 *"the flies are distinguishable"*: Alexandra Munroe and Jon Hendricks, eds., *Yes Yoko Ono* (New York: Harry N. Abrams, 2000).

118 *"Perplexing, thought provoking"*: Whitney Rose Graham, "Yoko Ono at MoMA—an Exhibition 50 Years in the Making," *Inside/Out* (MoMA blog), June 9, 2015, https:// www.moma.org/explore/inside_out/2015/06/09/yoko-ono-at-moma-an-exhibition -50-years-in-the-making/.

118 *"a feminist critique"*: Andrea K. Scott, "Yoko Ono Goes Solo," *New Yorker*, May 18, 2015, https://www.newyorker.com/culture/culture-desk/yoko-goes-solo.

CHAPTER 15

120 *The administration focused its efforts*: Jon Wiener, email to the author, February 27, 2024.

121 *"We were having our morning coffee"*: John Lennon and Yoko Ono, *Imagine John Yoko*, limited ed. (London: Thames and Hudson, 2018).

121 *"It was, perhaps, an early example"*: Ben Sisario, "How Sean Ono Lennon Helped His Parents Send a Message," *New York Times*, March 1, 2024, https://www.nytimes.com /2024/03/01/movies/john-lennon-yoko-ono-sean-ono-lennon-oscar.html.

122 *"My dad was in jail"*: Author interview with Kyoko Ono, May 11, 2022.

122 *"The bottom line"*: Author interview with Jon Hendricks, September 8, 2022.

122 *"And there was one private detective"*: Sheff, outtakes from the Playboy interview sessions, August and September 1980.

122 *"It was a classic case"*: David Sheff, *All We Are Saying: The Last Major Interview with John Lennon and Yoko Ono*, rev. ed. (New York: St. Martin's Griffin, 2020).

123 *forty million people*: Addie Morfoot, "'Daytime Revolution' Revisits the Remarkable Week John Lennon and Yoko Ono Co-Hosted 'The Mike Douglas Show' in 1972," *Variety*, January 15, 2023, https://variety.com/2023/film/news/day time-revolution-documentary-john-lennon-yoko-ono-co-hosted-mike-doug las-show-1235524252/.

123 *"It's become a cliché"*: Ibid.

123 *Yoko performed art pieces*: Kevin Concannon, "Yoko Ono's Touch Piece: A Work in Multiple Media, 1960–2009," *On Curating* (September 2021), https://www.on -curating.org/issue-51-reader/yoko-onos-touch-piece-a-work-in-multiple-media -19602009.html.

123 *"The audience's boisterous bewilderment"*: Cerene Dominic, "Mike Douglas Held Hostage!," July 9, 1998, https://www.phoenixnewtimes.com/music/mike-douglas -held-hostage-6422072.

123 *"We wanted to do the shows"*: Morfoot, "'Daytime Revolution' Revisits."

124 *"We used to ask"*: Sheff, *All We Are Saying.*

124 *"I'm always interested to know"*: Robin Blackburn and Tariq Ali, "Power to the Peo-

ple," *Red Mole*, January 21, 1971, https://www.johnlennon.com/news/revolution-build-around-it-you-better-free-your-mind-instead/.

124   *"to bring rock 'n' roll together"*: Jon Wiener, *Gimme Some Truth: The John Lennon FBI Files* (Oakland: University of California Press, 2000).

124   *Nixon would be renominated*: Wiener email.

125   *"When they described their plans"*: Sheff, *All We Are Saying.*

125   *"We won the court case"*: John and Yoko were on *The Dick Cavett Show* twice. Both times they spoke about Kyoko. This is from their second appearance (*The Dick Cavett Show*, ABC, aired May 11, 1972).

126   *"The editor of* Cosmopolitan*"*: Caroline Coon, "In Defense of Yoko Ono," Yahoo! Entertainment, July 2, 2012, https://www.yahoo.com/entertainment/rock-backpages-flashback-defense-yoko-ono-1974-132405253.html.

126   *The extent of the government's efforts*: Wiener wrote about the government's harassment of Yoko and John in the books *Come Together: John Lennon and His Time* (Chicago: University of Illinois Press, 1990) and *Gimme Some Truth.*

127   *Entitled "John Lennon"*: Wiener, *Gimme Some Truth.*

127   *The report recommended*: Ibid.

127   *"many headaches might be avoided"*: Ibid.

CHAPTER 16

129   *"So most people take methadone"*: Yoko Ono, "John Lennon Remembered by Yoko: 'We Were in Love Desperately,'" *Uncut* (September 2003), https://www.uncut.co.uk/features/john-lennon-remembered-by-yoko-ono-we-were-in-love-desperately-71166/.

130   *"phone pals"*: Author interview with Elliot Mintz, January 28, 2021.

131   *Craig Pyes, editor of* SunDance *magazine*: Craig Pyes, email to the author, May 30, 2024.

131   *"It was [Hong] who was"*: John Lennon, *Skywriting by Word of Mouth* (New York: It Books, 2010).

132   *"incipient artistic suicide"*: Stephen Holden, "Some Time in New York City," *Rolling Stone*, July 20, 1972.

132   *"Lennon, You're a Pathetic"*: Tony Tyler, "Lennon, You're a Pathetic, Ageing Revolutionary," *NME*, July 1972.

133   *"was spewing curses and screaming"*: *The Real Yoko Ono* (documentary), part 4 of 6, 2001.

133   *"There were few people left"*: Author interview with Bob Gruen, August 24, 2022.

133   *"I was just frozen, stuck there"*: *The Real Yoko Ono.*

134   *"It's a story of all of us women"*: Yoko Ono, *Onobox* notes (Rykodisc, 1992).

134   *"It was almost a mistake"*: Caroline Coon, "In Defense of Yoko Ono," Yahoo! Entertainment, July 2, 2012, https://www.yahoo.com/entertainment/rock-backpages-flashback-defense-yoko-ono-1974-132405253.html.

134   *after Nixon was reelected*: Jon Wiener, email to the author, February 26, 2024.

134   *"With a characteristic instinct"*: Laurie Johnston, "Lennon Sees a Wide Impact in Ouster," *New York Times*, March 4, 1973, https://www.nytimes.com/1973/04/03/archives/lennon-sees-a-wide-impact-in-ouster-voice-not-audible.html.

135   *"John was getting drunk"*: Gruen, interview.

135   *"I really needed some space"*: David Sheff, *All We Are Saying: The Last Major*

Interview with John Lennon and Yoko Ono, rev. ed. (New York: St. Martin's Griffin, 2020).

136 *"The affair was something that"*: Chrissy Iley, "Yoko Ono: 'John's Affair Wasn't Hurtful to Me. I Needed a Rest. I Needed Space,'" *Telegraph,* March 26, 2012, https://www.telegraph.co.uk/culture/photography/9160041/Yoko-Ono-Johns-affair-wasnt-hurtful-to-me.-I-needed-a-rest.-I-needed-space.html.

136 *"A typical day"*: May Pang, *Instamatic Karma: Photographs of John Lennon* (New York: St. Martin's, 2008).

136 *"Yoko came to me at 9:30"*: Tom Maxwell, "Shelved: Yoko Ono," *Longreads,* January 21, 2021, https://longreads.com/2021/01/21/shelved-yoko-ono/?share=cus tom-1422885119.

136 *"May Pang was a very intelligent"*: Callum Crumlish, "John Lennon's Mistress Was Hand-Picked by Yoko Ono During Marriage Breakdown," *Express,* February 18, 2023, https://www.express.co.uk/entertainment/music/1735618/john-lennon-yoko-ono-girlfriend-may-pang-the-beatles.

136 *"Can you imagine"*: Iley, "Yoko Ono: 'John's Affair.'"

137 *"Wherever we went"*: Gruen, interview.

137 *"One Beatle assistant"*: Sheff, *All We Are Saying.*

137 *"Before meeting John"*: Alexandra Munroe, "Spirit of Yes: The Art and Life of Yoko Ono," in *Yes Yoko Ono,* eds. Alexandra Munroe and Jon Hendricks (New York: Harry N. Abrams, 2000); excerpt at https://web.archive.org/web/20160307183246/http://www.alexandramunroe.com/spirit-of-yes-the-art-and-life-of-yoko-ono-2/.

137 *"When I met John"*: Sheff, *All We Are Saying.*

CHAPTER 17

139 *"When two people are separated"*: David Sheff, *All We Are Saying: The Last Major Interview with John Lennon and Yoko Ono,* rev. ed. (New York: St. Martin's Griffin, 2020).

139 *"Well, first I thought"*: Ibid.

140 *"I woke up one day"*: Ibid.

140 *"I was haunted"*: David Sholin and Laurie Kaye, "John Lennon's Last Interview," RKO Radio Network, December 8, 1980, http://www.beatlesarchive.net/john-len nons-last-interview-december-8-1980.html.

140 *"My body was shaking"*: *The Real Yoko Ono* (documentary), part 4 of 6, 2001.

141 *"There were some flashes of brilliance"*: Philip Norman, *John Lennon: The Life* (New York: HarperCollins, 2008).

141 *"Keltner and guitarist Jesse Ed Davis"*: Ibid.

141 *"Let us start with the premise"*: John Rockwell, "Yoko Ono's Contradictions," *New York Times,* October 26, 1973, https://www.nytimes.com/1973/10/26/archives/pop-music-yoko-onos-contradictions-frankss-melodies-quirky-and.html.

142 *"feminist manifesto"*: Madeline Bocaro, *In Your Mind: The Infinite Universe of Yoko Ono* (New York: Conceptual Books, 2016).

143 *"I'm the one that freaked out"*: Sheff, outtakes from the *Playboy* interview sessions, August and September 1980.

143 *"sort of halfheartedly promised"*: Sheff, *All We Are Saying.*

144 *"It was like Beatlemania"*: Author interview with Bob Gruen, August 24, 2022.

CHAPTER 18

145 *"very unscientific things"*: Author interview with Tadanori Yokoo, June 17, 2022.

146 *flew west with*: Author interview with Sara Seagull, September 6, 2022.

146 *"There will be times"*: Elliot Mintz, *We All Shine On* (New York: Dutton, 2024).

147 *"I didn't know she was there"*: Pete Hamill, "John Lennon: Long Night's Journey into Day," *Rolling Stone*, June 5, 1975, https://www.rollingstone.com/feature/john-lennon -pete-hamill-185277/.

147 *"In my whole career"*: Elton John, *Me* (New York: Henry Holt, 2019).

147 *"We looked at each other"*: Alan Clayson et al., *Women: The Incredible Life of Yoko Ono* (London: Chrome Dreams, 2004).

147 *"We dated"*: David Sheff, *All We Are Saying: The Last Major Interview with John Lennon and Yoko Ono*, rev. ed. (New York: St. Martin's Griffin, 2020).

148 *"'You'd better go now'"*: Ibid.

148 *"John [called and] said"*: Kim Willis, "John Lennon's Ex May Pang Says He 'Really Wanted' to Write Songs with Paul McCartney Again," *USA Today*, October 9, 2023, https://www.usatoday.com/story/entertainment/music/2023/10/09/john-lennon -girlfriend-may-pang-lost-weekend-movie/71115457007/.

148 *"Let the media"*: Author interview with Elliot Mintz, May 21, 2022.

148 *"I was the real pig"*: Sheff, *All We Are Saying*.

149 *"reorder our priorities"*: Ibid.

149 *"He was intelligent enough"*: Ibid.

149 *"When I was still drunk"*: Ibid.

149 *"performing flea"*: Ibid.

149 *"She was less restless"*: Author interview with Bob Gruen, August 24, 2022.

150 *"We had many miscarriages"*: Martin Torgoff, "Yoko Ono," *Interview*, January 1985, https://www.martintorgoff.com/yoko-ono.

150 *that court overturned the order*: Leslie Maitland, "John Lennon Wins His Residency in U.S.," *New York Times*, July 28, 1976, https://www.nytimes.com/1976/07/28 /archives/john-lennon-wins-his-residency-in-us.html.

150 *"Lennon's four-year battle"*: Arnold H. Lubasch, "Deportation of Lennon Barred by Court of Appeals," *New York Times*, October 8, 1975, https://www.nytimes.com /1975/10/08/archives/deportation-of-lennon-barred-by-court-of-appeals.html? searchResultPosition=1.

151 *"As usual, there's a great woman"*: Leslie Maitland, "John Lennon Wins His Residency in U.S."

151 *"I was there when it happened"*: Sheff, *All We Are Saying*.

CHAPTER 19

153 *"It's sort of a description"*: David Sheff, *All We Are Saying: The Last Major Interview with John Lennon and Yoko Ono*, rev. ed. (New York: St. Martin's Griffin, 2020).

153 *"I've never been so clear"*: Author interview with Bob Gruen, August 24, 2022.

154 *"At one point"*: Author interview with Klaus Voormann, June 2, 2022.

154 *"I am carrying the baby"*: Sheff, *All We Are Saying*.

154 *"If a father raises the child"*: Ibid.

154 *"She puts herself down"*: Ibid.

154 *"She can still allow him"*: Sheff, outtakes from the *Playboy* interview sessions, August and September 1980.

155 *"Yesterday, all of John Lennon's troubles"*: Leslie Maitland, "John Lennon Wins His Residency in U.S.," *New York Times*, July 28, 1976, https://www.nytimes.com/1976/07/28/archives/john-lennon-wins-his-residency-in-us.html.

155 *"Every lawyer had a lawyer"*: Sheff, *All We Are Saying*.

155 *"These lawyers were getting"*: Ibid.

155 *"It's a fascinating world"*: Peter Occhiogrosso, "Yoko Ono: Here's the Best of Me," *Soho News*, December 3, 1980, https://www.peterocchiogrosso.com/_files/ugd/d28fff_be28e76c24b54aa9aafc024ed7d85af6.pdf.

155 *"There was a bit of an attitude"*: Sheff, *All We Are Saying*.

156 *"The numbers weren't right"*: Joan Goodman, "The *Playboy* Interview with Paul and Linda McCartney," *Playboy* (December 1984), http://www.beatlesinterviews.org/dbpm.int3.html.

156 *"For instance, when I was going to Apple meetings"*: Barbara Graustark, "The Lost 1981 Yoko Ono Interview," *Rolling Stone*, October 1, 1981, https://www.rollingstone.com/music/music-features/yoko-ono-cover-story-john-lennon-death-1234681088/.

157 *"Buying houses was"*: Barbara Graustark, "The Real John Lennon," *Newsweek*, November 29, 1980, https://www.beatlesinterviews.org/db1980.0929.beatles.html.

157 *"People advised us"*: Ibid.

157 *"All that* mooing"*: Elton John, *Me* (New York: Henry Holt, 2019).

157 *"To make money"*: Sheff, *All We Are Saying*.

158 *"Why would I want to see"*: Craig McLean, "Yoko Ono: Back to Where She Once Belonged," *Times Online*, March 6, 2010.

159 *"He was just looking"*: Ibid.

159 *"The other one"*: Yoko Ono, interview with Michael Kimmelman, *TimesTalks*, October 5, 2012, https://www.youtube.com/watch?v=0WIosw1gv50.

159 *"lying in it, giggling"*: Yoko Ono, "The Lighter," 2000, https://www.facebook.com/story.php?story_fbid=293318785492522&id=100044432079529&paipv=0&eav=Afa6skHgxK2SQyCxBs7hwI2L0RJM212NtEVV_45z6edKjirzW2L61uH1y8ezd8iZ0-M&_rdr.

CHAPTER 20

161 *"We just stopped"*: David Sheff, *All We Are Saying: The Last Major Interview with John Lennon and Yoko Ono*, rev. ed. (New York: St. Martin's Griffin, 2020).

161 *"He was living close"*: Yoko Ono, ed., *Memories of John Lennon* (New York: HarperCollins, 2005).

161 *"Please call before you come"*: Sheff, *All We Are Saying*.

162 *"Daddy, were you a Beatle"*: Mark Binelli, "The Children of Rock," *Rolling Stone*, April 7, 2005, https://www.rollingstone.com/music/music-news/the-children-of-rock-99823/.

162 *"We have all seen the power of fame"*: Jerry Saltz, *Seeing Out Loud: The Village Voice Art Columns* (Great Barrington, MA: The Figures, 2003).

163 *"He didn't come out of my belly"*: Sheff, *All We Are Saying*.

163 *"She never wore most of it"*: Author interview with Sam Havadtoy, December 7, 2022.

163 *"Upstairs, they were playing disco"*: Jonathan Cott, "John Lennon: The Last Interview,"

Rolling Stone, December 23, 2010, https://www.rollingstone.com/feature/john-lennon
-the-last-interview-179443/.

164 *"The first night"*: David Sholin and Laurie Kaye, "John Lennon's Last Interview," RKO
Radio Network, December 8, 1980, http://www.beatlesarchive.net/john-lennons
-last-interview-december-8-1980.html.

165 *"Do not take Yoko's music"*: Yoko Ono, *Memories of John Lennon.*

165 *"I thought, If John"*: Barbara Graustark, "The Lost 1981 Yoko Ono Interview," *Rolling
Stone*, October 1, 1981, https://www.rollingstone.com/music/music-features/yoko
-ono-cover-story-john-lennon-death-1234681088/.

165 *"John said if they had her on one side"*: Author interview with David Geffen, May 9,
2023.

166 *"Here must be the world's first"*: Sheff, *All We Are Saying.*

CHAPTER 21

167 *"I knew it would be quite a coup"*: Yoko Ono, ed., *Memories of John Lennon* (New
York: HarperCollins, 2005).

168 *"The word is out"*: David Sheff, *All We Are Saying: The Last Major Interview with
John Lennon and Yoko Ono*, rev. ed. (New York: St. Martin's Griffin, 2020).

170 *"Well, we probably will"*: Ibid.

171 *"What inspired me"*: Ibid.

171 *Her gifts to John included*: Jay Fielden, "The Strange Journey of John Lennon's Stolen
Patek Philippe Watch," *New Yorker*, June 24, 2024, https://www.newyorker.com/maga
zine/2024/06/24/the-strange-journey-of-john-lennons-stolen-patek-phillippe-watch.

171 *On a quiet November morning*: Vicki Sheff and David Sheff, "The Betrayal of John
Lennon," *Playboy* (March 1984).

171 *number twenty-five with a bullet*: Billboard, December 6, 1980, https://www.bill
board.com/charts/billboard-200/1980-12-06/.

172 *"Not bad, eh, Mother?"*: Sheff and Sheff, "The Betrayal of John Lennon."

172 *"for John"*: Geffen, interview.

172 *"for him, not for her"*: Ibid.

172 *"Life begins at forty"*: Sheff, *All We Are Saying.*

173 *"I think you just"*: On the version of the song included on *Onobox*, John can be
heard remarking, "I think you just cut your first number one, Yoko."

PART THREE: YOKO ONLY

CHAPTER 22

177 *"John's been shot"*: Based on interviews and published accounts, I've reconstructed
the events of the night of December 8, 1980.

178 *"She just sat, frozen"*: Author interview with David Geffen, May 9, 2023.

178 *John's wedding ring*: Vicki Sheff-Cahan, "The Day the Music Died," *People*, December 10, 1990, https://people.com/archive/the-day-the-music-died-vol-34-no-23/.

178 *Speaking numbly*: Vicki Sheff and David Sheff, "The Betrayal of John Lennon," *Playboy* (March 1984).

178 *She also asked Geffen*: Sheff-Cahan, "The Day the Music Died."

179   *"An unspeakable tragedy"*: Eric Banas, "An In-Depth Look at Howard Cosell Announcing the Death of John Lennon," WROR, December 8, 2022, https://wror.com/2022/12/08/howard-cosell-breaking-news-of-john-lennon-death/.

179   *De Palma knocked*: Sheff and Sheff, "The Betrayal of John Lennon."

180   *"It was a crime scene"*: Author interview with Elliot Mintz, October 28, 2022.

180   *"Yoko-san is in her bedroom"*: Sheff and Sheff, "The Betrayal of John Lennon."

180   *"It's Elliot"*: Elliot Mintz, *We All Shine On* (New York: Dutton, 2024).

181   *"finish the job Chapman started"*: Sheff and Sheff, "The Betrayal of John Lennon."

181   *A man had been arrested*: Ibid.

182   *"When John died"*: David Sheff, "Yoko and Sean Starting Over," *People*, December 13, 1982, https://people.com/archive/cover-story-yoko-and-sean-starting-over-vol-18-no-24/.

182   *She asked that he be cremated*: Sheff and Sheff, "The Betrayal of John Lennon."

182   *household devoted to peace*: Ibid.

182   *"I know how you're feeling"*: Mintz, interview.

182   *"I just came downstairs"*: "Julian Lennon on Hearing of John Lennon's Death," Hudson Union Society, https://www.youtube.com/watch?v=o8_eJcAb00w, posted June 16, 2020.

183   *"Every person on that plane"*: Julian Lennon, interview by John Roberts, "The Murder of John Lennon," CNN, December 4, 2010, https://transcripts.cnn.com/show/se/date/2010-12-04/segment/02.

183   *"Take him around New York"*: Mintz, *We All Shine On*.

183   *"We were all afraid"*: Author interview with Sam Havadtoy, December 7, 2022.

183   *"I was like a person who was drowning"*: Barbara Graustark, "The Lost 1981 Yoko Ono Interview," *Rolling Stone*, October 1, 1981, https://www.rollingstone.com/music/music-features/yoko-ono-cover-story-john-lennon-death-1234681088/.

183   *"I remember"*: Author interview with Sean Lennon, August 26, 2020.

185   *"I recall Yoko mentioning"*: Julian Lennon, written answers to author's interview questions, June 9, 2024.

185   *"She wanted to avoid"*: Robert Hilburn, *Corn Flakes with John Lennon* (New York: Rodale, 2010).

186   *"There is no funeral for John"*: Elizabeth Aubrey, "What Happened on the Day John Lennon Was Shot," *Independent*, December 8, 2021, https://www.independent.co.uk/arts-entertainment/music/news/john-lennon-death-shot-killer-b1972428.html.

186   *When she was told*: Sheff and Sheff, "The Betrayal of John Lennon."

186   *"They asked me"*: Sheff, "Yoko and Sean."

186   *The sender was a woman*: Sheff and Sheff, "The Betrayal of John Lennon."

186   *"with the sheet off"*: Ibid.

187   *"the first one"*: Ibid.

188   *"When he died"*: Yoko Ono, "Yoko: John's Last Days," *Rolling Stone*, June 24, 2004.

CHAPTER 23

189   *"I never met anybody"*: Richard Williams, "John and Yoko Interview," *Melody Maker*, December 20, 1969.

190   *"the dirge"*: Author interview with David Geffen, May 9, 2023.

190   *Merry Christmas from Daddy*: Author interview with Dane Worthington, December 12, 2023.

190 *"the sudden trauma"*: David Sheff, "Checking In with Yoko," *People*, January 12, 1981, https://people.com/archive/cover-story-checking-in-with-yoko-vol-15-no-1/.

190 *"I asked him why"*: David Sheff, "Yoko and Sean Starting Over," *People*, December 13, 1982, https://people.com/archive/cover-story-yoko-and-sean-starting-over-vol-18 -no-24/.

191 *"I had good memories"*: Author interview with Sean Lennon, November 7, 2023.

191 *found it too painful*: Vicki Sheff and David Sheff, "The Betrayal of John Lennon," *Playboy* (March 1984).

191 *"I remember the janitor"*: Sean Lennon, interview.

191 *"My dad had just died"*: Ibid.

191 *Some supermarket chains*: Richard Cromelin, "Rolling Stones Gather a Little Moss," *Los Angeles Times*, January 9, 1981.

191 *"I promised John"*: Rick Vanderknyff, "Leibovitz Upset Over Yanking of Lennon Photo," *Los Angeles Times*, April 26, 1990, https://www.latimes.com/archives/la-xpm -1990-04-26-ca-442-story.html.

192 *an open letter*: Yoko Ono, "An Open Letter," *Washington Post*, January 18, 1981, https://www.washingtonpost.com/archive/politics/1981/01/18/in-gratitude /41fc1b80-de51-43f8-b641-45276b63d235/.

193 *"If I had had to sit"*: Barbara Graustark, "The Lost 1981 Yoko Ono Interview," *Rolling Stone*, October 1, 1981, https://www.rollingstone.com/music/music-features/yoko -ono-cover-story-john-lennon-death-1234681088/.

193 *"Music was my salvation"*: Yoko Ono, letter to fans, *Season of Glass*, May 6, 1981, https://www.johnlennon.com/music/with-yoko-ono/season-of-glass/.

194 *"It was a song John liked"*: Yoko Ono, *Onobox* notes (Rykodisc, 1992).

194 *"John was dead. I was alive"*: Ibid.

194 *"It was just too horrifying"*: Author interview with Bob Gruen, August 24, 2022.

195 *Gruen set up the lighting*: Ibid.

195 *"After Season of Glass was finished"*: Graustark, "The Lost 1981 Yoko Ono Interview."

195 *"They said it was in bad taste"*: Yoko Ono, *Onobox* notes.

195 *"Yoko has made a record"*: Mark Cooper, review, *Record Mirror*, June 13, 1981, https:// worldradiohistory.com/UK/Record-Mirror/80s/81/Record-Mirror-1981-06-13.pdf.

195 *"I remember Season of Glass"*: David Fricke, "Sean Lennon on His Father, Yoko Ono, and His Own Musical Career," *Rolling Stone*, June 11, 1998, https://www.rolling stone.com/music/music-news/sean-lennon-on-his-father-yoko-ono-and-his-own -musical-career-99562/.

195 *"People criticized her"*: Author interview with Sean Lennon, July 31, 2024.

196 *"Soon after John was killed"*: Sheff, "Yoko and Sean."

196 *"Each time he said these things"*: Ibid.

196 *"We were so stunned"*: Andy Warhol, *The Andy Warhol Diaries* (New York: Warner Books, 1991).

CHAPTER 24

199 *"I belong there"*: Author interview with Sam Havadtoy, October 13, 2022.

201 *"Sam really took over"*: Author interview with Jann Wenner, May 27, 2023.

201 *"When John died, I thought"*: Vicki Sheff and David Sheff, "The Betrayal of John Lennon," *Playboy* (March 1984).

202 *"Because of continuous and credible"*: Author interview with Dan Mahoney, June 28, 2024.

202 *One day a letter was delivered*: Ibid.

202 *found a razor blade*: Havadtoy, interview.

202 *"To fulfill the prophecy"*: Sheff and Sheff, "The Betrayal of John Lennon."

202 *"He was the most trusted person"*: Author interview with Sean Lennon, July 31, 2024.

203 *John and Yoko dolls*: Sheff and Sheff, "The Betrayal of John Lennon," and "Lennon Assistant Denies Cash Plot," CBS News, September 27, 2002, https://www.cbsnews.com/news/lennon-assistant-denies-cash-plot/.

203 *"That's what they did"*: Havadtoy, interview.

203 *"There is within me"*: Tom Junod, "Yoko Ono: What I've Learned About John Lennon, 30 Years On," *Esquire*, July 29, 2010.

204 *"I would always tell her"*: Havadtoy, interview.

205 *"One was just the barrel of a gun"*: Author interview with Elliot Mintz, September 23, 2023.

205 *In his book*: Elliot Mintz, *We All Shine On* (New York: Dutton, 2024).

206 *"Elvis was a pervert"*: Albert Goldman, *Elvis* (New York: McGraw-Hill, 1981).

206 *it was from Mark David Chapman*: Sheff and Sheff, "The Betrayal of John Lennon."

206 *Two days after that*: Ibid. and Mahoney, interview.

206 *he would be an orphan*: David Sheff, "Yoko and Sean Starting Over," *People*, December 13, 1982, https://people.com/archive/cover-story-yoko-and-sean-starting-over-vol-18-no-24/.

206 *"In Japan, when a woman"*: "Yoko Ono, a Year Later," UPI, December 7, 1981, https://www.upi.com/Archives/1981/12/07/Yoko-Ono-a-year-later/3981376549200/.

206 *"I think of John's death"*: Ibid.

207 *"This is where John and I"*: Sheff, "Yoko and Sean."

207 *"I thought it was too soon"*: Elton John, *Me* (New York: Henry Holt, 2019).

CHAPTER 25

209 *"We had a full life together"*: Author interview with Sam Havadtoy, July 18, 2023.

210 *"I carried a gun"*: Author interview with Elliot Mintz, May 21, 2022.

210 *"You can't tell her not to worry"*: Author interview with Bob Gruen, August 24, 2022.

210 *"I wrote the song 'It's Alright'"*: Yoko Ono, *Onobox* notes (Rykodisc, 1992).

210 *taking a bath*: Vicki Sheff and David Sheff, "The Betrayal of John Lennon," *Playboy* (March 1984). Also see David Segal, "Lennon's Disputed Days in the Life," *Washington Post*, April 17, 2000, https://www.washingtonpost.com/archive/lifestyle/2000/04/18/lennons-disputed-days-in-the-life/cf1770d0-48f2-4d57-adaf-4109f8739fb4/.

211 *broke into "and ransacked"*: Bob Rosen writes about the break-in on his website; see https://www.robertrosennyc.com/bio.htm.

211 *In April 1983, he pleaded guilty*: Andrew Jacobs, "Yoko Ono Sues Ex-Aide Over Photographs" *New York Times*, April 14, 1999, https://www.nytimes.com/1999/04/14/nyregion/yoko-ono-sues-ex-aide-over-photographs.html.

211 *Seaman's publisher dropped its plans*: Sheff and Sheff, "The Betrayal of John Lennon."

211 *"marriage counselor"*: John Green, *Dakota Days* (New York: St. Martin's, 1983).

212 *May Pang's book*: May Pang and Henry Edwards, *Loving John* (New York: Warner Books, 1983).

214 *"For God's sake"*: Author interview with Elliot Mintz, 1983.

214 *She and Stearns talked about John"*: Author interview with Nancy Stearns, July 15, 2022.

214 *"The bodyguards didn't"*: Author interview with Sam Havadtoy, December 7, 2022.

214 *The man was arrested:* Sheff and Sheff, "The Betrayal of John Lennon."

214 *It was the doorman:* Ibid. and Mahoney, interview.

215 *"living in this very, very high-stakes world"*: Author interview with Sean Lennon, July 31, 2024.

CHAPTER 26

217 *"You know the joke"*: Author interview with Sam Havadtoy, October 13, 2022.

217 *"We went in and"*: Andy Warhol, *The Andy Warhol Diaries* (New York: Warner Books, 1991).

218 *"When [Andy] brought me to Yoko's"*: David Sheff, "Keith Haring: Just Say Know," *Rolling Stone,* August 10, 1998, https://www.rollingstone.com/culture/culture-news /keith-haring-just-say-know-71847/3/.

218 *"the weird universe"*: Blake Gopnik, *Warhol* (New York: HarperCollins, 2020).

219 *"By 4 a.m. her normal workday"*: Barbara Graustark, "The Last Ballad of John and Yoko," *People,* February 20, 1984, https://people.com/archive/cover-story-the-last -ballad-of-john-yoko-vol-21-no-7/.

219 *Yoko, Sean, and a small entourage:* Author interview with Barbara Graustark, October 7, 2023.

220 *A photographer climbed into:* Author interview with Sean Lennon, August 25, 2022.

220 *"It was as if time"*: Yoko Ono, "The Lighter," 2000, https://www.facebook.com/story .php?story_fbid=293318785492522&id=100044432079529&paipv=0&eav=Afa6skHg xK2SQyCxBs7hwI2L0RJM212NtEVV_45z6edKjirzW2L61uH1y8ezd8iZ0-M&_rdr.

220 *ordered to pay:* "Yoko Ono Is Told to Pay Producer," *New York Times,* April 3, 1984, https://www.nytimes.com/1984/04/03/nyregion/the-city-yoko-ono-is-told-to-pay -producer.html.

221 *"The reason why"*: Barbara Graustark, *Yoko Ono: Then and Now* (documentary), 1984.

221 *"The problem in other people's eyes"*: Ibid.

222 *"I thought this"*: Havadtoy, interview.

222 *"60s hippie drivel"*: Rick Shefchik, "Yoko Ono: Old Hippie in New Package," *Charlotte Observer,* November 15, 1985.

222 *"the most balanced album"*: Robert Palmer, " 'Starpeace' Lets Yoko Ono Have Her Cake and Eat It," *New York Times,* October 13, 1985, https://www.nytimes.com/1985 /10/13/arts/starpeace-lets-yoko-ono-have-her-cake-and-eat-it.html.

222 *"The response of the audiences"*: Graustark, interview.

222 *"After Starpeace I was totally discouraged"*: Nick Johnstone, *Yoko Ono "Talking"* (London: Omnibus Press, 2006).

CHAPTER 27

225 *"I never even thought of the word widow"*: Sean O'Hagan, "Yoko Ono at 80: 'I Feel That I Am Starting a New Life, a Second Life,'" *Guardian,* May 25, 2013, https:// www.theguardian.com/culture/2013/may/26/yoko-ono-80-meltdown-john-lennon.

225 *"There are 150 trees"*: Maureen Dowd, "Strawberry Fields 'Garden of Peace' Opens Today," *New York Times*, October 9, 1985, https://www.nytimes.com/1985/10/09/nyregion/strawberry-fields-garden-of-peace-opens-today.html?searchResultPosition=2.

226 *"She had her own reasons"*: Author interview with David Geffen, May 9, 2023.

226 *Paul McCartney was alive*: Author interview with Jann Wenner, May 27, 2023.

226 *"The way I see it is"*: Mark Kemp, "Yoko Ono Reconsidered," *Option* (July 1992), https://beatpatrol.wordpress.com/2014/12/28/mark-kemp-yoko-ono-reconsidered-1992/.

227 *"simian-looking"*: Albert Goldman, *The Lives of John Lennon* (New York: William Morrow, 1988).

228 *Paul McCartney called for a boycott*: Allan Kozinn, "An Embattled Albert Goldman Defends His Book on John Lennon," *New York Times*, September 12, 1988, https://www.nytimes.com/1988/09/12/books/an-embattled-albert-goldman-defends-his-book-on-john-lennon.html.

228 *"It was a painful process"*: Author interview with Elliot Mintz, October 2, 2022.

228 *"He wasn't dangerous"*: Author interview with Dan Mahoney, June 28, 2024.

229 *"bizarre visitation"*: Jim Calio, "Yoko Ono's Ex-Husband, Tony Cox, Reveals His Strange Life Since Fleeing with Their Daughter 14 Years Ago," *People*, February 3, 1986, https://people.com/archive/yoko-onos-ex-husband-tony-cox-reveals-his-strange-life-since-fleeing-with-their-daughter-14-years-ago-vol-25-no-5/.

230 *"I felt as though"*: Helen Molesworth et al., "Yoko Ono a Kind of Meeting Point," Getty Research Institute (1990), https://www.getty.edu/podcast-transcripts/ono.pdf.

230 *"I realized that for something"*: Paul Taylor, "Yoko Ono's New Bronze Age at the Whitney," *New York Times*, February 5, 1989, https://www.nytimes.com/1989/02/05/arts/art-yoko-ono-s-new-bronze-age-at-the-whitney.html.

231 *she turned down the Pompidou Center*: Author interview with Sam Havadtoy, July 18, 2023.

231 *He hoped*: Author interview with Sean Lennon, November 7, 2023.

232 *Once, Michael Jackson visited*: Author interview with Dan Mahoney, June 28, 2024.

232 *a "normal" life*: Sean Lennon, interview.

232 *"Since he could get out"*: Havadtoy, interview.

233 *"as important as anything"*: Jann Wenner, "Lennon Remembers," *Rolling Stone*, February 1, 1971, https://www.rollingstone.com/music/music-news/lennon-remembers-part-one-186693/.

233 *"The uniformly favorable reviews"*: Rob Tannenbaum, "She Had Everything," *Newsday*, April 19, 1992.

234 Entertainment Weekly *gave the box*: Tom Carson, *Onobox* review, *Entertainment Weekly*, March 6, 1992, https://ew.com/article/1992/03/06/onobox/.

234 *"Yoko was holding court"*: Author interview with Cyndi Lauper, January 24, 2023.

CHAPTER 28

235 *"I remember them separating"*: Author interview with Kyoko Ono, May 11, 2022.

237 *"He literally kidnapped me"*: Ibid.

237 *"I heard people saying"*: Author interview with Sean Lennon, July 31, 2024.

238 *"I just felt terrible"*: Kyoko Ono, interview.

239 *"I'll never forget"*: Sean Lennon, interview.
239 *"I realized my mom"*: Kyoko Ono, interview.
239 *"When Kyoko came back"*: Author interview with Jon Hendricks, October 8, 2022.

CHAPTER 29

241 *"I wanted her to make"*: Author interview with Sean Lennon, August 25, 2022.
241 *"Sean was like a bridge"*: Author interview with Kim Gordon, October 3, 2022.
242 *"insanely gifted"*: Author interview with Thurston Moore, September 26, 2022.
243 *"I felt that Sean was very supportive"*: "Joy Press Interviews Yoko Ono," *Salon*, May 27, 1996, https://www.salon.com/1996/05/27/tibetlink960527_html/.
243 *"I'm an expert"*: Ethan Smith, "Sean Lennon," *New York*, May 18, 1998, https://nymag.com/nymetro/arts/music/features/2733/.
243 *"Sean Lennon is the most sympathetic"*: David Fricke, *Rising* review, *Rolling Stone*, November 30, 1995, https://www.rollingstone.com/music/music-album-reviews/rising-203964/.
244 *"It was a classic case"*: David Sheff, *All We Are Saying: The Last Major Interview with John Lennon and Yoko Ono,* rev. ed. (New York: St. Martin's Griffin, 2020).
244 *"I knew that taking them to court"*: Ibid.
245 *"Vertical Memory"*: See https://www.flickr.com/photos/mickeyono2005/5578886942.
246 *"a compressed retrospective"*: Author interview with Jeffrey Deitch, July 3, 2021.
246 *"The dots accumulated"*: "Yoko Ono: Drawings from Franklin Summer and Blood Objects from Family Album," Ubu Gallery, December 12, 1995, https://www.ubugallery.com/exhibition/yoko-ono-drawings-from-franklin-summer-and-blood-objects-from-family-album/.
246 *"Working with Yoko"*: Deitch, interview.
247 *"As a woman"*: Author interview with Mary Boone, June 14, 2024.
247 *never been acknowledged*: Author interview with Alexandra Munroe, September 16, 2022.
248 *"As a child in Japan"*: Yoko Ono, "All My Works Are a Form of Wishing," https://www.imaginepeacetower.com/yoko-onos-wish-trees/.
248 *Munroe recalled*: Munroe, interview.
248 *"Yoko Ono is really one of the most"*: Arthur Coleman Danto, "Work of Yoko Ono," *Nation*, December 18, 2000.
249 *"She always had a reputation"*: Author interview with Kyoko Ono, May 11, 2022.
249 *She even followed*: Author interview with Bob Gruen, August 24, 2022.
249 *"This is my reply"*: Yoko Ono, letter to parole board, October 6, 2000, https://www.tampabay.com/archive/2000/10/06/the-other-half-of-the-sky/.

CHAPTER 30

251 *"described in news accounts"*: William L. Hamilton, "From the Dakota to the Danube," *New York Times*, February 23, 2006, https://www.nytimes.com/2006/02/23/garden/from-the-dakota-to-the-danube.html.
251 *"I am not married"*: Glenn Plaskin, "Yoko Ono, a Decade After the 'Horrible Thing,'"

Los Angeles Times, May 6, 1990, https://www.latimes.com/archives/la-xpm-1990-05 -06-ca-245-story.html.

251 *"the shadow with"*: Author interview with Sam Havadtoy, December 7, 2022.

252 *"For me, [this relationship]"*: Ibid.

252 *"He's authentic"*: Elisabetta Provoledo, "A Hungarian Artist Comes Into His Own," *New York Times*, June 16, 2016.

253 *"Yoko was very smart"*: Author interview with Sam Havadtoy, July 18, 2023.

254 *Seaman released a book*: Frederic Seaman, *The Last Days of John Lennon: A Personal Memoir* (New York: Dell, 1992).

254 *"a sad portrait"*: Rosellen Brewer, *"The Last Days of John Lennon* review," *Library Journal*, 1991.

254 *Seaman settled the suit*: Terence Neilan, "Yoko Ono Wins Case Against Lennon Family's Ex-Assistant," *New York Times*, September 27, 2002, https://www.nytimes .com/2002/09/27/arts/yoko-ono-wins-case-against-lennon-familys-exassistant.html. Also see Aaron Moss, "Inside Yoko Ono's Copyright Lawsuit Against John Lennon's Former Assistant," *Copyright Lately*, October 3, 2020, https://copyrightlately.com /yoko-ono-copyright-lawsuit-against-former-assistant/.

254 *The* New York Post *described*: John Lehmann, "Best Book I'll Ever Burn," *New York Post*, September 28, 2002, https://nypost.com/2002/09/28/best-book-ill-ever-burn -lennons-son-slams-ex-aide-before-deal.

254 *Yoko's attorneys sued again*: Moss, "Inside Yoko Ono's Copyright Lawsuit."

255 *Seaman agreed*: Aaron Moss, "Yoko Ono Muzzles Former Lennon Assistant in Copyright Settlement," *Copyright Lately*, January 15, 2021, https://copyrightlately .com/yoko-ono-copyright-settlement/.

255 *he threatened to publish books*: "The Contents of Koral Karsan's Entire Blackmail Letter to Yoko Ono," WFMU, https://blog.wfmu.org/freeform/2007/01/the_contents _of.html.

255 *called the police*: Confirmed by Jonas Herbsman, attorney for Yoko Ono.

255 *threatened to kill*: Ibid.

255 *"on standby"*: Anemona Hartocollis, "Chauffeur Threatened Yoko Ono, Prosecutor Says," *New York Times*, December 14, 2006, https://www.nytimes.com/2006/12/14 /nyregion/15yokocnd.html.

256 *He agreed to return items*: Michael Wilson, "The Saga of Yoko Ono, Her Chauffeur and Lost Lennon Treasures," *New York Times*, November 24, 2017, https://www .nytimes.com/2017/11/24/nyregion/yoko-ono-john-lennon-lost-items.html.

256 *A decade later*: Andrea Codrea-Rada, "Man Arrested in Berlin Over John Lennon's Stolen Diaries," *New York Times,* November /212017, https://www.nytimes.com /2017/11/21/arts/music/john-lennon-stolen-diaries-berlin.html.

CHAPTER 31

257 *"Everyone was doing"*: Author interview with Sean Lennon, December 18, 2023.

257 *"I just want to say"*: Jean Teeters, "A Day in the Wife: Yoko Going Strong at 70," *New York Post*, February 16, 2003.

258 *"'Cut Piece' is my hope"*: "Crowd Cuts Yoko Ono's Clothing Off," CBS News, October 16, 2003, https://www.cbsnews.com/news/crowd-cuts-yoko-onos-clothing-off/.

258 *"When I first performed this"*: "Yoko Ono, 'Loving Cut, Spreading of Hope,'" Reuters, September 16, 2003.

258 *"That's not right"*: Yoko Ono: The Stanford Lecture 2009, part 4 of 4, January 14, 2009.

259 *"Lennon's Sister Calls for"*: Matthew Beard, "Lennon's Sister Calls for Yoko's 'Offensive' Art to Be Torn Down," *Independent*, September 25, 2004, https://www.independent.co.uk/news/uk/this-britain/lennon-s-sister-calls-for-yoko-s-offensive-art-to-be-torn-down-7906425.html.

259 *"I didn't understand"*: Michelle Robecchi, "Yoko Ono: Interview," *Contemporary* 84 (2006).

259 *"a living shrine, of sorts"*: Emily Karcher Schmitt, "Hirshhorn Visitors Fill Yoko Ono's 'My Mommy Is Beautiful' with Intimacy and Intensity," *Smithsonian Insider*, September 5, 2017, https://insider.si.edu/2017/09/yoko-onos-mommy-beautiful-brings-unfiltered-poignancy-net-media-hirshhorn-lobby/.

260 *"At a distance, the little strips of paper"*: Ibid.

260 *"specially coined"*: Yoko Ono liner notes for *Blueprints for a Sunrise*, https://www.imaginepeace.com/archives/3601.

261 *"women of all ages"*: Julia Zorthian, "Yoko Ono Invites Women to Share Their Stories for Her Next Art Installation," *Time*, September 12, 2016, https://time.com/4487920/yoko-ono-art-women-call/.

261 *Below are submissions*: Hilla Kerner, "Opinion: Yoko Ono Makes Space for Women's Testimonies at the Vancouver Art Gallery," Vancouver Is Awesome, April 26, 2022, https://www.vancouverisawesome.com/opinion/opinion-yoko-ono-makes-space-for-womens-testimonies-at-the-vancouver-art-gallery-5302101.

262 *"In a larger way, though"*: Holland Cotter, "Review: In 'Yoko Ono: One Woman Show, 1960–1971,' Text Messages from the Edge," *New York Times*, May 14, 2015, https://www.nytimes.com/2015/05/15/arts/design/review-in-yoko-ono-one-woman-show-1960-1971-text-messages-from-the-edge.html.

CHAPTER 32

265 *"the less we can talk"*: Author interview with Thurston Moore, September 26, 2022.

265 *"Pop media and fine art"*: Author interview with Pipilotti Rist, April 6, 2023.

266 *"She was beyond thrilled"*: Author interview with Danny Tenaglia, July 25, 2023.

267 *thirteen number-one dance hits*: Jason Farago, "Hearing Yoko Ono All Over Again," *New York Times*, June 25, 2015, https://www.nytimes.com/2015/06/28/arts/music/hearing-yoko-ono-all-over-again.html.

267 *hit number eleven*: "Greatest of All Time Top Dance Club Artists," *Billboard*, 2016, https://www.billboard.com/charts/greatest-top-dance-club-artists/.

267 *"She stood in front of the microphone"*: Author interview with Kim Gordon, October 3, 2022.

268 *"crate-digging"*: Author interview with RZA, January 26, 2023.

268 *"In my generation"*: Author interview with Sean Lennon, December 18, 2023.

268 *"When she sings simple songs"*: Author interview with Kate Pierson, November 22, 2022.

269 *"If suffering produces the best art"*: Madeline Bocaro, *In Your Mind: The Infinite Universe of Yoko Ono* (New York: Conceptual Books, 2016).

269 *"The computer"*: Alice Fisher, "This Much I Know," *Guardian*, September 19, 2009, https://www.theguardian.com/lifeandstyle/2009/sep/20/yoko-ono-this-much-know.

271 *"Dear Friends, I would like"*: Yoko Ono, Twitter, November 11, 2016, https://x.com /yokoono/status/797187458505080834.
271 *"All art activities"*: Ai Weiwei, email to the author, February 11, 2022.
271 *"I think her naïveté"*: Sean Lennon, interview.
272 *"Most people say"*: Amy Goodman, Democracy Now, October 16, 2007, https://www .democracynow.org/2007/10/16/exclusive_yoko_ono_on_the_new.
272 *"Some of us are here physically"*: Yoko Ono, unveiling speech for Imagine Peace Tower, Viðey Island, Reykjavík, Iceland, October 9, 2007, https://www.imaginepeace tower.com/unveiling/.

CHAPTER 33

275 *"Wildly"*: Author interview with Peaches, November 28, 2023.
275 *"Yoko Ono Turns 80"*: Angelica Leicht, "Yoko Ono Turns 80, Still Weird as Hell," *Houston Press*, February 15, 2013, https://www.houstonpress.com/music/yoko-ono -turns-80-still-weird-as-hell-6781196.
275 *"She's done more"*: Jon Wiener, "Oh Yoko! Ms. Ono at 80," *Nation*, February 20, 2013, https://www.thenation.com/article/archive/oh-yoko-ms-ono-80/.
275 *"Knocking on 80"*: Simon Schama, "Yoko Ono Talks to Simon Schama," *Financial Times*, June 1, 2012, https://www.ft.com/content/eca25228-a9eb-11e1-9772-00144 feabdc0.
275 *"I know you're not supposed"*: Nina Myskow, "Yoko Ono: I'm 80, I'm a Control Freak and I'm Going for It," *Times*, November 22, 2013, https://www.thetimes.co.uk/article /yoko-ono-im-80-im-a-control-freak-and-im-going-for-it-9n7qfglqr2t.
276 *"People tell me"*: Fiona Sturges, "'I Was Doing This Before You Were Born': Yoko Ono on John Lennon, Infidelity and Making Music into Her Eighties," *Independent*, August 30, 2013, https://www.independent.co.uk/news/people/profiles/i-was-doing -this-before-you-were-born-yoko-ono-on-john-lennon-infidelity-and-making-mu sic-into-her-eighties-8788694.html.
276 *"As always with Ono"*: David L. Ulin, "Yoko Ono Goes Back to the Future with Acorn," *Los Angeles Times*, April 12, 2013, https://www.latimes.com/books/jacket copy/la-et-jc-yoko-ono-goes-back-to-the-future-with-acorn-20130411-story.html.
278 *he confirmed*: "Paul McCartney: Yoko Ono Didn't Break Up the Beatles," *Rolling Stone*, October 29, 2012, https://www.rollingstone.com/music/music-news/paul -mccartney-yoko-ono-didnt-break-up-the-beatles-178309/.
278 *"She's badass"*: "Paul McCartney Can't Slow Down: Inside *Rolling Stone*'s New Cover Story," *Rolling Stone*, October 23, 2013, https://www.the-paulmccartney-project.com /interview/paul-scenes-from-a-nonstop-life/.
278 *"the most miserable session"*: Stuart Miller, "'Let It Be' Was Never the Beatles' Breakup Movie. Peter Jackson's New Doc Shows Why," *Los Angeles Times*, November 25, 2021, https://www.latimes.com/entertainment-arts/tv/story/2021-11-25 /the-beatles-get-back-disney-plus-let-it-be-peter-jackson.
278 *"She never has opinions"*: Keith Zubrow, "How the Documentary 'The Beatles: Get Back' Recasts Old Narratives," *60 Minutes*, CBS, June 26, 2022, https://www.cbsnews .com/news/beatles-get-back-documentary-peter-jackson-60-minutes-2022-06-26/.
279 *"The World Owes Yoko an Apology!"*: Andy Welch, "The World Owes Yoko an Apology! 10 Things We Learned from The Beatles: Get Back," *Guardian*, December 2, 2021,

https://www.theguardian.com/music/2021/dec/02/the-beatles-get-back-peter-jackson
-documentary.

279 *"She is always at John's side"*: Takashi Murakami, email to the author, June 27, 2022.

279 *"I have always been drawn"*: Lindsay Zoladz, "Yoko Ono and the Myth That Deserves to Die," *Vulture,* May 13, 2015, https://www.vulture.com/2015/05/yoko-ono-one
-woman-show.html.

279 *"I get thank-you notes"*: Nick Johnstone, *Yoko Ono "Talking"* (London: Omnibus Press, 2006).

280 *"Yoko Ono–ing"*: Nicki Cox, "Taylor Swift Compared to Yoko Ono as Chiefs Lose Again Amid Travis Kelce Romance," Page Six, December 26, 2023, https://pagesix
.com/2023/12/26/entertainment/taylor-swift-compared-to-yoko-ono-as-chiefs-lose
-again-amid-travis-kelce-romance/.

280 *"Hey guys it was only rumors"*: Jessica Chia, "Health Fears for Yoko Ono, 83, as She Is Hospitalized for 'the Flu' in New York City," *Daily Mail,* March 8, 2016, https://www
.dailymail.co.uk/news/article-3466704/amp/Yoko-Ono-83-hospitalized-flu-New
-York-City.html.

280 *"Dehydration and feeling tired"*: "Yoko Ono Hospitalized in New York with Symp-toms of 'Serious Flu,' Rep Says," ABC News, February 26, 2016, https://abcnews
.go.com/Entertainment/yoko-ono-hospitalized-york/story?id=37237215.

280 *Yoko insisted on walking*: Author interview with Dane Worthington, December 12, 2023.

280 *accompanied by an assistant*: "Frail Yoko Ono, 83, Raises a Smile as She Visits Central Park with Her Assistants and Chats with a Young Man in Her First Public Outing in Months," *Daily Mail,* April 14, 2017, https://www.dailymail.co.uk/news
/article-4412804/Frail-Yoko-Ono-visits-Central-Park-s-strawberry-fields.html.

280 *"I've learned a lot from having this illness"*: National Music Publishers Association's Centennial Song Award, YouTube, 2017, https://www.youtube.com/watch?v=ZK
_aaqEIReI.

281 *"She was sitting"*: Author interview with Bob Gruen, August 24, 2022.

281 *"an enduring hymn of solace"*: "500 Greatest Songs of All Time," *Rolling Stone,* De-cember 11, 2003, https://www.rollingstone.com/music/music-lists/500-greatest
-songs-of-all-time-151127/john-lennon-imagine-38368/.

281 *"While things may have been different in 1971"*: Steve Marinucci, "NMPA Honors John Lennon's 'Imagine' with Centennial Song Award, Surprises Yoko Ono by De-claring Her Co-Writer," *Billboard,* June 15, 2017, https://www.billboard.com/music
/music-news/nmpa-john-lennons-imagine-centennial-song-award-yoko-ono-783
3025/.

282 *"You can find a direct link"*: Author interview with Sean Lennon, August 25, 2022.

282 *highest-paid dead celebrities*: Marissa Dellatto, "The Highest-Paid Dead Celebrities of 2023," *Forbes,* October 31, 2023, https://www.forbes.com/sites/marisadellatto/2023
/10/30/highest-paid-dead-celebrities-2023-michael-jackson-elvis-presley-whitney
-houston/.

283 *"The thought of New York"*: Anna Kodé, "Yoko Ono and the Dakota," *New York Times,* July 24, 2023, https://www.nytimes.com/2023/07/21/realestate/yoko-ono
-dakota-apartment-nyc.html?searchResultPosition=1.

283 *"She literally believed"*: Author interview with Kyoko Ono, May 11, 2022.

EPILOGUE

286 *"a beautiful and exploratory instrumental project"*: Darryl Sterdan, "Albums of the Week: Sean Ono Lennon, Asterisms," *Tinnitist*, February 16, 2024, https://tinnitist .com/2024/02/16/albums-of-the-week-sean-ono-lennon-asterisms/.

286 *"I feel like as my responsibilities"*: Author interview with Sean Lennon, December 18, 2023.

286 *"I used Cox for years"*: Author interview with Kyoko Ono, May 11, 2022.

286 *"intended to demonstrate"*: Rachel Aroesti, "Various Artists: Ocean Child: Songs of Yoko Ono Review—Tribute to Brilliance of Rock Icon's Music," *Guardian,* February 18, 2022, https://www.theguardian.com/culture/2022/feb/18/various-artists -ocean-child-songs-of-yoko-ono-review-canvasback-music-atlantic-records.

286 *"The song was so Yoko"*: Author interview with David Byrne, October 10, 2022.

INDEX

ABOUT THE AUTHOR

DAVID SHEFF is the author of multiple books, including the #1 *New York Times* bestselling memoir *Beautiful Boy*, which was turned into a movie in 2018 starring Steve Carell and Timothée Chalamet. His work has appeared in *The New York Times, Rolling Stone, Wired, Fortune*, and elsewhere. His piece for *The New York Times* "My Addicted Son" received an award from the American Psychological Association for Outstanding Contribution to Advancing the Understanding of Addictions.